Praise for *Capturing New Markets*

"*Capturing New Markets* is a compass for business transformation. The book combines fascinating stories with clear takeaways that enable readers to chart their long-term courses and to begin with concrete steps tomorrow morning."

—Greta Metts, Head of Global Marketing Innovation and Business Transformation, Boehringer-Ingelheim Pharmaceuticals

"Entrepreneurs are barraged with urgent issues, and it is easy to lose sight of strategy. Amidst all the pressing things you have to do in building a business, make it a priority to read *Capturing New Markets*. This book gives succinct and powerful advice that can save you immense amounts of time and money while substantially boosting your odds of success."

—Suneet Wadhwa, Cofounder of Snapfish.com and Serial Entrepreneur

"Wunker has created a valuable tool for anyone seeking to drive meaningful change in a market or an organization. Bridging theory to case studies, he creates effective, practical and actionable advice for those seeking opportunity within change."

—Meredith Baratz, Vice President, Market Solutions, UnitedHealthcare

"In fast-moving markets, leaders can never rest. *Capturing New Markets* lays out a clear and convincing route for how big companies can act like nimble entrepreneurs in building new sources of growth."

—Ingrid Johnson, CEO, Retail and Business Banking, Nedbank

CAPTURING
NEW
MARKETS

Bob,

I hope you enjoy it!

I hope you enjoy it!

CAPTURING
NEW
MARKETS

How Smart Companies
Create Opportunities
Others Don't

STEPHEN WUNKER

New York Chicago San Francisco Lisbon London Madrid Mexico City
Milan New Delhi San Juan Seoul Singapore Sydney Toronto

1 2 3 4 5 6 7 8 9 10   QFR/QFR   1 6 5 4 3 2 1

ISBN: 978-0-07-176744-6
MHID: 0-07-176744-4

e-ISBN: 978-0-07-176752-1
e-MHID: 0-07-176752-5

This publication is designed to provide accurate and authoritative information in regard to the subject matter covered. It is sold with the understanding that neither the author nor the publisher is engaged in rendering legal, accounting, securities trading, or other professional services. If legal advice or other expert assistance is required, the services of a competent professional person should be sought.
　　　　　—From a Declaration of Principles Jointly Adopted by a Committee of the
　　　　　　American Bar Association and a Committee of Publishers and Associations

Library of Congress Cataloging-in-Publication Data

Wunker, Stephen M.
　　　Capturing new markets : discover how smart companies create opportunities ohters don't / by Stephen Wunker. —1st ed.
　　　　　p.　　cm.
　　　Includes bibliographical references and index.
　　　ISBN: 978-0-07-176744-6 (alk. paper)
　　　1. Marketing.　　2. Creative ability in business.　　I. Title.

　　HF5415.W87　　2011
　　658.8—dc22　　　　　　　　　　　　　　　　　　　　2011008987

*To Jessica, Wyatt, and Cyrus—a growing family
every bit as dynamic as a new market*

CONTENTS

PREFACE

Hero of Alexandria had a great idea. In the first century AD, Hero's design of the first steam engine was ingenious and workable. Indeed, classical scholars have argued that it could have been combined with other inventions of the era to create a steam locomotive and railroad, transforming commerce and military affairs in the ancient world.

But Hero's invention lay in a sketchbook, unused. Roman Egypt lacked an effective network of fellow inventors to improve on his device, and it had few immediate commercial applications for basic steam technology. Hero's brilliant and potentially earthshaking concept became irrelevant to history.[1] It was not until around 1712, when Britain's Thomas Newcomen created an engine capable of pumping water from mines, that steam power started to catch on, and it took another 50 years for James Watt to invent what is commonly regarded as the first modern steam engine.

Very soon, this technology enabled the spread of railroads, revolutionized shipping, enlarged factories, and transformed agriculture. In turn, these developments led to the massive economic growth of the industrial revolution. Without the steam engine, large factories and the cities to support them could not have existed.

The steam engine was a classic new market.[2] The business of producing these engines became a large one, and the industries made possible by this platform became larger still. Following a seemingly endless period of early tinkering, the steam engine rapidly emerged to displace alternative sources of power and vastly expand the power industry. The fast growth of the steam engine after Watt's invention did not result from a firm battling entrenched waterwheel competitors for market share but rather from the technology revolutionizing the use of power and transforming it beyond all recognition.

The integrated circuit may be the steam engine of our day, and few companies have been more successful in leveraging its potential than Apple. Often the rise of Apple to become one of the world's most valuable firms is credited to the elegant simplicity of the products envisioned by its cofounder and CEO, Steve Jobs. But the roots of Apple's accomplishments lie deeper—like the pathfinders of the industrial revolution, Apple visualizes how technology can lead to new markets. Rather than slog it out by battling low-cost computer makers cloning IBM's personal computer (PC), Apple created a new market segment with the Macintosh that it has dominated for over 15 years. As growth in the computer industry began to slow, Apple redefined the music industry with its iPod. More recently, it has generated explosive growth in smartphones and mobile applications with the iPhone and initiated a totally new product category with its iPad. Apple has not beaten its competitors at the industry game—it has consistently changed the game to one where competitors seemed irrelevant.

As Apple has shown, new markets are potent sources of growth. Not only do they generate new revenues, but they also often create opportunities for firms to lead new industries, earning a price premium for their offerings while building up strengths that limit competitors' ability to make inroads.

Credit cards, air travel, video games, and television—all giant industries today—were once new markets. Big companies often get their start this way. In fact, 42 of America's 50 largest firms[3] are based on exploiting markets that once were new. The list includes a huge range of industries: high tech, consumer products, energy, pharmaceuticals, and many more.

The Challenge of Pursuing New Markets

While it is attractive, growth through tapping new markets is difficult, particularly for older and larger firms. This book explores in detail how the strategies that companies pursue in established industries often do not apply when markets are nascent. Indeed, many of the best strategies for new markets—targeting nonconsumers, entering narrowly, avoiding sales channels, and other key moves—at first can seem counterintuitive. For established firms, success in new markets may also require acting in unfamiliar and entrepreneurial ways. These challenges are addressable. Through understanding the patterns of new market development and structuring internal efforts appropriately, established companies can win in these spaces.

Many well-known companies have thrived repeatedly in developing new markets. Since Thomas Edison created it, General Electric (GE) has profited by consistently trailblazing industries, from the lightbulb to electric utilities, the garbage disposal, and commercial finance. However, many other established firms have missed out on new markets that they might have led. For example, newspaper groups could have leveraged ample advantages from their relationships with readers and advertisers had they been early movers in the online classified advertising industry. Yet these companies sat out those critical first years. Upstart entrants such as Monster.com, eBay, and Craig's List pioneered and continue to lead these multi-billion-dollar markets, whereas many major newspapers have seen their traditional business shrink considerably.[4] Success in new markets can power growth, and failure to recognize the impact of these markets may lead firms to neglect critical chances for corporate renewal.

For firms already in business a while, pursuit of new markets requires intelligently leveraging existing competencies while leaving some engrained orthodoxies behind. GE today may appear to be a conglomerate consisting of dozens of seemingly distant businesses, but these ventures began through deliberately capitalizing on the company's strategic position. For example, GE entered the power-generation business and invented the first dynamo because Edison needed a neighborhood-based source of electricity for his new lightbulb. It made sense for GE to pioneer this field because it could make money from both dynamos and lighting. The company then used its brand, sales channels, and electrical engineering competencies to create a wide range of new markets, such as for the electric stove. The company subsequently took advantage of its appliance engineering and manufacturing capabilities to create high-speed kitchen equipment that facilitated the rise of the fast-food industry. Each of these endeavors required new competencies, but the ventures also made judicious use of capabilities and strategic positions staked out in the past.

For entrepreneurs, the mission is more straightforward. New companies have a very poor success rate when they target established firms in existing industries. One study found that 85 percent of these entrants fail within five years.[5] In new markets, the picture is different; many of these industries, from dog waste removal to commercial space travel, are led by new companies. Entrepreneurs look to new markets not just to grow but also to survive. Through better understanding the dynamics of new markets, they can focus money and people on the handful of endeavors that may make or break the business. Equally, they can compete more effectively against rivals who are following the wrong playbook.

My Link to the Subject

Since I was 15 years old and decided to create a planetarium for my high school (I was a real nerd), I have spent my life imagining how people could enjoy new products, services, and experiences. Before I had graduated from business school, I had helped to set up student debating leagues in several countries, establish nonprofit organizations in Eastern Europe after the end of communism, and create renew-able-energy ventures in emerging markets. Subsequently, I led a team designing one of the first mobile Internet devices, created some of the world's first mobile marketing campaigns, and launched the first mobile commerce business in Africa. In each of these endeavors, I was surrounded by people who envisioned all that could be possible; we were bewitched by the possibilities.

Unfortunately, we were befuddled about when demand might materialize. In the business ventures, we had little idea about how competitors might emerge and behave. There were no tools for systematically assessing these new markets. We tried to adapt methods commonly used in established markets, but the results were unconvincing or even misleading. Ultimately, we were toiling for a dream.

Some of these endeavors muddled through, whereas others succeeded quite well. I began to wonder if there were patterns and methods that could predict when new markets will arise and how companies can best profit from them. Harvard Business School Professor Clayton Christensen, through his groundbreaking research and creative yet rigorous logic, influenced my thinking greatly. I was very fortunate to have him as a mentor and colleague in consulting over many years. Drawing from his theories, other academic research, a decade of findings from consulting, new case studies, and my past experiences, I have sought in this book to decode what leads to firms' successes and failures in new markets.

Content of This Book

This book explains how to find, enter, and win in new markets. It also explores how to create a corporate competency to generate growth from new markets over and over again. It provides a broad perspective on how to view new markets while also supplying a toolkit that can be deployed immediately.

The content draws from dozens of interviews with leading venture capitalists and firms as diverse as Siemens, Corning, and The Hartford. While it is rigorously grounded in research,[6] the text is free-flowing, directing the reader who is seeking data to figures or other reading to the Notes. The objective has been to create an easily read guidebook to the patterns displayed in new markets and the methods that can lead to success.

Chapter 1 explores what new markets really are and why they are critically important for corporate and economic growth. It examines how new markets can become big and renew firms' growth trajectories. It also delves into how ignoring new markets has led to the decline of some companies that inhabited even seemingly stable industries.

Chapter 2 focuses on how to find new markets—it explores both how to assess latent demand and what sort of events can trigger market formation. Drawing on examples including George Eastman's Kodak camera and Panasonic's Mobile Clinical Assistant, Chapter 2 looks at how to find markets that do not yet exist.

Chapter 3 turns to how companies can assess these markets. Given that there are no reliable data regarding market size, growth rates, and competitor shares for markets in their earliest stages, how can firms gauge their potential? This chapter concentrates on how to scope the value at stake in a market, how quickly a market can blossom, and whether a firm can create a defensible position. This chapter also addresses several pitfalls that can derail companies during market assessment. It draws on several past and present examples, including entry by the textbook-publishing giant Pearson into online tutoring.

Chapter 4 looks at how to enter new markets. Counterintuitively, the fastest route to winning broad dominance of a market is often to start narrowly, laser-targeting a foothold that can provide fast traction, customer feedback, and reference accounts. This chapter lays out the role footholds play and how firms can quickly evolve their strategy with this approach. It draws from my own experience in starting Africa's first mobile commerce business.

Sales channels are essential to innovation, yet market pioneers often overlook their importance. Seized by the power of an idea and how customers should grab onto it, the creators of new markets can neglect the ability of sales channels to sink or supercharge the proposition. Chapter 5 concentrates on channels by exploring two distinct strategies for gaining market penetration. Delving into examples that include the creation of the mobile marketing industry, this chapter lays out how to tackle sales-channel issues that can matter enormously for new ventures.

In business as in comedy, timing is everything. Chapter 6 assesses when to be the first in a new market versus when to follow others in. This chapter examines video gaming, where Atari fast established a dominant position only to utterly lose its way, whereas Nintendo twice played the role of the late entrant that revolutionized the industry. This chapter will consider how different business models in an industry can help to predict when it is most profitable to enter.

Developing countries are a huge source of new markets, yet few Western firms do a large proportion of their business in these environments. Chapter 7 focuses on how companies can profitably tackle the challenge of creating new markets in these contexts.

An executive once told me, "Just about everyone here recognizes our problem. A few people think they have the answer. No one knows how to implement it." Building a corporate capability to tackle new markets is difficult. The task often requires distinct approaches to decision making and project governance. Chapter 8 looks at these issues and recommends how to change internal processes, structures, and culture when attacking new markets. This chapter also provides advice from leading practitioners in the field, including both corporate executives and venture capitalists.

Chapter 9 addresses how public policy can support or hinder the growth of new markets. Drawing from examples that include health-care information technology, mobile phones, and renewable energy, this chapter illustrates how low-cost and apolitical policies can generate big returns.

As illustrated in Figure P-1, this book is organized in the same way that it suggests attacking new markets. It begins with corporate strategy, definition of latent demand, and assessment of the opportunity. It then proceeds into selection of the first customers and sales channels. Subsequently the narrative moves into choosing the right timing for entry as well as the right place, focusing on the potential of emerging markets. Only then does it address how to align the organizational and public policy context. Too often, explorations of new markets begin instead with a company assessing its core competencies and the demands of its current businesses, or with wishful thinking about government incentives. Those efforts reverse the direction of the arrows in the figure, and that orientation typically leads to conceiving markets as they are today, not as they might be. Conversely, the most creative thinking about new markets often stems from intense concentration on marketplace needs, linked to the strategic reasons why a company should invest in this source of growth.

The end of each chapter features a brief summary of key points, and several chapters also contain tables and figures highlighting major take-aways. An Afterword explores 10 critical differences between new

Figure P-1   Flow of the book.

1. Strategize
2. Define Markets
3. Assess Markets
→
4. Target First Customers
5. Choose Right Channel
→
6. Choose Right Time
7. Choose Right Place
→
8. Enable the Corporation
9. Enable Public Policy

and established markets that are explored in the book. The Afterword also addresses how companies can begin their journeys toward growing in these directions.

———⟫◦○◦⟪———

New markets can be deceiving. While they can create vast new growth, they may seem small and irrelevant today. Much as the principles of Newtonian physics begin to break down on a nanoparticle scale, strategic planning tactics appropriate for established markets fail to account for the opportunities and challenges of these nascent industries. Winning in new markets requires taking a disciplined, dispassionate view of where opportunity lies. It may necessitate embracing new ways of engaging with customers, channel partners, and other stakeholders. Frequently, it entails adopting an unfamiliar way of making decisions. Yet the payoffs can be immense. Let us explore how success happens.

ACKNOWLEDGMENTS

A book that bridges academic theory and everyday practice owes debts to many people. I have learned from some of the best. While all errors and omissions are my own, I must acknowledge the people who affected this book most.

Foremost, my thanks go to Harvard Business School Professor Clayton Christensen. I first read Clay's works in 2004, just before joining the consulting firm he had started, Innosight. For the first time, I could see clearly why various ventures of mine had succeeded and struggled. I deeply wished I had read his thinking earlier. Over the next five years, it was my honor to collaborate with Clay and others to bring his theories to life at dozens of clients. I also was privileged to write with him; invariably, he would pull lucid and insightful theses from seemingly hopeless complexity. I have unending admiration for Clay as a scholar and as a person. His thinking is foundational to this book in many respects.

In that consulting practice, I worked with some outstanding people who also taught me about how to put forth intricate arguments in straightforward ways. Scott Anthony and Joe Sinfield, my former partners there, had a particularly strong influence on how I communicate concepts now.

I also have had the privilege of interacting with other leading academics in this field. Vijay Govindarajan of Dartmouth's Tuck School of Business provided a rigorous view of how to build organizational capabilities to execute new market strategies. Chip Heath of Stanford's Graduate School of Business influenced my approaches to both organizational change and how to make ideas memorable. Rita Gunther McGrath of Columbia Business School was instrumental in developing a method of sequencing risk-reducing activities.

I have worked with more talented executives than I could possibly count or thank. However, two deserve special mention. Ken Dobler at Johnson & Johnson has translated academic thinking around new markets into highly actionable and methodical processes. Colin Watts at Walgreens has been exceptionally thoughtful about how to create new ventures and competencies in an enterprise of almost 250,000 people that has to provide error-free service to millions of customers a day. I have learned much from their creative and disciplined minds.

Many executives lent their time to be interviewed for this book, and their real-world perspectives help to make this book's recommendations actionable. Thanks go to Greg Fleming of Air Liquide; Tom Polen of Becton, Dickinson and Company; Deb Mills and Daniel Ricoult of Corning; David Aronoff of Flybridge Ventures; Karen O'Reilly of Lexington Insurance; Patrick Supanc of Pearson; Willy Hoos, Mary Sargent, and Linda Trevenen of Philips Healthcare; James Wang of Sercomm; Russ Conser of Shell; Gernot Spiegelberg of Siemens; Brad Gambill of Singapore Telecom; Jacqueline LeSage Krause of The Hartford; Meredith Baratz and Bill Whitely of UnitedHealthcare; and Charles Warden of Versant Ventures.

Several people have taught me how to approach a book such as this, but particular thanks go to three. Stanley N. Katz was my thesis adviser at Princeton, and there is nothing quite like having a past president of the Organization of American Historians critique your chapter on historical analysis. I lived through the experience and became a clearer thinker as a result. Tony Jaswinski taught me how to write, although I imagine that his omnipresent red pen could show how this volume might have been considerably improved. More recently, Danny Stern gave savvy advice to a first-time author.

Knox Huston, my editor at McGraw-Hill, provided excellent input. I am very thankful for the strong team there that supports this book. In addition, Evgenia Eliseeva did her usual first-class job with photography.

My team at New Markets Advisors gave indispensible assistance. Darren Coleman in the United Kingdom and Pramod Mohanlal in South Africa offered valuable thoughts, and Kate Bonamici Flaim did much of the quantitative research.

Two people read every word of this book through many drafts. My father, Robert Wunker, is an outstanding writer and suggested changes to both phrasing and structure that made this a better book. My wife, Jessica Wattman, not only improved the writing but also imposed the discipline of her MIT Ph.D. to make my arguments as robust as possible. Alongside her detailed suggestions, she provided the moral support that made this project happen.

CAPTURING NEW MARKETS

Chapter | 1

WHY NEW MARKETS MATTER

On April 3, 1973, Martin Cooper turned the heads of even jaded New Yorkers as he strolled the sidewalks while talking into a brick-like device. Cooper, head of Motorola's Communications Systems Division, was placing the world's first call on a cellular phone. In his triumphant moment, he mischievously dialed his archrival at AT&T's Bell Labs. A new market was born.

Cell phones are representative of new markets and their huge potential. Like the steam engine discussed in the Preface, they had been years in gestation. People with money to burn could use primitive car phones with an operator's help in setting up calls. Humphrey Bogart used one playing the mogul Linus Larrabee in the 1954 movie *Sabrina*. But there were many problems that prevented systems from being scaled—for several years, Britain's Prince Philip had the United Kingdom's only mobile phone.[1] Motorola's technology removed these issues. It allowed many people to use a network simultaneously, traveling between cells, calling through a totally automated process. The dawn of a new era finally seemed at hand.

In a press release issued that historic day, Motorola confidently projected that cell phones would be in public use by 1976.[2] Yet it took until 1979 for the first commercial cell phone networks to be deployed, in Bahrain and Tokyo, and a U.S. network did not exist until 1983. Motorola's sales of cellular equipment were exceptionally small for over a decade after that first call was made. The first handsets cost $3,500, weighed 28 ounces,[3] and appealed to a sliver of the population. As is frequently the case in a market's early days, the future seemed uncertain.

In 1980, AT&T commissioned a study to project the total number of cell phones in use worldwide by 2000. The study's answer: 900,000. The company decided to sit out as others built the first U.S. cellular networks. The correct number for the year 2000 ended up being 750 million,[4] and by 2010, worldwide users stood at 4.6 billion.[5] AT&T was forced to pay $11.5 billion in 1994 to buy McCaw Cellular, one of the early movers in the industry.[6] Motorola had been too optimistic, but AT&T had been expensively pessimistic. Both had severely misjudged the market.

Following the pattern of many new markets, the cell phone spawned several other industries. Wireless networks became a business exceeding $150 billion in the United States alone.[7] Mobile mapping has taken off so rapidly that Nokia recently spent $8 billion to acquire a navigation company. The iPhone has created a market for over 400,000 software applications, and that number keeps growing. The cell phone enables mobile marketing campaigns by giant brands such as Coca-Cola and Adidas. People using this small device now transact nearly 5 percent of Zambia's gross domestic product (GDP).[8]

Perhaps the most astonishing thing about these markets is that they were latent for years. The potential for over 400,000 applications of a mobile device existed long before the iPhone came around to unlock that demand. For millennia, people have wondered about tomorrow's weather, played games, and sent messages to friends. The cell phone allowed that latent demand to be channeled into a commercial transaction.

As often happens, the cellular industry did not so much cannibalize an old one as create an entirely new source of growth. Think about the calls you make today on your cell phone—how many would never have been placed if your only option was a landline handset? Think too about the leaders in the cellular business—giants such as Nokia and Vodafone were not present in traditional telecoms.

Cellular telephony also was typical in other respects. Initial take-up was slow. Expensive and bulky handsets hindered the industry's expansion, yet the tiny market seemed not to warrant big investment to make these devices significantly better. Competition generated awareness but also created problems as companies rolled out conflicting technical standards and offered pricing plans that made it costly for customers of one carrier to interact with subscribers on rival networks. Behavior change at first took root through leveraging existing habits, such as checking the weather, and then rocketed into new directions, such as finding friends' locations. The industry shifted from a handful of vertically integrated players to today's gaggle of competitors. Advances in component technologies, like digital photography, enabled totally new and unexpected uses of the device.

Given the criticality of new markets to business growth, it is essential for companies to pursue these opportunities in an appropriate manner. Unfortunately, when firms assess and enter new markets, they often cross-apply the principles, strategies, and analytical tools used by mature industries. The results can be profoundly misleading. As we shall see throughout this book, there are clear patterns that govern the creation and growth of new markets, and these principles contradict common behavior in established fields.

In this chapter, we will look at

- What defines a new market
- How new markets create big industries
- How new markets build great companies
- Why ignoring new markets is perilous
- How new markets can become a source of corporate renewal
- What trends make new markets particularly critical today

What Is a New Market?

The words *new market* are often used loosely. Google references over 8 million pages with the term. This book does not focus on new technologies catering to existing markets (Blu-Ray replacing DVD), ways to enter an industry by seizing a share of existing customers (Walmart becoming America's leading grocer), or new competitors entering an existing territory (South African winemakers rising to equal France's share of the British wine market). These other topics involve different customer and competitive dynamics than the creation of new markets.

This book's focus is on markets that have not existed previously. It is concerned with tapping latent demand to create new sources of consumption, much as the cell phone did. A new market might cannibalize some of the old, but it also expands overall consumption—cars significantly hurt the makers of buggy whips, but they greatly expanded the use of transportation. If fighting competitors for share is a zero-sum game, new markets are about positive sums that create economic growth.

There are two general ways in which new markets create growth:

- *New customers.* A new market often will lead to people or institutions buying products or services that they had not purchased before. Sometimes these products may be new-to-the-world, such as Apple's iPad, whereas in other circumstances they might be newly affordable or accessible, like cell phones have become in developing countries.

* *New consumption occasions,* A new market also may result from new consumption occasions. Colgate created a new market with its Wisp toothbrush, an ultraportable single-use brush meant to be used on the go. E*Trade enabled consumers to trade stocks far more frequently than they could with traditional brokers.

New products, services, or technologies do not necessarily lead to new markets. The key distinction is whether they ultimately lead to new consumption.

As with many definitions, there are gray areas. Wind energy is not a new market for electric utilities because it does not materially change the amount of power that people consume. However, for turbine companies, it is clearly a vast new market. This book does not dwell on exploring fine definitional distinctions. Unless otherwise noted, each example of the 181 used qualifies as a new market under the basic definition given earlier.

New Markets Create Big Industries

Over the past 50 years, the U.S. economy has gone through waves of transformation. An agriculturally oriented nation had already given way to one focused on manufacturing. Services then became predominant. Information and communication became vastly larger components of GDP than before. As Figure 1-1 illustrates, the makeup of the economy and size of key industries have shifted enormously.[9]

Sometimes the rate of change has caught the statisticians off-guard. The Census Bureau has counted nationwide sales of greeting cards since before World War II. However, the biotechnology industry, with

Figure 1-1 Economic transformation over five decades.

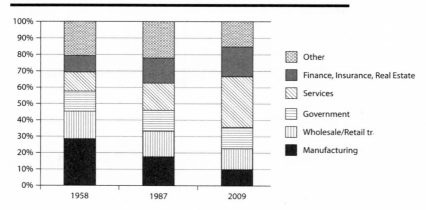

annual revenues now exceeding $60 billion in the United States alone, was not tracked as recently as 1997.[10]

Indeed, the most recent Census of the U.S. economy lists myriad industries that scarcely existed 20 years ago—satellite communications, Internet publishing, data hosting services, and more. These new technology-related industries constitute nearly 8 percent of today's economy.[11] Moreover, a look within preexisting industries shows the growth that new markets can create. Hotel accommodation was an industry before Rome was a city, but the rapid growth of extended-stay hotel chains over the past 20 years has led to their becoming almost 7 percent of all U.S. hotel rooms.[12] People have cleaned their homes since the dawn of civilization, but innovations such as Procter & Gamble's Mr. Clean Magic Eraser recently have grown this industry in totally new ways.

While many observers grasp the potential of new technologies to create industries, one of the most stunning facts about new markets is that some of the greatest successes have come from relatively low-tech offerings. General Electric (GE) makes nearly one-third of its $158 billion in revenue from capital finance, thriving in once-obscure niches that banks largely overlooked.[13] Overnight package delivery was feasible long before the creation of Federal Express in 1971, yet the company pioneered a market that today is worth $74 billion.[14] One wonders about what the next great industries will be that have nothing to do with new technologies.

New Markets Build Great Companies

Table 1-1 shows the top 10 U.S. firms by market capitalization. Eight of these 10 firms have become giants through repeatedly finding and dominating new markets.[15] Several of these companies' stories will be explored in this book. Let us look at two of them now.

Table 1-1 Most Valuable Companies in the United States and a Few of Their New Markets

Company	Example New Market
ExxonMobil	Kerosene, gasoline, components of lithium batteries
Apple	PCs, laser printers, MP3 players, smartphone hardware
Microsoft	PC operating systems, PC application software
Berkshire Hathaway	N/A
Walmart Stores	N/A
Procter & Gamble	Disposable diapers, fabric softener, safety razors
IBM	Mainframe computers, magnetic tape, PCs, information technology services
Johnson & Johnson	Sterile sutures, dental floss, stents, laparoscopic surgery
General Electric	Commercial finance, electric toasters, moldable plastics
Google	Paid searches, smartphone operating system

Google was born in 1998 (its incorporation took place in a garage, one not even belonging to the two founders).[16] In its early days, a venture capitalist considering investment counted 17 other search engines that seemed just as good.[17] Internet search was growing rapidly, with Yahoo, Netscape, and Excite leading the pack.[18] Yet no one was making much money because these firms had not figured out how to derive significant revenues from the millions of hits they were generating every day. It was late-coming Google that created a new market, as opposed to a new product, through pioneering the now-commonplace practice of paid search—having a company's laser-targeted ads appear alongside the results provided by the search engine. Paid search opened up new consumption among Internet searchers as well as new advertising spending from businesses that finally could target customers with pinpoint accuracy but without ad production cost. These concepts became an immense business for Google, generating over $22 billion in revenue during 2009 alone.[19]

Google moved on to have higher aims—to organize the world's information and make it universally accessible and useful.[20] This mission led the company to launch services such as Google Reader, which allows users to organize their favorite blog and news feeds into a customized magazine-like experience. The service created many more consumption opportunities for the company's advertising-powered business model. It produced Google Maps, a compelling way to find local resources that opens up new possibilities in location-based search and advertising.

The company did not stop there. It understood the potential of its dominance on the PC desktop and the threat as well as the opportunity of the cell phone usurping much of the PC's functions. It invested heavily to launch Android, a rapidly ascendant cell phone operating system that creates countless more consumption opportunities for highly targeted advertising. It has experimented in other markets as well, such as using Internet technologies to radically change the way that television ads are targeted and sold.

While Google is clearly a technology-based company, its ascent has had little to do with any scientific breakthrough. The firm succeeded by recognizing the new markets that technology can open up rather than from creating breakthrough technologies that subsequently generate markets on their own. In other words, we should not be deterred by Google's ranks of engineers—any company can follow in Google's footsteps.

The stock market believes in the potential of Google to create further new markets. Analysts have attributed over 20 percent of the company's value, a sum worth over $30 billion, to businesses outside paid search.[21] The analysts are not sure about exactly which new market will be a blockbuster, but Google's portfolio of initiatives is enticing.

As noted in the Preface, Apple also provides a powerful story about the potential of new markets. The company famously helped to create the PC market in 1977 with the Apple II.[22] In the 1980s, the company was the first to harness the PC's power for graphics applications. It produced not only the Macintosh in 1984 but also one of the first laser printers in 1985.[23] While the rest of the PC industry raced toward commoditization, Apple cornered a market willing to pay high prices for its compelling offerings.

More recently, the firm has had a string of successes in building new markets. Its iPod was launched three years after Diamond produced the first portable MP3 player,[24] yet Apple was able to energize and own that market by offering consumers an ecosystem of device, software, and music that worked brilliantly together. Similarly, the iPhone was a very late entrant into the mobile phone market yet now captures over 30 percent of the profits in the total handset industry.[25] It revolutionized how people thought about a mobile device. In 2010, the company launched the iPad, selling nearly $5 billion in the product's first six months as it created still another new market.

One might think that Apple spends enormous sums on technology to create these magnificent devices. Incredibly, the firm devotes only 3.1 percent of its sales to research and development (R&D),[26] considerably under the industry average of 7.1 percent.[27] The firm does not rely on gee-whiz products emanating from years of colossally expensive technology projects. It is the vision of new markets that drives this company's huge success.

New Markets Are Dangerous to Ignore

Some firms choose to stick to their core markets—American Greetings has been a market leader in the greeting card industry for decades, with revenues of about $1.6 billion in 2009. Unfortunately, those revenues have shrunk since 1990 at an annual rate of 3 percent after inflation. Despite the company rebranding its business as "social expression products," the stock market seems to find little potential for growth in the company. If Apple's stock traded at American Greetings' earnings multiple, $140 billion would be knocked from the company's value.

Another outcome of ignoring new markets is illustrated by Blockbuster, the video rental retail chain that once controlled nearly 40 percent of the industry.[28] The firm skyrocketed with the spread of VCRs and DVD players. The company seemed unassailable, with over 9,100 stores by 2004.[29]

Yet, during Blockbuster's best days, the seeds of its demise had already taken root. In 1997, a California film buff named Reed Hastings paid a $40 late fee when he returned Apollo 13 to his local video store and had an epiphany. Hastings started a company called Netflix to capture a totally new entertainment market. Rather than compete for spur-of-the-moment rentals to people on their way home from work, Hastings targeted a market that was small because it was poorly served. Netflix renters had to order DVDs in advance over the Internet, receiving them in the mail a couple days later. The benefit was that they could keep them as long as they wanted, paying only a monthly subscription fee and no late charges. This was a terrible proposition for impulsive renters but a great idea for people such as busy parents who had no time to stop at a store and who could never predict which night their kids would choose for that blissful event—early bedtime. Netflix took off, shipping over 100,000 units a week before it reached its second anniversary of operations.[30] The company went public, and the stock soared.

In 2003, a business called Redbox attacked Blockbuster from a different direction. It targeted customers who might be so impulsive that they did not even know they wanted to rent a video. Redbox's business model was influenced by one of its earliest financial backers—the McDonald's restaurant chain.[31] Placing small, fully automated kiosks in locations such as fast-food restaurants and grocery stores, it offered shoppers a very limited selection of popular videos at the bargain-basement price of $1 a night. The company quickly succeeded and installed more than 22,000 kiosks across the United States. Like Netflix, it is also growing quickly into the video-on-demand market.[32]

For much of this time, Blockbuster did . . . nothing. It enjoyed its highly profitable business and ignored these seemingly insignificant markets. Only in 2004 did the company launch a subscription-based service of its own, with the option of either in-store or mail pickup and delivery. Giving consumers the choice of store or mail theoretically was a superior offering to Netflix, but the service had hidden late charges that created outrage sufficient to prompt lawsuits by the attorneys general of several U.S. states.[33]

In 2009, Blockbuster Express was launched as a response to Redbox. Its kiosks rent DVDs at $1 a night, just like its competitor. There are a few extra bells and whistles, such as the ability to reserve a DVD online, but these features may be irrelevant to the target market for the machines. Redbox has already established itself in many of the best locations, and it may be a tough firm for Blockbuster to beat.[34]

While Blockbuster pondered how to fight for these new markets, its core business declined. The target customers the company had addressed found that Netflix and Redbox were more convenient and often better value. Blockbuster was stuck with a high-cost business model due to its retail outlets and so had trouble cutting prices. It became harder and harder for the company to support big stores in prime locations as the number of renters declined. Without big, convenient selection, still more renters defected. The firm entered a downward spiral and ultimately filed for bankruptcy.

Many firms endure a cycle similar to Blockbuster. Dell grew from a dorm room startup in 1984 to a giant $107 billion market capitalization 15 years later through its innovative build-to-order business model.[35] Dell's approach enabled it to have lower costs than competitors selling through retail channels. Yet the company now seems like a one-trick pony, and its stock trades at less than 40 percent of its value in 2005. Hewlett-Packard, Acer, and other firms emulated Dell's model while being faster to partner with cheaper suppliers. Dell continued to focus on desktop PCs while the market moved to laptops and eventually to inexpensive netbooks. Competitors also upped their game in customer service even as Dell was said to neglect this function because of its cost. In short, competitors copied Dell where they had to, beat it on providing overall value, and embraced new markets that drove industry growth. Dell is still a winner in Intel-based desktop PCs but missed what matters. The industry has moved on.

Some industries seem to have few prospects for such spectacular growth, but often this perspective stems from defining a market in traditional ways.[36] Even firms in seemingly static sectors can miss out on major sources of growth by ignoring new markets. Coca-Cola, for example, holds a 42 percent share of the U.S. carbonated soft-drink industry[37] but got started late in the nearly $5 billion market for energy drinks,[38] where the best it has been able to muster is a 10 percent share.[39] Hertz dominates the airport rental car industry yet largely missed out on the business model embraced by Enterprise Rent-A-Car, which targeted the distinct market of neighborhood-based rentals. Enterprise now holds a 53 percent share of the overall U.S. rental car market, whereas Hertz has only 23 percent.[40] As this book will make clear, business history is packed with examples of new markets arising alongside seemingly staid ones.

Whether the outcome of ignoring new markets is stagnation or decline, the moral is straightforward—firms ignore new markets at their peril. Figure 1-2 shows the total shareholder return (stock price change plus dividends) since initial public offering (IPO) of three hugely successful firms: Dell, Home Depot, and Southwest Airlines.[41] After a period of rapid growth as they tackled a new market, these companies stalled. Like Dell, many firms have only one trick up their sleeve; they are great at doing what they do, even when that thing becomes less and less relevant to where growth in the market is continuing to occur.

Figure 1-2   One-trick ponies?

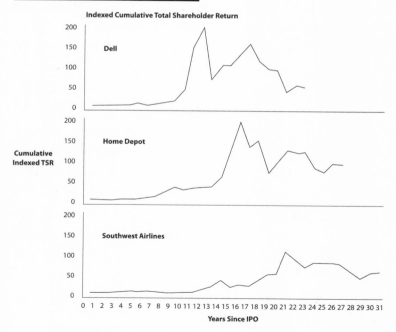

Note: TSR = (closing price + dividends) opening price; prices are adjusted for stock splits and special events
Source: Yahoo Finance

The Potential for Corporate Renewal in New Markets

On the other side of the coin, some companies have mastered the art of repeatedly identifying and conquering new markets. Netherlands-based Royal Philips Electronics is one such firm. Founded in 1891 as a producer of light bulbs, the company quickly succeeded and by 1910 was the country's largest employer. Philips continues to be a global leader in the lighting business today, selling $8.3 billion annually. Yet the firm quickly sought to leverage its electronics expertise into new markets. It produced its first medical x-ray tube in 1918. The company targeted certain sectors very aggressively; for example, it entered the nascent radio industry in 1927 and became the world's largest radio manufacturer within five years. It also created new technologies to transform industries, introducing the compact audio cassette in 1963, the compact disc in 1983, and the DVD in 1997.[42] Lighting now constitutes only 28 percent of company sales, whereas health-care electronics—an industry that did not exist when the company was founded—contributes 34 percent of revenues.

Philips believes in targeting applications, not industries, which creates a dynamic view about what business the company is in. By evolving to meet customers' shifting needs, the firm keeps pioneering new markets. For example, the company has gone beyond offering home health-care devices—where it is a market leader—to providing health-related services for consumers and their employers. Its new DirectLife business provides a mobile monitor to track physical activity, a Web site personalized with data from the monitor, online coaching, and employer-based motivational programs to improve workforce fitness and health.[43]

Philips is far from unique. Many firms have established a capability to repeatedly create new markets:

- Fidelity Investments pioneered the concept of mutual funds back in 1930. It also created the first discount brokerage in 1978.[44] The company's innovations enabled consumers to do new things with their money, even if it sometimes meant paying Fidelity higher fees than for a traditional bank savings account. Along the way, Fidelity became one of the world's biggest money managers, responsible for $1.5 trillion.[45]
- After Medtronic invented the portable pacemaker, it also pioneered the implantable cardiac defibrillator and many other devices to extend and improve the lives of people suffering from heart disease.[46] Its cardiac rhythm business unit now generates $4.9 billion in annual sales.
- Johnson & Johnson has brought us the Band-Aid, disposable contact lens, modern hip replacements, and dozens of other market-creating innovations.[47]

The ability to create new markets has led to the sustainable success of these enterprises. Even as established markets slowly declined, new markets have helped to fuel the overall growth of the businesses. These market-creating firms are not one-hit wonders but rather giants that repeatedly throw competitors off balance by redefining their industries.

Why New Markets Matter Now

New markets are particularly relevant in today's economy. As firms emerge from the "great recession," they are seeking new ways to grow. The downturn has left little appetite to take on the high costs of competing head-on against entrenched competitors, and so it is compelling to pioneer businesses with low costs of entry but high potential rewards.

Aside from the short-term economic climate, several long-term trends are also converging to force new markets onto companies' strategic agendas:

- *Globalization.* For many firms, emerging markets are new territory. With 80 percent of the world's population and 40 percent of the global economy, emerging markets account for just 12 percent of sales for the Standard & Poor's (S&P) 500.[48] While companies may understand at a gut level that they need to play in these settings, they often lack a road map for upending their long-standing business models to attack these new markets. Worse, they fear that enterprises that triumph in this setting may leap into developed markets and threaten incumbents on their home turf. If firms do not play offense in emerging markets now, they soon may be playing defense against globalization's winners.

- *Information.* Thanks to innovations such as the Internet, e-mail, social networks, and cheap telecommunications, information flows far more rapidly today than ever before. The easy availability of information enables markets to form quickly. Niche communities can discover highly relevant new offerings, share experiences, and give confidence to later adopters about the value of these solutions. Yet information also can lead to transparency of competitors' pricing, easy comparison shopping, and commoditization. Industries can rise and decline fast. In this situation, it is imperative to discover new markets that will generate future growth.

- *Virtual sales channels.* As well as enhancing information flows, the Internet has created virtual channels that link pioneers with target customers, bypassing the middlemen who often neglect new markets because of their focus on short-term sales quotas.

Through Google's paid-search advertising, LinkedIn's microtargeting of demographics, and blogs that generate attention virally, the companies creating new markets now can reach nontraditional sets of customers in hyperfocused ways. Moreover, they can communicate their message directly without reliance on channels that can have their own agendas.

- *Open platforms.* Many new markets build on innovations that originally had an entirely different purpose. Global Positioning System (GPS) technology underlies industries such as car navigation devices, vehicle tracking, and location-based advertising. The technology was originated to aid in targeting submarine-launched ballistic missiles.[49] GPS is an example of an open platform—a technology that is freely available for others to build on. The steam engine, integrated circuit, Internet, radio, and electric grid are other examples. Open platforms can trigger innovation in completely unexpected directions, and the constant acceleration of technical progress generates these platforms at a growing rate.

- *Discontinuities.* Traditional tools for marketing and strategy are predicated on continuous trends from the past to the future. Businesspeople can extrapolate market growth rates, project competitors' shares, estimate profits, and more confidently plan long-term investments. All this information is comforting. Unfortunately, as AT&T discovered in its projection of a global market in 2000 of 900,000 cell phones, these approaches can be profoundly wrong when an industry is experiencing rapid change. Discontinuities seem to be occurring at an ever-faster pace. Competitors from emerging markets, new technologies disrupting traditional industries, concerns about environmental sustainability, dramatic improvements in life expectancy, new communications tools, and a host of other factors are moving the economy in radically new directions. While change can shut down growth prospects for some firms, such as Blockbuster, it can open up potential for others willing to embrace new markets, such as Netflix.

━━━━◦◦◦◦━━━━

The economic history of the twentieth century frequently was the story of new markets.[50] Industry after industry arose to expand consumption, from household cleaning products to information technology services. If this was the case over the past century, what will happen in this one? The trends that made new markets a powerful engine of growth are even stronger today. Businesses that seize the opportunity of new markets may grow enormously. They also can stay vibrant as the economy changes around them.

Summary

- New markets tap latent sources of demand to create new consumption. They arise from creating either new customers or new opportunities for consumption by existing customers.
- New markets are a critical source of both economic and company growth. They have created huge new industries, such as cellular communications, and big firms.
- Even companies in seemingly stable industries jeopardize their future by ignoring new markets. Markets that can seem uninteresting, irrelevant, or invisible can quickly power the success of emerging rivals.

- Some firms, such as Philips, Fidelity Investments, Medtronic, and Johnson & Johnson, have shown that repeated discovery of new markets can power sustained corporate success over decades or longer.
- Several current trends make new markets particularly important today. These include globalization, the free flow of information, the rise of virtual channels, the fast introduction of new open platforms, and economic discontinuities.

Chapter | 2

FINDING NEW MARKETS

F inding the unknown used to be a mission for the very brave or the
very foolish. When Christopher Columbus sought India, he simply
sailed west and hoped for the best. Fortunately, our era is different.
When today's explorers seek oil or minerals, they sift through enormous data repositories with sophisticated algorithms. Their rigor cuts
risk, lowers costs, and vastly increases the scale of searchable territory.

These principles apply to business explorers on a quest for new markets. Rigorous research and analysis can point to new ways for firms
to grow. Inspiration and good fortune—while always welcome—are
hardly necessary. Companies can define target customers and map
their latent needs, creating detailed portraits of problems to be solved.
Firms then can match these needs to typical triggers of market formation to understand when new markets might arise.

This chapter begins by recounting how George Eastman, the
founder of Eastman Kodak, found new markets through genius, intu-
ition, and a good deal of luck. It then explores how companies can
accomplish these tasks through a much more deliberate method. This
chapter covers

- How Eastman created a huge new market in photography
- How firms can follow a six-step process to uncover latent needs
- What triggers the formation of new markets where latent needs exist

Creating the Photography Market

When George Eastman bought his first camera on November 13, 1877,[1] many Americans had already seen a photograph. The first one was taken in France in 1826.[2] By 1877, professional and amateur photographers had sprung up around the world, but the market still was tiny. Within 10 years Eastman had unleashed the industry from the forces holding it back, and his Eastman Kodak Company quickly accounted for more than 40 percent of all photography sales in the United States. What happened?

The camera that Eastman bought in 1877 was no Instamatic. He had to develop its pictures quickly, before emulsions on glass plates dried out. He needed a tent to ensure darkness while he applied the emulsions and developed the photos. The camera was the size of a microwave oven and required a large tripod. Eastman also needed glass tanks, a water carrier, and a heavy device to hold the plates. Moreover, he needed "a small chemistry laboratory—nitrate of silver; acetate soda; chlorides of gold, sodium, and iron; collodion; alcohol; litmus paper; a hydrometer; graduate; an evaporating dish; a funnel; a bristle brush; scales and weights; and washing pans."[3] The materials cost him almost $50. He also spent $5 on lessons to understand how to use all this paraphernalia. In today's money, it all cost over $1,100.[4] Photography was expensive, time-consuming, and difficult.

Eastman became interested in photography at a time of intersecting technological developments. In 1871, an Englishman had invented a process for making premanufactured photographic plates that did not require extensive preparation prior to picture taking. Eastman eagerly read publications from both sides of the Atlantic in which experimenters boasted of improvements to this process, and he spent countless nights tinkering to come up with a better method himself. His result, created in 1878, was both a better plate and the machinery to make it. Amateur photographers embraced the new plates, but picture taking remained costly and hard. Eastman was still far from his goal of making photography "as convenient as a pencil." He knew that photography was fun and appealing for the masses, particularly in an era when leisure activities such as bicycle riding, professional sports, and vaudeville were changing lifestyles. Eastman just needed to get photography to the point where it could be consumed easily.

Eastman drew on a range of emerging technologies to create a celluloid film on a continuous piece of paper. After exposure, the photographer stripped the paper and developed the film. Eastman thought that this invention would be embraced by photographers the world over, but it did not work out that way in part because the picture retained the grainy pattern of the paper. For these enthusiasts, the product was not good enough. As Eastman later put it, "When we started out with our scheme of film photography, we expected that everybody that used glass plates would take up film, but we found that the number that did this was relatively small and that in order to make a large business we would have to reach the general public and create a new class of patrons."[5] To achieve this goal, Eastman not only would need to remove any worry about the film, but he also would have to shrink the camera.

In 1888, after years of toil, his dream came to fruition. The Kodak camera was less than half the size of alternatives. It was sold for $25 preloaded with film for 100 exposures. Once the pictures were taken, the owner sent the camera back to Kodak's headquarters in Rochester, NY, paying $10 to have the photos developed and the camera returned to him or her reloaded with film. Taking advantage of the explosion of catalogues, periodicals, and newspapers around this time, Eastman created a compelling marketing campaign to educate the public about his invention, complete with a timeless slogan, "You press the button, and we do the rest." It was an enormous success. In 1900, he followed up with the Brownie camera, which cost only $1.00 plus 15 cents for six exposures of film. Photography truly had gone mainstream.

Eastman's story contains many lessons about how new markets come about. They seldom blossom from nothing but rather can stew in a half-formed state for long periods until conditions become right. Customers may require time to become aware of new offerings and their benefits. The initial adopters in a new market may have preferences very distinct from the great bulk of potential customers. Technological advancements may have to intersect for solutions to work effectively and inexpensively enough for mass adoption. While technology can be an important trigger for new markets, success may require a complementary business model and network of firms that facilitate the industry taking root.[6] Once conditions do eventually align, growth can occur rapidly.

Lessons from new markets such as photography show how to find new markets through a disciplined process, as the remainder of this chapter explains.

Finding Latent Needs

How can companies spot markets that do not exist? The key is to focus not on the industry or what is being sold but rather on the underlying customer need. Of course, customers are always hounding companies for product improvements, and firms usually are quite aware of what their most important customers want. These are not the needs that give rise to new markets; they typically lead to extensions from what has come before, given that current customers are already partly satisfied by existing offerings. This is why they are already customers!

Instead, demand in new markets frequently comes from the latent, often unexpressed needs of customers who scarcely participate in the existing markets. This is what makes the markets new.

People were not knocking on Eastman's door demanding a camera for the masses—they probably did not know it was conceivable, nor did they imagine its benefits. As Henry Ford reputedly said of his industry, "If I had asked customers what they wanted, they would have said a faster horse." The fallacy in much "voice of the customer" research is that it can be rooted in the markets of today, asking current customers for ideas about improvements rather than identifying future customers and trying to intimately understand their world.[7]

Clayton Christensen has put forth a distinct way of understanding innate demand.[8] Rather than asking what potential customers want, firms need to find out what jobs these people are trying to get done in their lives. This approach focuses on "why," not "what." For example, consumers might not have said that they were in the market for a tiny automobile—particularly before the Mini was relaunched in 2001. However, they could talk about their need to express individuality, their desire for easy parking in urban areas, their wish to display consideration for the environment, and so on. Some of these jobs could be addressed in totally distinct ways, such as through the clothes people wear. Consumers were likely not asking for a car that was as tailored to their personalities as a piece of clothing. Once the product existed, though, the idea quickly clicked. More than half of early U.S. buyers custom ordered their Minis and waited three months for delivery.[9] Many Mini drivers were city residents who otherwise might not have owned a car. While rival carmakers were eking out sales by defining markets on product-oriented terms (midsized sedans and so forth), Mini sought individualists. Mini's follow-on products, such as the Countryman sport utility vehicle (SUV), are not particularly small but are still firmly targeted toward this individualist market. By defining potential customers in this unique way, Mini has avoided the price-based competition gutting much of the car market and has become a handsomely profitable brand.[10]

In contrast to Mini's experience, some firms are in markets where the jobs that people want to get done are quite functional in nature. The jobs of hospital nurses include taking down patient information, obtaining records from central files, consulting guidelines, and sharing data with physicians. Nurses did not often complain about long-standing methods of getting these jobs done—paper records, frequent trips to their ward's nursing station, and paging doctors. Panasonic, however, saw an opportunity. In 2008, the company introduced the Toughbook H1, the first "mobile clinical assistant," targeted at addressing these jobs in a completely different manner. The H1 allows stylus-based input of patient data, contains a high-resolution camera, and synchronizes data wirelessly. A strap on the back allows nurses to hold the device easily. It can be dropped from a height of six feet. Its batteries have a long life and are hot-swappable, enabling the device to be constantly on and never plugged in. One reviewer has called the device the "anti-iPad."[11] It is bulky, rugged, highly focused on one market, and six times as expensive as Apple's creation. For some nurses, it wins hands down because of its tight focus on their most important jobs to be done.

Through defining the jobs that target customers are trying to get done, companies can create detailed problem statements. As summarized in Table 2-1 and detailed below, these problem statements draw on a process quite distinct from the norms in established markets. Once firms have rigorously defined the problems to address, they can match the problems against typical triggers for market formation to understand whether the potential for a new market exists.

To start, first define the customer types you wish to target. Get granular. The customer segmentation you have today probably averages out a lot of variation in order to make the scheme simple. There will be a time later to create a succinct summary of customers you

Table 2-1 Moving from Product Definition to Problem Definition

Established Markets—Product Defintion	New Markets—Problem Definition
Market as product or service	Market as jobs that people are trying to get done
Current competitors	Current approaches and pain points
Benchmark against industry competitors	Benchmark full range of competing offerings and analogies
List of marketing requirements	List of performance criteria used to assess offerings
Define competitive differentiation	Define what prevents new solutions from being adopted
Determine target price	Determine value that can be created

wish to pursue, but beginning the process with an abstract customer segment can lead to abstract solutions—and who buys those? Create a detailed profile of a few customers that you really can understand in depth. The targeted customers, of course, should relate to strategic priorities, but you should not see them from your company's perspective. Rather, stand firmly in their shoes and see the world as they do. Now you are ready to understand their problems.

As laid out in Table 2-1, a good problem statement consists of at least six components:

1. What Jobs Are People Trying to Get Done?

This question is not as straightforward as it sounds because most people or institutions have a hard time being comprehensive in recounting what they are trying to get done. You cannot just ask them. If the target is a particular circumstance, such as nurses on the move, then it is best to observe these people in action so that you can understand their everyday inconveniences. By all means, ask for details around why they are doing something, but do not let these questions interfere with their workflow. It is also important to use running dialogue with the customer to capture what people are choosing not to do because it is too inconvenient.

Emotions can be hard to observe, so gently probe at psychological motivation. Make customers talk about their feelings proactively rather than leading the witness. Often an interview about emotional jobs succeeds best by taking an oblique tack, first prompting people to open up about themselves and then moving into specific topics related to the researcher's objectives. This approach ensures that people are not filtering their thoughts but rather speaking from the heart.

Some things cannot be observed, like the purchase of a mortgage or datacenter software. In these cases, disaggregate a purchase process into its many steps, using an in-depth interview or a diary kept during the process to probe in detail about what occurs at each step. Rather than having customers edit and organize their thoughts for the interviewer or having them talk about an average purchase occasion, explore a specific purchase decision. When examining a particular decision in detail, the narrative likely will take many twists and turns that involve unexpected influencers, waiting time, and complicated series of events. Capture these faithfully, perhaps using a simple process-flow diagram (see Figure 2-1 for an example). The messiness of many purchase decisions can lead to critical findings about hidden influencers and ways in which customers are silently frustrated.[12]

Focus groups can be extremely misleading when trying to probe for jobs to be done. People may edit themselves when speaking with others, focusing on functional aspects of their jobs over emotional aspects. Also, groups of six to eight people are too big for individuals to speak at length and in depth. Moreover, a jobs-based conversation can be extremely wide ranging, and it offers many possibilities for the group to go off on tangents that a moderator

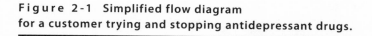

**Figure 2-1   Simplified flow diagram
for a customer trying and stopping antidepressant drugs.**

will have difficulty restricting lest he shut down discussion of a potentially fruitful topic.

Occasionally, small group discussions of two to three people can be well suited for probing jobs to be done. This is the case, for instance, when discussing social phenomena among peers, such as teenagers talking about text messaging or bad breath. The format is also useful when understanding a group decision, for example, having two influencers and a decision maker all in the room when speaking about how a company buys expensive equipment.

Customers' jobs often occur in hierarchies. A car owner, for instance, may care about the status of her vehicle. Probing further, we would find that she is concerned about status because her coworkers see what she is driving, as do her neighbors. The car owner cares about her coworkers' feelings because they rate her professional prospects that way, whereas her neighbors matter because she is jealous; she has the ugliest house on the block. By understanding this hierarchy, we can uncover hidden levers for innovation; for example, perhaps we could create a Web-based application the car owner can check at work to examine her car's performance (and show off to her coworkers).

As you capture information about the jobs that people are trying to get done, probe for what is really important. Customers may have reasonably similar jobs but view the importance of individual jobs quite distinctly. These differences will be a key factor in determining what market segments emerge from this process.

2. What Are the Current Approaches and What Pain Points Result?

Through scoping out the jobs that customers are trying to get done, you may have created a good catalogue of what people do today. Capture the details of those activities and their consequences—they can provide important clues about the pain points that new solutions can address. For example, the nurses targeted by the Toughbook H1 would be scurrying between the nurses' station and patient rooms dozens of times a day to retrieve information. How long did each of those walks take? What did that do to the nurse's productivity? What was the impact on the wait time of patients and physicians to see the nurse? Were certain tasks not done because the information was not immediately at hand? Were central hospital facilities such as radiology occasionally overwhelmed because nurses did not know about the length of the queue?

The list of pain points goes on. A large number of people need to communicate about patients and hospital activities, and it is not ideal to leave voicemails or wait for a physician to come by on his rounds. Records may be dispersed between the patient's room, the nurses' station, and central recordkeeping. Work occurs by the bedside but also in radiology, pathology, and other specialized locations throughout the hospital. As if coordinating all this information was not already challenging, some decisions need to be made fast. Lives literally can be at stake.

Sometimes this analysis can show that demand for a new solution might stem from unexpected sources. For instance, if tablet computers helped to better schedule doctors' rounds, expensive time could be saved. If the devices could smooth the flow of prescriptions to the hospital's pharmacy, the staff there could work more efficiently. Physicians and pharmacists may not use the devices but could be key stakeholders advocating for their adoption.

3. What Benchmarks Exist in the Full Range of Competing Offerings and Analogies?

It is a bad idea to start the analysis of latent needs by looking at competitors because they are probably focused on the market as it is today (which is why we view them as competitors). Benchmarking too early can put blinders on a project team; the concreteness of competitive offerings grabs attention more than a statement of jobs to be done and so orients thinking in that direction. Worse, looking at competitors before understanding the jobs landscape can lead teams to misdefine who the worthiest competitors might be. The car owner discussed above is being wooed not just by Jaguar and Lexus but also by Samsung and Gucci. She has many options in choosing how to project her status.

However, once you understand the jobs landscape, it is useful to evaluate all the competing offerings. Frequently, these will go well beyond classic industry definitions—Mercedes is competing with Samsung, Mini is competing with fashion, and the Toughbook H1 is vying with shoe leather. This is a critical point. *Customers may define competition very differently than vendors do.* Particularly in the case of new markets, a customer's choice is often not between vendors but between consumption of a new solution and sticking with the old approaches. Eastman's rival was not a photography firm but oil portraits and bicycles. Panasonic's rival is not so much Apple or Toshiba as walking and paper. Naturally, Panasonic still should compare its offering to the iPad and be prepared to sell against it, but it should understand that its real competitor in the marketplace is customer inertia.

When companies understand their true competition, they can position new offerings appropriately. Eastman knew this. His advertisements made no mention of other cameras or film makers. He emphasized Kodak's ease of use, knowing that photography might seem complex compared with other leisure activities like bicycling. He also understood that his lower-priced cameras, such as 1900's $1 Brownie, would make good gifts. The Brownie was marketed with the slogan "so simple they can easily be operated by any school boy or girl," and Kodak formed Brownie camera clubs that gave children prizes for good photos.[13]

During expansive benchmarking, firms may benefit from looking at how other firms in analogous industries or overseas markets approach similar jobs to be done. This endeavor can provide clues to underlying jobs that may have been missed in the first two steps of this process. For instance, retail banks might borrow some ideas from leading-edge goods retailers such as the U.S. grocery chain Whole Foods, which educates consumers about needs they may not have realized they had and creates an immersive experience totally distinct from the average supermarket. Life insurers in developed markets might learn from a niche player in South Africa called AllLife, which offers life insurance only to people who have HIV infection or diabetes—customers need to prove compliance with treatment regimens to continue qualifying for coverage. Consumer products firms might learn from Japan, where hundreds of new beverages are introduced each year. Some of these drinks may seem bizarre, but they can speak to latent demand. For example, Suntory recently launched Love Mode Ginger—a pink diet ginger ale with a label that unzips![14]

4. What Performance Criteria Do Customers Use?

Once you have fully mapped customers' jobs, their current approaches, and the full range of competitors, it is possible to list the performance criteria customers use in evaluating alternatives. The sequence of these steps is important—the jobs landscape is the baseline and then a scoping of what people do today and what are competitive solutions. Each of these items provides valuable input into understanding what are the true performance indicators. It is not only what people profess when you probe about their jobs, but it is also how they evaluate current and potential future offerings in practice.

Be comprehensive. A list of performance criteria can easily run into the dozens. For the Toughbook H1, the criteria will compare the device with existing alternatives (such as on ease of use and error-free data entry) and against direct rivals (such as on simplicity of data integration and portability). Under each of these headings, there may be further criteria; for example, portability is a function of weight, size, and design. It is ideal to understand what people want to minimize or maximize.[15] Sometimes this is not feasible; as in the case of mobile devices, designers live in a world of tradeoffs—they can make a device lighter, but it will have to be more expensive. In such circumstances, researchers should try to capture what are acceptable parameters; for example, the smaller the better, but it needs to fit into a shirt pocket.

Eventually, these criteria may translate into a traditional list of "marketing requirements" for engineers to fulfill, but too often this list is a logical leap by marketers into familiar territory from the poorly delineated world of how people actually assess new offerings. Rigorously captured performance criteria enable marketers and product developers to have a cogent discussion about the "why" of design, not just the "what." This is essential in reconceiving categories and making tough calls about what features to include and trade off.

An objection to this approach might be that it is too rational. Behavioral economists and psychological researchers have outlined the irrationality in how people make many decisions.[16] A list of performance criteria is appealingly logical, but sometimes it does not explain why people purchase the things they do. For instance, gambling is a giant industry built on irrational behavior.

For most businesses, the principles of behavioral economics only confuse matters. Nurses and hospitals can judge the Toughbook H1 on its merits, based on a reasonably clear list of criteria. The importance of individual criteria may vary between customer types, but the overall list will be quite consistent. This is good. This exercise is not one that will define the exact features that will go into the H1 versus its successor and which market segment should be emphasized by which product. An extensive quantitative survey can provide that input later. Up front, we simply need to scope out what the overall "medical clinical assistant" market might look like. We do not need to overcomplicate things.

5. What Prevents New Solutions from being Adopted?

If paper and shoe leather pose so many problems for hospital nurses, why do these solutions continue to dominate the market? The technology that brings computers to the nursing function is not all that complicated. Unfortunately, many obstacles stand in Panasonic's way.[17]

First, the H1 is most useful if the rest of the hospital is on a coordinated information technology (IT) system. If radiology cannot talk to the emergency room, and neither can communicate with obstetrics, then the hospital has some priorities that need to be worked through before it can consider bringing these devices to the nursing ward. Nurses would not be able to access much of the information they need and so would be awkwardly forcing together paper and H1. This could be worse than the status quo because people in a hurry may not know where to look for key patient data.

Another concern is the security of the hospital's wireless infrastructure. Government regulations require close guarding of patient data for privacy reasons. While hospitals do run encrypted wireless networks, purchasers would want to ensure that the system is completely bulletproof. They may receive little credit for improving nurses' productivity with the H1 but much blame if something goes wrong.

The hospital also might be concerned about the possibility of spreading infections by transporting a device from bedside to bedside. Never mind that a nurse's clothes and shoes also move from bedside to bedside—these are the sorts of objections that people can raise during the purchasing process. In fact, a Panasonic promotional video shows the H1 being wiped down with alcohol between each patient encounter.

Who will train the nurses on how to use these devices? While the H1 is designed to be intuitive, a hospital cannot afford for nurses to make mistakes with data entry or interpretation. Panasonic or its partners will need to have training personnel dedicated to ensuring that the devices are used properly. The H1 ultimately should save nurses' time, but initially there will be a productivity decrease as the nurses learn to use it.

A further challenge is the sales channel. Who is going to sell this device to the hospital? Vendors of computer equipment are not accustomed to making their case to nurses, nor to talking about how an overall change in staff workflows will improve patient care. Software firms are not used to selling physical devices, nor do they tend to deal with issues such as servicing a broken unit.

Cost is also a significant issue. The H1 sells for over $3,000. While hospitals are big businesses, they tend to work on very thin profit margins. Many are nonprofit enterprises. There is not a lot of excess cash socked away for discretionary purchases. Even if the H1 promises substantial savings because of better staff productivity, those benefits are largely theoretical until they occur. Whose budget will this purchase come from? What will the hospital have to give up in exchange for buying these devices?

All these objections might be raised for a device that is purchased largely on functional rather than emotional criteria and that really makes a great deal of sense to buy. Other new markets have to travel a much rockier path to win their first customers.

6. What Value Would Success Create for Customers?

Through understanding customers' jobs and current activities, the full set of competitors, performance criteria, and what impedes consumption, you should have a good view of what value new solutions might generate. The economic value created by success on functional criteria can be quantified, such as through time and labor savings and reduced use of other products. Emotional value also can be estimated through understanding how competitive solutions are priced—how much would someone have to spend on new suits to equal the status bump acquired by driving a Mercedes to work? Of course, there may be a great margin for error in these estimates, and the figures may differ considerably from customer to customer. The point is that you can establish a general range of value that firms can create.

With those numbers, you can better picture what sorts of new markets are feasible. If $20,000 is at stake for customers, there are many more degrees of freedom than if the potential value is substantially less. For example, a health insurer might save $20,000 by preventing a hospitalization because of an exacerbation of emphysema. For severe sufferers of this disease, it may make sense to give patients relatively costly home monitoring equipment to reduce the chances of such an event occurring. For other patients who are less at risk of hospitalization, the economic value associated with improving the condition is the savings from a patient taking an older drug versus a new one that costs $200 more. There may be far greater numbers of these people, but if home monitoring costs $200 per patient, it is not going to save the insurer any money. For these patients, a new market of home monitoring equipment is not in the cards, but possibly the insurer could provide an Internet-based program that asks patients to provide daily input on their breathing difficulty, amount of exercise, and other important factors.[18]

This is not to say that a company should determine prices at such an early stage. We have not even defined what is being sold! Moreover, it can be useful to retain flexibility in pricing during a market's early stages. Early customers will reveal a lot about the value inherent in a solution.

After determining the value at stake, the company is ready to create a full jobs profile of the target customer. The profile should note questions that this process has generated so that subsequent research can focus narrowly on those issues. A simplified form of such a profile is shown in Table 2-2.

Defining Target Customers

The great virtue of this approach to finding latent needs is that it takes a very expansive view of a potential marketplace yet ends up with highly detailed portraits of where opportunity lies. The challenge is that the analysis can become unwieldy unless it is focused. Customer types and their needs can be diffuse.

Firms need to focus their lens twice during this process. Starting off, they need to choose whom they will assess. The target customer has to be linked to the company's overall strategy—pursuing the moderately poor, rural consumer in India, for example. A company can arrive at that target through traditional methods such as estimating

Table 2-2 Simplified Jobs Profile for Target Nurse

Profile Element	Target Nurse	Outstanding Questions
Jobs	Take down patient information Obtain records from central files Consult guidelines Share data with physicians	How important is accessing images? How much are these jobs standardized between nurses, patients, and hospital types?
Approaches and pain points	Paper records Paging Nurses' station	How much are pain points recognized? How broadly?
Competition	Shoe leather Awkward work-arounds iPad	Do people recognize the dangers of work-arounds? Who is adopting the iPad?
Criteria	Fast Easy	Must we be faster or equal to existing systems? What training period is permissible?
Obstacles	Risk Channel Decision-making process	What customer types present the fewest obstacles?
Value	>$3,000	How much does this value range? Can we differentiate pricing via service contracts?

purchasing power, market growth, competitive intensity, and so forth. Importantly, it should be wary of focusing on its current big customers because these people are more likely to be already somewhat well served by existing offerings. As Clayton Christensen has profiled in great depth,[19] the best source of growth may be people who are underconsuming or are nonconsumers altogether. Few firms may be targeting those people, leaving room for a company to grow in ways that are asymmetrical to its usual competition.

After the company has profiled latent needs in this customer group, it needs to focus again. The detailed picture likely will show that customers who once seemed similar can vary greatly in their job profiles. The challenge then is to group customers by those profiles. Occasionally, statisticians will run sophisticated analyses to establish clusters of customers who may be distinguished by half a dozen characteristics each, summarized by catchy names such as "Hopeless Harry" and "Studious Sally." It seems wonderfully scientific, but the result can be too complex to act on. Marketers need to strike a balance between subtlety and simplicity that suits their firm. However, it is useful to anchor even the most complex segmentation schemes in a handful of distinguishing jobs so that the framework can be used rapidly in the course of everyday work.

Triggers for Market Development

Sometimes a scan of latent needs using a process such as the one outlined in the previous section will identify markets waiting to be formed. For example, the Colgate Wisp is a single-use toothbrush meant to be used without water. A breath-freshening bead is embedded in a small, very lightweight brush. At nearly 50 cents per use, the Wisp is an extremely expensive device. Yet just a year after its 2009 launch, it claims nearly 5 percent of the U.S. toothbrush market,[20] bringing in more than $100 million in annual sales.[21] One might have thought that needs for toothbrushes were well satisfied. After all, the Chinese invented the first bristle toothbrush in 1498.[22] The Wisp does not use any fundamentally new technology. Colgate recognized a latent need—for fast, basic cleaning and freshening on the go—and intelligently created a solution.

In other cases, a number of factors need to converge to make a market possible. This was Eastman's experience and luck. Chemistry, mass production, leisure time, catalogue retailing, and a handful of other elements combined to make the 1880s an ideal time to create the Kodak camera.

The precursors for any market will depend greatly on the idiosyncrasies of that industry. Generally, there are six categories to monitor, which are quite distinct from the factors to monitor in established markets (see Table 2-3):

Table 2-3 Monitoring New Factors for New Markets

Established Markets—Shifting Power	New Markets—Shifting Demand
Competitor intellectual property and patents	Emerging platform technologies
New sales channels	New business systems
Changing pricing	Changing customer capabilities
Changing market share	Changing customer behavior
Changing sales channel margins	Changing business partner incentives
Regulations' downside	Regulations' upside

1. Platform Technology

Given the accelerating rate of technological advancement,[23] platforms are constantly emerging to enable new markets. These platforms can build on each other to create expanding frontiers of potential. For instance, the integrated circuit made the cell phone possible. Integrated circuits gradually took on more computing functions until they became microprocessors. As microprocessors gained increasing power, and cellular standards made fast transmission speeds feasible, the smartphone was born. As smartphone operating systems such as Google's Android took root, software developers could develop hundreds of thousands of applications for these machines. As these applications enable smartphone users to interact in new ways, still more new markets will bloom. As shown in Figure 2-2, new platforms build on previous ones, and they also enable a cascade of future platforms and associated new markets. The number of new markets keeps expanding as a result.

The technologies enabling new markets need not be platforms with multiple uses, but they frequently are. Technologies are seldom invented for just one application. If that happens, it is usually because a big, existing market proves that there will be a good return on investment for creating the technology. Gillette patented a near-nanoscale coating process[24] for steel blades to make the Fusion razor because it knew the product would be a massive hit. The uncertainties surrounding new markets tend not to inspire such large bets.

The multiuser nature of platform technology does have downsides. For instance, new standards can be less uniform than they might appear. Because companies have not yet built new products on these standards, people may not have thought through exactly how they will be implemented. When Wireless Application Protocol (WAP) first appeared in 2000, mobile Internet pages would function differently depending on whether the handset was from Nokia, Motorola, Sie-

Figure 2-2 Platforms beget platforms.

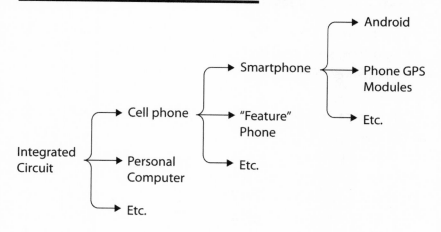

mens, or other manufacturers. No one really knew why. This was one reason why early users were disappointed by WAP applications, giving the new industry a poor reputation while it was just getting started.[25]

Platforms also may bring vulnerabilities, technical or otherwise. While these can hinder take-up of the platforms, they also lead to more opportunities for market creation. Microsoft's operating system facilitated the fast expansion of the PC market, but the uniformity of computers also made it far easier to spread viruses and hack into systems. Antivirus software developed in response. Credit cards generated greater consumer debt, leading, in turn, to credit counseling services.

A final issue with platform technologies is that they are usually available to competing firms. Companies can overrate this danger. It is unusual for two companies to be eyeing the same technology to create the same market through the same approaches.

Occasionally, firms can focus overly on new platform technologies when declaring the birth of a new market. While they are critical triggers, platforms often must be complemented by some of the other factors explored below to generate rapid market growth.

2. New Business Systems

George Eastman was a skilled amateur chemist, but his invention of celluloid film was not sufficient to make photography mainstream. Consumers were worried about how to handle the film—the original Kodak camera, while relatively inexpensive, still cost consumers over $5 in today's money to develop a single exposure. Eastman's coup was inventing a business system in which consumers never had to touch the film. The camera was sent back to Rochester for the film to be removed, developed, and reloaded. Eastman also depended on the mass marketing enabled by the rapid growth of newspaper and periodical publishing during this time; the business model of a relatively cheap camera sent to Rochester for developing may not have provided local dealers with big motivations to create the market on their own.

Sometimes these systems can arise in unexpected places. SunPower Afrique, in West Africa's Togo, is a modern example. Confronting the challenge of financing solar panels and ensuring appropriate installation in a desperately impoverished country, this organization has opted to target microfinance institutions (MFIs). MFIs can lack reliable power at their facilities, creating innumerable problems such as preventing them from running accounting software consistently. SunPower Afrique is providing panels to these institutions and then is leveraging them to provide loans to finance panels for their client businesses. MFIs are also partnering with the organization to educate customers about solar power and provide training for installers. [26]

3. Changing Customer Capabilities

Almost 11 percent of the world's population, or 740 million people, live in India's countryside. Collectively, they spend about $148 billion on consumable products each year, including both food and nonfood items such as clothing. Their per-capita consumption is growing at about 2.2 percent per year. While this translates into a little over $16 per person per month, the sums add up to significant amounts. In urban India, it is a different picture. There, 420 million people—a mere 6 percent of the people in the world—spend $160 billion per year—almost $32 per person per month. Moreover, consumer spending in urban India is growing by 5.4 percent per annum.[27] These are already large markets, and they are quickly getting bigger.

As Indian consumers grow wealthier, new markets form. Nokia understands this well. With 60 percent of the Indian mobile phone market,[28] the company sells over $3 billion of handsets annually.[29] India is Nokia's second-largest market, behind only China. The country is adding 10 million new cell phone connections every month, and Nokia is competing for them aggressively. For people unable to afford a basic handset, it has created a microfinance scheme where it will sell a phone for 25 weekly installments of $2. When Nokia wins new customers, it is in a good position to offer accessories and value-added services such as providing alerts about changing market prices for seeds and fertilizer.[30] New markets beget new markets.

Wealth is one sort of changing customer capability, and its effects are making developing nations a compelling source of new markets.[31] However there are also many other capability types. For instance, customers may begin to better understand a category; it is hard to convince people of the value of text message alerts about agricultural prices if they have never used a cell phone. Alternatively, they may have acquired a platform like a household refrigerator that enables them to consume new products. New sales channels also may make it far easier for customers to become acquainted with and consume a product (channels are the focus of Chapter 5).

Changing capabilities also have an impact on business-to-business (B2B) transactions. Two decades ago, some banks in emerging markets experimented with using retail stores as points to collect and disburse cash. Unfortunately, fraud could be rampant, and many banks halted this strategy. The emergence of smartcards and wireless payment processing devices now has changed the environment. A bank such as Brazil's Bradesco can vastly extend its reach into poor *favela* townships, Amazonian villages, and far-flung provinces. Technology helps to prevent fraud, and retailers are leaping at the chance to earn fees on banking transactions.

4. Changing Customer Behaviors

One of the most difficult market triggers to scout for is a change in customer behavior. The challenge lies not in finding new behaviors— they can be readily observed—but in resisting the urge to proclaim optimistically that the tipping point is at hand. Behavior change takes a while, and it is hard to rush.

In 2000, the first mobile "friend finder" services were launched.[32] These applications allowed people in a social network to find the current physical locations of their friends and to broadcast their own locations. While the whole idea seemed appalling to many adults, teenagers and university students responded enthusiastically. Mobile networks such as Vodafone loved the concept. Location finding was imprecise because handsets did not contain GPS technology at the time, and the services were accessed via text message or WAP rather than slick Web pages on phone screens. But the systems basically worked.

These services won many industry awards yet few customers. They were just too early (a topic to be explored in Chapter 3). Before people would feel comfortable using friend finders, they had to get accustomed to using mobile services in general. The first popular mobile services were weather reports, horoscopes, and other simple extensions of things people viewed in other contexts.[33] People also needed to become comfortable with how their handsets enabled location tracking, such as through using mapping applications—again, an extension of preexisting behavior. Moreover, they needed to form online social networks. In hindsight, customers needed more impetus to create these networks than the promise of finding their friends barhopping one hazy night.

Today, friend-finder services like Foursquare have become quite popular. Foursquare was established only in 2009 and within one year was declining takeover offers of $125 million.[34] It seems like the market was just waiting to be created. However, the founders of Foursquare started a similar service, called Dodgeball, back in 2000. In 2005, they sold the business to Google, which shut it down four years later. The founders' timing was off in 2000, but it was ideal the second time around.

5. Changing Business Partner Incentives

Sometimes the incentives within an industry's ecosystem of firms can change to make companies more receptive to buying a new category of products. For example, doctors have long had the ability to buy health-care IT systems that computerize their medical records and enable them to download data from other physicians and even patients' home monitoring equipment. These systems have the potential to improve care, make medical practice more efficient, and save money by helping to avoid duplicative testing and unnecessary referrals to specialists. Yet the U.S. market has emerged slowly. Practices have to invest sizable sums for these systems and take substantial time to train staff, only for some of the cost savings to accrue to health insurers.

Recently, the market has changed. Medicare—by far the nation's largest health insurer—will now pay physicians bonuses if they meaningfully use electronic records in their practices. Private health insurers are starting to pay doctors for achieving certain quality metrics, such as reduction of patients' blood pressure or blood sugar levels, giving physicians new reasons to download data from home monitoring devices. For doctors, investment in health-care IT is now looking a lot more attractive. As a result, this industry is expected to grow at over 10 percent per annum for the next several years.[35]

6. Changing Regulations

Coal is one of the dirtiest forms of energy, but it is far and away the leading source of global electricity consumption. Fully 41 percent of the world's electric power comes from coal.[36] In the United States alone, coal is responsible for generating 1.5 billion tons of CO_2 per year.[37] As the costs of climate change become clearer, demand is growing for regulations that will lead to coal-fired power plants capturing more of the carbon they produce.

The market for carbon capture and storage (CCS) is now in its infancy. However, the Norwegian energy giant Statoil[38] has captured 10 million tons of CO_2 from North Sea gas fields since 1996.[39] The motivation for its efforts was not purely environmental—the firm needed to remove unusually high levels of CO_2 from this natural gas so that the gas could burn properly. With the right price applied to carbon emissions, initiatives like these could multiply, and the industry could become huge. One group of researchers from the Massachusetts Institute of Technology has estimated that the CCS industry could be worth $30 per ton of carbon sequestered, a potentially enormous number.[40]

Regulations can change quickly and affect the fortunes of new markets overnight. While lobbyists sometimes focus on the costs of regulations to existing businesses, this money can go into the coffers of firms prepared to lead the newly formed markets that result due to these changes. This point is not lost on Statoil, which is investing to become the world leader in the nascent CCS industry.[41]

New markets can seem to spring up fast, but close observers can spot the foundations of growth well in advance. By creating detailed portraits of latent need in the marketplace, focusing on a handful of early target customers, and scanning for typical triggers of market creation, firms can put themselves ahead of the curve. They can then assess these markets carefully, a subject that is the focus of Chapter 3.

Summary

- Companies can spot new markets through carefully mapping latent needs and scanning for triggers of market formation. This can be a disciplined process.

- George Eastman's experience with popularizing photography shows how several trends can converge at one time to suddenly enable a market to blossom. There are patterns to what must come together to fuel industry growth.

- Latent needs are found through creating precise problem statements for target customers. Often customers cannot articulate these needs themselves, but appropriate techniques can elicit a fine-grained view of where opportunity lies. A six-step process, followed in sequence, allows firms to obtained detailed portraits of hidden demand.

- Triggers for market formation can vary considerably by industry. However, there are generally six factors to evaluate. Observers can focus overly on one of these factors, new technology platforms, but other elements frequently are critical as well.

Chapter | 3

ASSESSING WHAT DOESN'T EXIST

How can you evaluate something that does not exist? Borrowing techniques used in established markets is often folly. Past trends cannot be extrapolated, growth estimates are wild guesses, and competitors are unknown. Additionally, potential customers may think new business ideas to be a bit weird. Like the movie characters Austin Powers and Dr. Evil, who emerged 30 years into the future, we should recognize the initial oddity of so many things that people now take for granted, such as microwave ovens, automatic teller machines (ATMs), and lasers. I attended early concept tests of DVDs and flat-screen televisions—customers showed scant interest.[1]

While some firms can move fast to launch experiments in a market, others require more intensive cost-benefit assessment. This is most true when the investment must be front-loaded, such as when cellular networks bid for spectrum licenses or life sciences companies investigate new therapies.

This chapter examines how to perform detailed assessments of new markets.[2] In it you will learn

- How the publishing company Pearson found a new market and went about assessing it
- How to gauge a new market's potential value
- Which factors to assess in judging how fast a market can grow
- What indicates whether a market is ready to take off soon
- How to assess competitive advantage when competitors are unknown
- What are the common pitfalls in new market evaluations

Pearson Assesses a New Market

London-based Pearson PLC is a publishing juggernaut. The company may be best known for producing *The Economist*, the *Financial Times* newspaper, and Penguin books; however, fully 62 percent of its revenues come from educational publishing. Pearson is a leading vendor in the kindergarten to grade 12 textbook market with imprints such as Scott Foresman, Prentice-Hall, and Addison-Wesley. The business generated revenues of over $5 billion in 2009 and is growing smartly at 22 percent per annum.[3]

Many firms in Pearson's position would focus narrowly on this attractive sector. The company has developed unique skills to serve this market, employing hundreds of former teachers and selling to thousands of school systems. Yet, fittingly for a firm whose roots are over 150 years old,[4] Pearson has taken a long view about how the market is changing and what the company should do to prepare for the future.

Textbook publishing is on the cusp of upheaval. A great deal of educational research[5] has shown that students vary considerably in their learning styles, and the old one-size-fits-all method of teaching is starting to be supplanted by customized approaches. Textbook publishing is following suit, creating online modules paired with book sections to make learning more configurable and interactive. Simultaneously, school systems are placing heavier emphasis on student assessment, and the trend toward more personalized content must be coupled with appropriately tailored approaches to testing.

While these changes are exciting, Pearson recognizes that they are occurring in a deeply troubled environment. In the United States, 30 percent of students entering ninth grade do not finish high school, and 82 percent of ninth graders will not go on to finish college within 6 years of postsecondary education. Efforts to supplement basic high school education tend to be bimodal. Guidance counselors, funded by school systems, focus on the most troubled students. Tutoring services such as Sylvan or Kaplan, funded by parents, tend to concentrate on high achievers. The great mass of students flows through a poorly performing educational system with little intervention.

In this context, Pearson's CEO, Marjorie Scardino, created an incubator for new businesses serving the education market. To lead the unit, she tapped educational entrepreneur Patrick Supanc, who had spent several years helping to build an education-related startup called Blackboard.com and more recently led Pearson Education's product management.

Supanc saw all the signs of latent need, particularly among B- and C-grade students who do not make it from ninth grade through to college graduation. He looked at how this market was currently served and came to some important realizations:

The industry is in silos, organized around traditional ways of working with the customer in a given point of time. The educational experience for a student is much more a continuum; they don't see it as content, data, and assessment. If we're to transition to an outcomes-oriented business, we have to start with the learner and think about how to build services around that learner.

Supanc's team decided to focus on the critical points where a comprehensive, integrated service could make a significant difference. The development of markets overseas stimulated thinking:

In India and China, the limitations of the public system are more obvious and acute, and there is a flourishing market that almost serves as a second parallel education system. You get tutoring whether you are an A+ or a C student. In the U.S., tutoring at a place like Sylvan can cost $3,000 a semester. This seemed like an interesting nonconsumption opportunity.[6]

Based on this analysis, Supanc formed a series of problem statements, such as, "How do we help eighth grade girls who like math to decide what should be next for them?" The team developed a series of still-confidential (as of this writing) concepts to address these needs. But how could they assess this nonexistent market? Supanc says:

We did some of the traditional things, such as talk to a lot of people, survey parents, and collect quantitative data. With 24 million middle and high school students in the United States, we knew we needed to slice that down to get to a more addressable market. So we got a sense of the demand curve and characteristics around certain populations. We also tested the strength of existing brands in personalized education, guidance, and support, and we confirmed that the brands just aren't there.

This research had its value, but the traditional approaches did not provide enough pertinent information about Pearson's concepts. According to Supanc:

> I felt like we weren't getting enough data. We were getting point-in-time feedback instead of ongoing feedback and true interaction with the concepts. We were getting false user behavior. So over a few months we launched several applications in a stealth fashion, driving users through low-cost social media tactics like advertising on Facebook. This was much more cost-effective than traditional market research. It tested our underlying assumptions around the core value proposition, pricing, customer acquisition, initial registrations, and actual student participation. We had to be creative in how we built these experiments. For example, to see how good students are at math, it would be great to do a 20- to 40-minute assessment, but students won't do this. So we brought together math testing and games that students could complete in 2 to 3 minutes.
>
> We were surprised by many things. For instance, we thought that the most interested students would be from higher income suburban families. That wasn't true; there was broad interest across socioeconomic, geographic, and ethnic groups. This was encouraging, because current tutoring and test prep services are driven by referrals, and we wanted to think about product design and marketing strategy in a way that would create referrals within social groups.

Pearson's approach to the opportunity was inexpensive, fast, and impactful. This chapter details how firms can do as Pearson did—using a small number of approaches suited to their circumstances to assess what does not yet exist.

Gauging a Market's Value

To get to the stage of detailed assessment, a new market should seem significant. It may provide either a modest value to a large number of customers (social networks) or a large value to a modest number of customers (biotech drugs). Ideally, it will do both.

To determine the number of target customers, the value created by a new offering, and the extent to which a firm can capture that value, companies should take traditional approaches as far as they can. For instance, the medical device manufacturer Becton, Dickinson and Company (BD) was able to estimate the potential market for health-care worker safety at over $500 million based on the number of workers using needles as well as the cost and consequences of infection through accidental needle sticks. This estimate helped to justify a hugely successful product-development program to make the company the new market's leader.[7]

As in Pearson's case, market data may only go so far; quantitative information might give a sense of the total addressable market—24 million students—but fail to provide an accurate sense of whom to target within that population, how enthusiastically they will react to a concept, and how much value a new solution could create. To achieve these latter objectives, firms can undertake a fast set of actions distinct from how they would assess established markets (see Table 3-1).

Table 3-1 Valuing the Unknown

Established Markets—Extrapolating from Data	New Markets—Modeling Demand, Scenarios, and Risks
Project market size	Gauge interest level via use of prototyping, customer conversations, and social media
Determine feasible price	Establish what value is at stake
Estimate likely share	Plot scenarios for market evolution
Create financials focused on projections	Create financials focused on assumptions

Prototyping

Pearson shows the potential of a quick-and-dirty approach to trialing services. Nothing gives truer results about market potential than actually trying to sell something. Campbell Soup also takes this approach, setting up "lemonade stands" in groceries to see if customers are interested in new products. Best Buy puts up card tables in their stores to try out new service propositions, taking a scientific approach through assessing a very small number of variables at any one time, paired with a "control group" store that caters to similar buyers.

Of course, prototyping is easiest when firms can quickly create small batches of products or services. The barrier can seem higher in industries such as high tech and health care, where investment needs or regulations prevent early sales of a new offering. Yet, even in these fields, scrappy prototypes are possible. Soon after he cofounded Palm Computing, Jeff Hawkins shaped a block of wood to fit into his shirt pocket (the target size for the device), and he took it out whenever he felt a need to check or record contact details, appointments, or notes. He carried it for months. This simple "prototype" proved to him that many users would be happy with a small, simple device that did a handful of things extremely well.[8]

Early Customer Conversations

Keeping in mind the points in Chapter 2 that customers cannot necessarily tell you what they want and that customers in new markets may be distinct from those in existing industries, people still can react to concepts and prototypes. In the cell phone business, for instance, suppliers frequently share their product road maps with carriers to gain early reactions. Taiwan's HTC shared two versions of its Droid Incredible handset with Verizon Wireless, gaining fast feedback and then doubling down on the winning device.[9] Services can be mocked up into storyboards or even can be replicated in empty warehouses, creating opportunities to shadow customers through experiences.[10]

The challenge lies in having productive conversations around concepts that are so novel that they seem a bit strange. In these situations, it is critical to mimic actual usage as much as possible. For example, Israel's InterCure makes a device called Resperate that plays musical tones matched to a person's rate of breathing, as measured by a strap that goes around the chest. The device first gauges the person's breathing rate and then slowly alters the tones to coach the person into slowing his or her breaths. The drops can be dramatic, from 20 breaths per minute to less than 10. Through reducing breathing rates, the device can lower blood pressure by as much as some medications. In focus groups, potential customers thought the idea to be pretty far out there. After 2 weeks at home trying the device, though, many became fanatically loyal and offered very specific feedback about the design and experience. This sort of reaction convinced the company that it could create the market via direct-response ads in newspapers featuring a money-back guarantee.

Social Media

Pearson used social media advertising to good effect, and sites such as Facebook and LinkedIn can offer excellent ways of finding micro-targeted customer groups at a modest cost. As Pearson demonstrated, the full service does not need to be live to get basic feedback from these groups.

Ambitious marketers may seek to get direct customer involvement in product design through these sites. For example, Pepsi's Mountain Dew brand recently completed a program called "DEWmocracy" that encouraged people to provide specific feedback on concepts and to vote for their favorite new flavor. The champion was called White

Out, a clear soda with a neutral taste.[11] Its adherents liked the concept because it was so distinct from the current lineup.

Undoubtedly, Pepsi generated customer loyalty through this program and primed demand for early sales. However, this tactic may work best in exactly these sorts of situations—where customer groups already exist, are highly brand-loyal, and care enough about a brand to get involved in an online program. In other words, they may be a poor fit for new markets unless a nonconsuming customer group can be minutely targeted and will quickly understand the proposed offering. Even in those circumstances, it may be more useful to engage customers in live, interactive conversations that can probe ideas deeply and avoid peer pressure based on rushed judgments reached online. Social media may offer a way to recruit those target customers, such as through following social tags and bookmarks.[12]

Value Creation

Air Liquide, based near Paris, is a nearly $15 billion leader in the supply of industrial gases that has provided industry with molecules such as oxygen and nitrogen since 1902. It specializes in cryogenically stored gases, offering the molecules, cryogenic tanks, and trucking fleet needed to supply gases reliably in a vast array of applications ranging from semiconductor manufacturing to mining.

While Air Liquide customers typically are concerned with gases that are at least 99.99 percent pure, the company wondered what new markets could exist for less pure gases. New technology from DuPont enabled the creation of gas-separation membranes that could extract nitrogen and oxygen from air at a typical purity of 98 percent. Not only could this process be much cheaper than providing liquefied gases, which must be frozen to unfathomably cold temperatures, but it also could eliminate the need for large and heavy cryogenic tanks.

Given the lower price and smaller physical footprint of the technology, Air Liquide reasoned that the market potential was substantial.

Working in partnership with DuPont, the company leveraged its salesforce's connections to have conversations in a huge range of industries, from manufacturers of aircraft fuel tanks to makers of beer keg taps. One large potential customer it uncovered was the food-transportation industry. With produce worth billions of dollars spoiling annually, Air Liquide found a way to mount the gas-separation membranes on trucks so that, for example, apples could be transported in an inert atmosphere of nitrogen instead of in regular air. The company could calculate the value of extended shelf life and price its technology at a level that made sense for this new market.[13]

Scenario Planning

When there are substantial regulatory, competitive, and technical uncertainties, the value of a new market may swing hugely depending on a host of factors outside a company's control. In these circumstances, firms can create discrete scenarios about how events might transpire, leading to a clear view of markets' value and the company's strategic position in those settings. Scenario planners usually have to make a number of simplifying assumptions about how events will bundle together in order for there to be a comprehensible number of scenarios to assess.

Sweden's Ericsson AB, the world's leading producer of cellular telecom infrastructure, put this methodology to work in envisioning how its industry might look in 2020. It started with certainties and then layered on uncertain factors, evaluating how those unknowns were interdependent. Then it created a range of scenarios, including one in which telecom carriers become "dumb pipe" utilities and one where the world has 50 billion connected devices ranging from cell phones to machine sensors. The firm thought through implications for devices, applications, and the company's carrier customers.[14] Scenario planning like this can occur for a broad industry, as in Ericsson's case, or more narrowly regarding the evolution of a targeted market.

Focusing on Assumptions, Not Projections

It is astonishing that many executive meetings to discuss new markets presume the same degree of certainty as management has in existing markets. The executives will ask for pro forma projections going 10 and sometimes 20 years out. Then they may look at the net present value (NPV) of the projections compared with the NPV of a totally dissimilar and better understood market to decide whether the opportunity merits investment.

This is madness. Executives usually understand that the new market is inherently uncertain. However, rather than focus their analysis on the major risks, they instead may raise the discount rate for future profits, providing less weight to income further out in the future. Because new markets tend to have most of their potential a few years out—they are new!—this approach leads to these opportunities looking especially unattractive. Worse, it focuses management attention on an NPV figure that is certain to be fiction. It buries the impact of critical assumptions within complex financial models, turning the emphasis of the discussion away from what is truly important.[15]

I have firsthand experience with this. In January 2004, I was asked by Celtel BV—a Netherlands-based firm that was one of Africa's largest cellular carriers and is now owned by India's Bharti—to evaluate whether it should build a network in Liberia. The country had emerged from civil war just four months previously, but Celtel had a history of building hugely successful enterprises in countries where other investors feared to tread. A Liberian entrepreneur had purchased a license to a large amount of cellular spectrum (exclusive use of spectrum is absolutely essential for a cellular network to function) and was offering to make us business partners in challenging the current carrier's highly profitable monopoly.

Liberia was difficult to assess. We did not know how many people were still in the country. We had no recent economic data. What I had thought initially was a pleasant atrium in the telecom ministry was the result of a shell exploding in the building. The telecom minister had no telephone service.

Celtel had certain thresholds that it asked new networks to meet. Rather than estimate an exact NPV for this venture, I looked at what we would need to do to hit those numbers. I started with the level of investment, which was reasonably straightforward to estimate based on the number of cellular towers we would need to erect in major population centers and what we typically spent for a new network on information technology, sales, and administration. Then I looked at what revenues would be necessary to hit revenue, NPV, and other financial targets. I assessed the few factors that would really drive those figures, such as the number of potential competitors and the extent of cell phone penetration into the population, which was one of the world's poorest.

As a result, the discussion focused on the most important factors rather than on fictional estimates. In the end, we passed on the opportunity because of a risk that I had not modeled: The ministry had sold the same bloc of spectrum to at least four different companies![16]

Signs That an Industry Can Quickly Grow

Why is it that some great ideas take forever to take root, whereas others flourish fast? What lessons do these patterns of struggle and success hold for new markets today?[17]

Several great innovations took exceedingly long to become popular. The Indus Valley cities of Harappa and Mohenjo-daro, located in present-day Pakistan, contained the world's first known flushing toilets some 4500 years ago.[18] A king of China's Western Han dynasty (which ended in 24 AD) placed one in his palace as well.[19] Britain's Queen Elizabeth I had one installed at Richmond Palace.[20] Yet this exceptionally good idea did not take off in earnest until the middle of the nineteenth century.[21] In another vein, the first American sushi restaurant appeared in 1966,[22] but it took decades for the cuisine to become popular. Similarly, prior to wildly successful Internet services that enable subscribers to listen to music through their computers, there was Tel-musici. The firm offered subscribers the ability to listen to music on demand through their telephone wires, which were attached to special speakers that could be used for the occasion. This was in 1909.[23]

Of course, many other innovations have caught fire fast. Radio, energy drinks, and the bicycle[24] each become popular within five years. Eight factors explain the difference (see Figure 3-1). Lacking any of these variables can be enough to retard a market. In combination, their absence can be devastating.

1. Physical Infrastructure

If an innovation relies on others laying the groundwork, a firm might wait a long time for change to happen. This was literally the case

Figure 3-1   Eight drivers of fast market growth.

Few Dependencies	Relative Advantage	Low Perceived Risk
1. Physical Infrastructure	4. Need & Performance	6. Speedy Sales & Use
2. Business Infrastructure	5. Little Behavior Change	7. Low Switching Cost
3. Few Decision Makers		8. Low Cost of Failure

with indoor plumbing, which is scalable only if there is a water supply system. Perhaps domestic servants could have brought well water to each toilet, but it would be a labor-intensive chore involving things that the upper classes did not like to discuss. Families also would need to design their new houses for indoor plumbing from the ground up, and prior to the nineteenth century, new housing stock for the wealthy was not built very frequently—social immobility kept the same wealthy families in the same places for long periods. The industrial revolution started to change things. Mobility increased, and densely packed cities demanded infrastructure such as water being pumped to neighborhoods.

By contrast, in the 1920s, it was easy to set up an amateur radio station, and receivers needed no infrastructure except the ubiquitous electrical socket. There was no dependency on new infrastructure, only on the growth of transmitters and receivers that were inexpensive, fast to install, relatively simple to operate, and fun.

2. Business Infrastructure

Groundwork can be economic as well as physical. Sushi needed no building projects, but it did require (at least initially) a restaurant with highly trained sushi masters, almost all of them Japanese. It also needed an adequate supply of appropriate fresh fish. Local demand for the food and the supply of both sushi masters and fish were sufficient in Los Angeles' Little Tokyo for the first sushi restaurants to emerge in the 1960s, but the situation was quite different in most of the United States. Energy drinks faced no such obstacles. Nightclubs—the first foothold for these drinks—exist everywhere, and they were motivated to sell high-priced mixers that kept people dancing longer. Groceries and convenience stores also liked the small physical footprint and high margins of these drinks.

3. Few Decision Makers

World War II U.S. Rear Admiral Robert Copeland once said, "To get something done, a committee should consist of no more than three people, two of whom are absent." Alas, indoor plumbing required an army of decision makers to agree on a need and a solution. Urban planners, architects, builders, and families all had to align. Trying to coordinate diffuse decision makers is very difficult. In a modern context, when makers of intriguing energy-efficient technologies target automakers, they often have to work with electrical engineers, mechanical engineers, designers, marketing, finance, and many other functions—it is exceptionally hard to get traction. This sort of situation often occurs in selling to businesses, which is why the initial customer in many corporate contexts is not a company as a whole but an isolated department with a small, flexible budget and a willingness to try new things.

4. Depth of Need and Relative Performance

To get noticed, a new offering has to excel over competitors on at least some important criteria. Tel-musici was an intriguing idea with a supportive physical and business infrastructure in place, but it had stiff competition in the phonograph and live music. There was an advantage in being able to choose the music type you wished and in paying per listen—3 cents for popular recordings and 7 cents for grand opera[25]—but the proposition was unattractive in other ways. Subscribers were constrained by the extent of the company's music catalogue, and they had to guarantee to spend at least $18 per year. Competitive offerings did not face these issues. Once the radio emerged roughly 15 years later, listeners had a wide variety of choices for free listening, and the bar for any competitive service rose quickly.

Would-be inventors of the bicycle struggled for decades to create a workable design—something light and with minimal rolling resistance. Once this design finally emerged in France in 1864, it took off very rapidly.[26] The bicycle met a clear need for transportation, and it beat the competition—it was inexpensive, easy to maintain, and did not require feeding. While the device took some training to use, potential consumers could readily see others riding this contraption and became inspired to try it themselves.

5. Behavior Change

As Chapter 2 illustrated, behavior change can be vital for new markets to emerge, and it is very difficult to rush. This was unfortunate for sushi, which violated several taboos. After all, this stuff is raw fish wrapped in seaweed. Many prospective diners heard about this idea and had the identical thought: "Yuck!" In contrast, energy drinks built on existing familiarity with athletic drinks such as Gatorade, and some were consumed initially in place of soda mixers. They required almost no behavior change to adopt. Indeed, smart marketers try to link fundamentally new offerings to existing behaviors—Procter & Gamble's Swiffer looks like a mop and the company's Febreze looks like air freshener, but they are not. Customers often start using a new offering by applying current behaviors and subsequently discover that it enables new behaviors as well.

6. Speedy Sales and Use Cycle

An innovation's penetration into the market is directly related to how fast prospective customers can understand whether it is really useful for people like themselves. Often these prospects cannot be convinced by marketing materials—they need to see the innovation in action.

The resulting imperative for fast sales and use of an innovation has big implications for selecting target markets. For instance, automakers typically require four years to design and build a car, making them a poor choice of target market for innovative devices. By the time other customers can see the device being used in a mass-produced car, the industry may well have moved on. The infrastructure for indoor plumbing had a longer sales cycle, to the extent that one even existed. In contrast, the bicycle was quickly purchased and used, as were radio receivers and Red Bull.

The late Everett Rogers compiled a wide array of academic studies on market penetration in his classic work, *Diffusion of Innovations* (Fifth Edition, 2003).[27] His influential list of traits of quickly adopted innovations included trialability, as well as observability and the homogeneity of a customer group (because potential users can quickly cross-apply the experience of a current user). While trialability continues to be a significant barrier to market penetration, the importance of observability and customer homogeneity may be declining. Mass-media advertising, the Internet, digital cameras, social networks, and other technologies have improved communication dramatically since the decades when many of these studies were conducted, and good marketers can leverage these mechanisms to help ensure that people trying a new offering can provide quick endorsement to relevant peers.

7. Low Switching Cost

Switching costs make it more difficult for potential adopters of an innovation to sign on. Tel-musici required the listener to install a speaker in the home in addition to spending $18 annually. These were high barriers. Indoor plumbing was so hard to retrofit into existing homes that the viable market was confined to new construction.

8. Low Risk of Failure

Customer trial also will proceed slowly if the result of an innovation's failure would be far worse than its potential benefit, no matter how slight the risk of that event might be. There were dire consequences if indoor plumbing failed. As many of the early adopters of this technology learned, leaks, poor ventilation, or improper sloping of pipes could end the allure of this idea in a hurry. If a person invested in Tel-musici but was disappointed in the service, he was out a relatively significant sum of money. A bad sushi experience . . . we need not explore. Risks like these make potential customers want to see others adopting the innovation first, lengthening the overall penetration process.

When Is a Market Ready to Grow?

A market may have all the ingredients for fast growth yet not be ready to take off. CompuServe, the first major Internet service provider (ISP) in the United States, was founded in 1969 but struggled for over two decades before the market skyrocketed.[28] Chapter 2 pointed to several triggers for market formation. Here we take a closer look at specific attributes of a market ready to start growing fast. Table 3-2 outlines how these factors are distinct from what strategists seek in established markets.

Table 3-2 Jockeying for Share versus Creating a Market

Established Market—Seeking Share	New Markets—Growing the Industry
Offerings with broad benefits	Offerings with a killer application
Support of an established ecosystem of firms	Power to shape the industry
Competitors as the enemy	Competitors as allies

Killer Application

It can be extremely tempting to see all of a platform's potential and push headlong into a new market, neglecting to emphasize its killer application—the one thing that the platform does exceptionally well. Don't fall prey. While new markets can radiate outward from new technology platforms, they tend to begin in narrow areas where the platform offers substantial advantages for addressing a need that a few customers realize is unsatisfied.

I learned this lesson the hard way. I started my first day at Psion PLC, the leading British consumer electronics company, by participating in a secret meeting with top staff from Motorola. The meeting's purpose was to scope out a joint initiative in which the companies would develop what we hoped would be the world's first smartphone.

Psion had invented the personal digital assistant (PDA) back in 1984, and by 1999, it had created a loyal, mainly European user base. In addition to being an organizer, a Psion PDA could create spreadsheets and documents. It even could send faxes. The devices were large, and users often displayed them prominently on conference tables as signs of their importance. They were complicated. When I first got mine, I had to consult the owner's manual to figure out how to turn it on. And they were expensive.

Psion understood that its technology was leaps ahead of Palm, an emerging American upstart in this industry. Through a marriage with Motorola's telephony expertise, it was poised to underlie the first example of the smartphone.

We had great visions. We created exciting plans. We thought the potential market would be huge and immediate. Eventually, these dreams were realized; in 2010, about 300 million smartphones were sold.[29]

However, these huge ambitions obscured the immediate opportunity. During our meetings, I was annoyed by the Motorola staff
incessantly using two-way pagers to send quick notes back and forth,
sometimes even to people in the same room. These machines would
be buzzing constantly with new messages and proved a distraction to
everyone. I wished we could just focus on creating the future.

Of course, the future was right in front of me, had I understood
how to look for it. While today's smartphone is indeed a remarkable
device, these handsets first got traction through being outstanding at
one killer application—e-mail. Rather than produce a lower-cost, relatively simple device focused on this killer app, as Canada's Research
in Motion (RIM) then was doing with the introduction of its new
BlackBerry, we pulled out the stops. The project developed extensive
technical dependencies on component suppliers, and when some of
these soured, the initiative ended.[30]

This was not a mistake born of stupidity; the Psion and Motorola
people on this project were incredibly bright. We simply did not realize how new markets typically start. Rather than assessing the overall potential of the smartphone industry, we should have chosen one
killer application and evaluated the potential size and rate of penetration of that specific market instead.

Taiwan's Sercomm has taken this route. Moving from a legacy of
producing both servers for telecom carriers as well as Wi-Fi equipment, Sercomm has become an early leader in the new market for
femtocells. These devices provide a direct connection to the cellular
network within extremely small confines, such as a home. Sercomm
has thought intensely about killer applications for this technology.
According to the company's CEO, James Wang:

We knew that cellular carriers wanted to improve coverage without building expensive new towers. But another factor that really
made the femtocell market exciting was the explosion of smart-

phones. Many people are using these devices in their homes, and carriers want to offload that traffic to the fixed line network as early as possible. This is driving big demand.[31]

Power to Shape the Industry

As Psion's smartphone example showed, technical partners can sink ambitious projects. Business partners are another major risk. Three-dimensional (3D) filmmaking was long tarred with the brush of 1950s monster movies, even though technology existed to improve the experience substantially.[32] Yet it was difficult to align movie equipment makers, producers, directors, and studios to move forward concertedly. Even if they had, there were few theaters equipped to show these films. It took the power of James Cameron, who had already directed the world's top-grossing movie of all time, *Titanic*, to align these forces behind *Avatar*. Its enormous success convinced companies to make many more 3D movies and to build out 3D theaters as fast as possible.

Most of us are not James Cameron. If a new market requires established players to collaborate, a firm should have the power to force this change through for at least a highly targeted set of customers or projects. Otherwise, the company should define its strategy so that it does not rely on the fickle goodwill of business partners (sales-channel strategy is the subject of Chapter 5).

Supply-Led Growth and the Benefits of Competition

In some industries with long product-development cycles, an uptick in activity can be a precursor to firms entering aggressively a few years later. Companies filing patents, venture capitalists funding startups, and scientists publishing academic papers are indications that new offerings are coming. Firms behind these offerings will be investing to educate customers and establish the market.

This observation leads to a maxim that runs counter to effective strategy in well-established markets: In new markets, *competition can be good*. A company trying to create a market on its own has a great deal of work to do in building awareness about a new offering, educating the market about how to use it, and prompting initial purchases. Competitors can be allies in this quest.

Of course, a downside of competition is that other firms may lock in their initial customers, or they may drive down pricing to win the business. These are real dangers, but they can be overrated. The first customers to try a new offering are wary of lock-in; they are dabbling and know it. While the first company to serve them may have an inside track on future purchases, it also has the first crack at making the mistakes that are almost inevitable when doing something new. Competitors can swoop in with a more refined offering and win the repeat business (Chapter 6 explores when it makes sense to be a pioneer versus a fast follower). As for pricing, a new market can be dominated by steep discounts from companies attempting to establish a track record, but this condition does not last. Firms cannot afford to do this for long, and serious buyers usually understand that they get what they pay for. When people are looking to make extensive use of a new offering, they are unlikely to gravitate toward free trials.

Assessing Competitive Advantage and Adaptability

A company will, of course, want competitive advantages over potential rivals. These can stem from several sources, such as established customer relationships, reference accounts proving the firm's excellence, intellectual property such as patents, deep partnerships with leading suppliers, scale economies, a strong hold over distribution channels, and intangible assets like a brand.

A key strength in new markets is specific to nascent industries—a company's ability to adapt rapidly as it learns about what it can reliably supply and what customers actually demand. This adaptability is one reason why upstarts can triumph in new markets that incumbents are also targeting—witness the dominance that America Online (AOL) quickly established in the U.S. ISP market while initially fending off competition from CompuServe, General Electric, IBM, and others.

It can be useful to deconstruct the business model that you believe the new market will require (see Figure 3-2). At the center of the model is the offering—not just a product, for example, but all the services and support that go around it to stimulate market acceptance. The offering should be led by strategy, such as which customers you are targeting and why you will win against competitors. Unlike in established markets, where strategy should be the "due north" of the compass that guides offerings even while "magnetic north" occasionally drifts, in new markets the strategy and offering need to shift in

Figure 3-2 Deconstructing the business model.

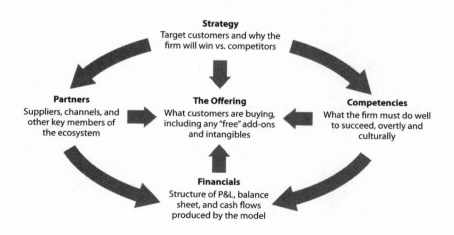

Strategy
Target customers and why the firm will win vs. competitors

Partners
Suppliers, channels, and other key members of the ecosystem

The Offering
What customers are buying, including any "free" add-ons and intangibles

Competencies
What the firm must do well to succeed, overtly and culturally

Financials
Structure of P&L, balance sheet, and cash flows produced by the model

tandem. Customer feedback about the offering may require many iterations of strategy. Indeed, the entrepreneur's lore is that strategy for successful ventures will shift an average of four times.[33]

As strategy and the offering shift, consider how the three other elements of the model must change. In established firms, these can be poorly linked. Partnerships—with suppliers, sales channels, complementary firms, academic institutions, and others—may be either immutable or driven by a business-development function loosely tied to strategic planning. The structure of a venture's income statement may be written in stone, such as a need for gross margins of at least 60 percent. Competencies can be so engrained that they are often not even written down. For new markets, far more flexibility is needed in each of these three variables.

Chapter 8 explores how firms can create a corporate capability to repeatedly tap new markets. Here it suffices to say that a company should believe that it has the ability to align the elements of the business model around a shifting target. If it lacks this flexibility, it should very carefully assess how other advantages, such as intellectual property, will succeed in fending off nimble attackers.

A final point concerns making strategy for the right industry. Value often can migrate between stages of an industry's *value chain*—the series of activities that makes an offering possible.[34] When George Eastman invented the film camera, distributors made the lion's share of the money in the photography industry[35] because heavy glass plates and the huge assortment of equipment needed to take pictures required local firms to serve as critical resources to photographers. Eastman seemed to understand that his creation would change those dynamics, making the camera and film manufacturer the champion. Firms assessing new markets should think about where the power will lie in the new value chain—what will create the most value for customers and be the most proprietary. Assessment should focus on the viability of that link in the value chain.

Pitfalls in Market Assessment

This chapter has touched on numerous potential hazards in assessing new markets—running traditional concept tests, creating standard NPV estimates, ignoring corporate adaptability, and many others. A few additional ones deserve mention:

Market Size Estimates

Market research firms often trumpet their predictions for a new market's overall size through press releases and client events. Less visible is any comparison of these estimates between firms. They can vary hugely. Consider, for example, current forecasts for the size of the wireless health-care market—using wireless devices to monitor and assess patients' health. As of 2010, leading firms varied in their estimates for the market in 2014 from $1.9 billion to $5 billion.[36]

It is enticing to provide management with a single estimate of market size in any summary of a new market's potential. However, these estimates can be deceiving, and they do not matter terribly. What is truly important is how much revenue the company can ultimately realize for itself and its profit margins. Those numbers are driven more by eventual competitive advantage than by a market's overall size.

In 1997, my consulting caseteam was in the unlucky position of having a client ask, "How big will the Internet be?" We had no idea. But this was the wrong question. If the Internet was big enough to be interesting (it was!), then the right question was, "Do we have advantages that can make us winners somewhere on the Net?"

Competitive Snapshots

Strategy consultants excel at creating slides that summarize competitors' strengths and weaknesses. Unfortunately, these can be inherently backward-looking and focused on what is observable. For new markets, it can be more important to understand competitor motivations and capabilities. A firm might have many innate advantages in serving a new market, but if it that will cause conflict with existing sales channels, distract manufacturing facilities focused on scale economies, or call for new technological capabilities, then the incumbent may fail.

There is every reason to have thought that one of the leading automakers would dominate the market for electric vehicles. Instead, today a market leader is Tesla Motors, a Silicon Valley–based startup with no previously established plants, dealerships, brand, or anything else. The large automakers were slow to attack the market, but a competitive snapshot taken in 2005 might have made Tesla seem irrelevant.

Internal Feedback

One of the worst things a firm can do when assessing new markets is to let the company's staff vote with their feet. If projects receive a lot of internal support from people wanting to volunteer their time, then they become major initiatives. This can be a terrible idea.

The staff of a company usually has been chosen to execute well on the current business model. At Psion, we had outstanding technologists who thought deeply about what sophisticated, deep-pocketed technology enthusiasts would want to buy. They loved the idea of a highly advanced smartphone. A lone industrial design consultant argued for an inexpensive device focused on sending messages, but alas, he had no support.

Internal marketplaces can work well when considering innovations that serve existing markets that value current competencies. For new markets, they can bear little relation to what the market needs.

Assessing new markets is challenging. Alongside traditional tools, companies need to use both different methods and a distinct mindset. Even if the market calls for substantial upfront investment, it can be impossible to predict demand accurately. Planners instead should focus on whether the market meets criteria laid out in this chapter, and they should retain flexibility to iterate the offering, its strategy, and the overall business model. Humility matters.

Summary

- Several traditional tools of market assessment can lead firms astray when considering new markets.
- Pearson shows how even large firms can evaluate markets in a fast and nimble fashion.
- Companies can gauge the overall value at stake in a market through approaching an opportunity like an entrepreneur, experimenting rapidly and understanding their offering's true value to customers.
- It is critical to assess both the potential speed of a market's growth and whether now is the time for the market to take off.
- Ultimate competitive advantage can be more important than a market's size and is driven by adaptability to evolving learnings as well as more traditional factors.

Chapter | 4

THE FIRST CUSTOMERS

The open-air markets in Lusaka are crowded, noisy, and chaotic. As the capital of Zambia, in southern Africa, Lusaka is the country's commercial hub. Ancient delivery trucks pull up along dusty streets to entrepreneurs manning steel containers by the roadside, unloading goods by hand that are then picked up by vendors on bicycles. The cyclists push their creaky, overloaded bikes to stores throughout the vast townships where the city's poorer residents live. Shoppers line up there to purchase small amounts of goods that they bring to their homes on foot.

At first glance, the poverty is inescapable. Almost all these actors in the commercial scene are struggling, and purchases typically are small simply because the buyers have little cash to spend. But then it strikes you—there is all this *cash* being exchanged. The delivery driver is paid in cash, as much as $4,000 in small bills for a truckload of beer. The lean men powering the bicycle delivery network might pay $50 for their loads. The women in their shops, beautifully dressed in their flowing robes, can have hundreds of dollars stashed in their drawers. Consumers have large quantities of small bills—the largest-denomination note in Zambia used to be worth about $2—stuffed into their pockets.

I arrived in Lusaka in 2002, sent by Celtel, one of Africa's largest cellular networks, to create a new business using cell phones to exchange money. We called it Celpay (imaginative branding was not our strength). We knew we wanted to replace cash with electronic commerce, but where should we begin? We had millions of subscribers on the Celtel network; should we reach out to them first? Thousands of market vendors sold our scratchcards for prepaid airtime; should we try to get them on board? What about the other firms supplying those vendors with everything from toothpaste to cement; would they be interested?

We could not target all these parties at once. We could spend a few million dollars launching the business, but our funds were not limitless. No one had tried building this kind of business in Africa before, and our parent company was not about to plunge headlong into the unknown. If we were to establish partnerships with banks, we had to pick among many competing institutions. Regulators also wanted to understand what our business was, and I could not plausibly explain that it would be all things to all people. Moreover, we had little staff and had to focus people on a clear target. We had to make a choice. We could not just leap to the top of the mountain that we needed to climb. First, we had to find a foothold.

This chapter focuses on why footholds are critical to new markets. Firms pursuing new markets are often seeking fast growth, and their impulse can be to enter with massive strength. Counterintuitively, the quickest route to success is often through entering narrowly in a foothold segment. The chapter explains

- Why visions of ultimate success can push companies in hazardous directions

- What are the advantages of foothold strategies
- What hazards to avoid when selecting the foothold

The Strengths and Dangers of Vision

Firms sometimes deny the need to choose a foothold. Having spent years in the core business, where markets are well understood and competitors are quick to copy, managers are used to launching new offerings with bold moves and large scale. After all, a major virtue of being a big company is the ability to push out offerings speedily.

I certainly listened to many advocates of that approach back in Celtel's head office in Amsterdam. "Just send our subscribers a text message that offers them some free airtime to sign up—you'll get tens of thousands to do it." These people were right; many people would jump at that offer, but would they become loyal users of the service? Where could they spend their electronic cash? Would consumers change their long-established payment behaviors so quickly? What if we gave away millions in free airtime and six months later we had little business?

Launching into a new market is different from pumping out offerings in the core of an established company. Usually, people being honest with themselves will recognize that there is a tremendous amount they do not know. Do people really want our product? Will they use it as intended? Will they pay what we require? Did we plan our costs correctly? How will the competition evolve in a year's time?

Only the very brave will sally confidently into such murky waters. They may be under substantial pressure from senior management and investors to get big fast. Or, in other contexts, they may have grown used to creating detailed project plans and executing them ruthlessly.

Sometimes the roulette wheel comes up 32 red, and everyone celebrates the bold winner. We tend to remember those victors, such as oil wildcatters or technology seers who took huge risks and had them pay off big. These stories are exciting, and we want to believe in the power of human genius to peer confidently through the mists and find the riches.

We also remember the biggest failures, when huge sums were staked on misguided ventures. Take Motorola's $5 billion mistake during the 1990s with Iridium, a satellite-based system that enabled people to place a call from anywhere on earth, even the middle of the ocean. While the system worked as intended, it turned out that people were not willing to pay exorbitant sums for handsets that were truly valuable only in extreme circumstances. As one technology executive told me at the time, "This project never would have gotten off the ground if it was a $50 million effort pushed by middle management. But because it was a $5 billion project championed by senior management, it was a *vision*, and no one wants to argue against vision."[1]

The dot-com era of the late 1990s was replete with this kind of vision. Who could argue with the vision of a company selling dog food by mail with its advertising led by a sock puppet?[2] Because no one really knew how the Internet would evolve, and because everyone was in a hurry to get big fast, companies spent billions in a vast land grab. The biggest winner out of the Internet era? Google, established at modest cost well after the land grab was underway, in 1998.

More typically, bold efforts launch with a bang, struggle, and then fade away quietly. Management hesitates to kill projects that once appeared promising, so they linger in a zombie-like state before patience ultimately runs out.

Look at General Motors' experience with its Saturn line of cars. Launched in 1990 as a totally new brand within the GM portfolio, Saturn was touted as a "different kind of car company." Its iconic plant in Spring Hill, Tennessee, became famous for its collegial working relationships and high-quality output. Yet, after a first burst of buyer enthusiasm, sales began to disappoint. Gradually, the finance people in Detroit insisted that more costs be shared with the core business. With cost sharing came conformance. Saturn became a less expensive company to run but also turned into a near clone of other GM badges such as Chevrolet. Car buyers saw through the tactic and began treating Saturn just like its GM brethren. GM eventually shut down the brand in 2010.[3]

When the "visionaries" come knocking, hide. It is entirely good to have a long-term vision of what a business can become and the way in which it should act along that path. As noted in Chapter 1, Google's vision is "to organize the world's information and make it universally accessible and useful." This statement pushes staff to imagine new markets and gives their efforts an overall coherence. Yet it is also wise to be humble. Google tries out dozens of new ideas as beta tests every year, and it can prune failed efforts mercilessly. As Harvard Business School Professor Willy Shih is fond of telling his students, "I can tell you we're going to California and that we're going to drive. But I can't tell you where we'll stop to have lunch on Tuesday."

To find inspiration, people tasked with creating new growth platforms should look to the world's experts at the task—venture capitalists (VCs). VCs are known for staging their investments. They may take a first nibble with a $3 million series A investment. If the business meets key milestones, they may follow their money with a $10 million series B investment, often in concert with another VC firm. By the time the business is really scaling up, they may lead a $30 million series C investment, syndicating the deal among many investors. At each stage, the VC will look to turn major assumptions into facts and be more certain of the ultimate route to success. VCs recognize that any new business is replete with risks, that often those risks are poorly understood, and that surprises do happen.[4]

The Power of Footholds

Staging growth is an element of a foothold strategy, but it is not the same thing. Firms could limit their investment in a business while spreading small bets across diffuse market segments. They could focus solely on research and development (R&D) up front and defer actual product launch. By contrast, a foothold approach focuses investment on creating an offering for a very small number of market niches, and it seeks to get out into the marketplace early to obtain the sort of real-world feedback that countless hours at a whiteboard never can achieve.

Speed

While getting big fast is a hazardous proposition, new businesses do need to move quickly. The return on investment (ROI) earned by a venture is a direct function of how fast profits are realized. Footholds accelerate action. By focusing money and people on a small, well-defined target, footholds enable rapid decision making. Offerings will not accumulate hundreds of features but rather need to be just good enough to appeal to initial target customers. Sales efforts can be concentrated, so first customers may sign up more quickly. If some part of the proposition does not work for a key stakeholder, the negative feedback will be loud and specific.

At Celpay, time was limited. The core telephony business was growing by over 20 percent per year, and it was hungry for capital. Skilled staff in a place such as Zambia can be hard to find, and if we did not find success quickly, our technology and sales teams would be hired away by others. Fast decisions were needed.

My first day on the job, I gathered with my direct reports in a musty conference room with a chalkboard of the kind I remembered from grade school (while we shared a building with the cellular network, we did not get the fancy offices). We did some simple math. What commission could we earn from a street vendor receiving cash from consumers? Maybe 4 percent. How much would the firms supplying township-based depots be willing to pay us for money received? Maybe 1 percent. And so on. Then, how big would a transaction be at each stage of that chain? What sort of penetration could we achieve in the first year?

Math can provide a wonderfully clear compass heading. We quickly concluded that a 1 percent commission on a $4,000 truckload of beer, delivered daily, could lay the foundation for a successful business. A 4 percent commission on a bottle of beer, bought occasionally, could not.

We decided that Celpay's foothold market should consist of multinational firms distributing goods to supply depots that lacked electricity and Internet access. These multinationals had substantial sales, and they were constantly in fear of fraud and theft. They had the capital to have their own fleet of trucks. But because their depots had no power or online access, they had few, if any, other options for electronically transferring funds.[5]

Focusing on these distributors would require few sales staff and no advertising expense. It was not a slam dunk; these customers would need to change their financial procedures, and they required some features that our software did not have. However, out of an eight-hour delivery run, distributors spent three hours counting cash. Cash was counted seven times between when it was paid and when it was banked. The companies delivering to the supply depots were desperately eager for a solution, and we could penetrate those accounts in a matter of months.

Gaining "Scale"

One of the iron laws of business is that firms are more profitable the larger they are relative to their competition in a given marketplace. Scale allows companies to save through purchasing more cheaply. It spreads costs such as technology, marketing, and management across a larger sales base. Scale also can enable firms to price higher because customers like to buy from a leader in the industry, and the leader can afford to create product features that followers lack.

The laws of scale apply equally to new markets, provided that scale is achieved within narrow groups of customers. The new business likely has relatively large overhead as a percent of sales, and focusing the offering on a particular foothold enables the company to limit the complexity that drives that expense. Furthermore, when firms are pioneering new propositions, they need to get known for *something*. Customers are used to thinking of firms as doing specific things, not as fuzzy entities that could morph in dozens of directions. If the company can be the *leader* in providing *something*, even to a very limited market, it may be able to charge the prices it requires to make money. It also can deter would-be competitors, who may start with less recognition in that space and fewer capabilities.

At Celpay, we competed against both the engrained habit of using cash and a planned system for interbank electronic transactions between companies. A working group of banks had been outlining such a system for two years and was starting to implement it. Aside from the hindrances of management by committee, that system suffered from lack of scale. Its mandate was to serve as a one-size-fits-all mechanism for executing transactions. As such, it could not afford to build capabilities tailored to specific markets, such as the ability to export sales records into inventory-management systems or the ability to conduct transactions via cell phones in street markets where PCs were impossible to operate. Judged as a whole, the interbank system had far more functionality than Celpay, but it was not targeted at a foothold. Celpay, on the other hand, was very good at serving the needs of a specific foothold customer set.

The Sociology of Innovation

Sociologists have long studied how innovations diffuse within a population. Starting with a 1943 landmark examination of how Iowa farmers adopted novel seed corn from 1928 to 1941,[6] they have traced how innovations tend to take root in a small sliver of a population that is prone to consider new approaches because they are desperate for a solution, have processes to assess these offerings, or are simply intrigued by new things. Many of these lessons underlie the attributes of fast-growth markets put forth in Chapter 3.

In a foothold market, customers often will know each other, even if they compete. They may hire people from rival firms, meet at industry events, or golf at the same country club. Even if they do not know each other personally, they will be keenly interested in what their competitors are doing. They will not want to be outdone by fast-moving rivals, and they will not want their bosses asking why they missed a chance to understand a competitor's newly acquired capability.

Zambia had a small economy, with a gross domestic product (GDP) of about $3 billion at the time of these events in 2002. There were not many multinational firms to target as our foothold; however, the finance directors of these companies tended to live in Kabulonga, a leafy neighborhood of Lusaka near the presidential mansion, and they often knew each other socially. We realized that if we could get the beer company on board, we would have an excellent chance of winning the cement company's account, and then the oil company's, and so on.

By focusing on a foothold, a company creates reference customers. Firms or individuals who are not the first adopters of an offering can peer over the shoulder of people who have taken the plunge and can understand the relevance of that experience.[7]

Competitive Signaling

While it is illegal in many countries for companies to collude on price, it is well-established practice to signal intent to lead a particular market. In this way, firms can limit their head-to-head, price-based competition and instead can dominate particular market segments based on their unique offerings for that customer set.

Through becoming known for *something*, market pioneers can tell their would-be competitors, "Back off. There are many other small sets of customers that you can penetrate, but with this one you are going to be a follower." Then the leader has some time to iterate its offering for its chosen market and to further entrench its position.

Some companies worry that they will tip off competitors to the existence of enticing markets before they have the scale to exploit them effectively. As noted in Chapter 3, competitive fears in new markets are frequently exaggerated. Others often have thought about a market but may have decided to pass for a host of internally focused reasons, such as lack of synergy with the core business or scarcity of funds. Conversely, if the existence of a new market truly had not occurred to them, the followers can be strongly tempted to wait and see how the entrant does before seeking to emulate it.

Hazards within Footholds

While footholds are critical to success, there are a number of hazards for firms entering new markets.

Choosing the Wrong Foothold

Few strategies in business lack downsides, and this principle extends to footholds. One significant danger is that the trailblazer will choose the wrong foothold. Given that much remains unknown at the time a foothold is picked, a firm might invest its resources in pursuit of an illusory goal. Indeed, we almost encountered this issue with Celpay. We had not thought through the entirety of the process that customers would need to follow, and we neglected to realize that it would be difficult for the supply depot entrepreneur to put his cash in the bank—enabling the electronic transaction—if he did not have a car. While banks were not terribly far from the markets, the entrepreneur was understandably reluctant to walk through the streets carrying thousands of dollars in small bills! We solved the problem by having two trusted drivers provide a free, very low-key taxi service for this network of entrepreneurs.

Firms can help themselves avoid wrong footholds by staying wary of marquee accounts. Project sponsors often push new businesses to land prestigious initial customers so that they can convince investors to provide further funding. The problem is that marquee accounts understand their status, and they milk it. These firms are used to being demanding and having their suppliers do whatever it takes to keep them happy.

Celpay required a banking partner to accept cash deposits and inform us of the amounts. Otherwise, there would be no way to get money into the electronic system. We had discussions with most of the local institutions. Large multinationals had precise specifications that did not align with how our software was configured. Their technology centers were in distant countries, and working with a Zambian startup was definitely not on the priority list. So we started business in partnership with the African Banking Corporation (ABC), a small Zimbabwe-based bank that had a grand total of three branches in Zambia. ABC was not prestigious and had limited computer systems. But it was looking for some sort of advantage in the marketplace, and its processes were eminently flexible. For Celpay, it was a perfect fit.

Time Frame

Occasionally, a firm considers a foothold approach but concludes that it will take too long. Senior executives support new platforms because they need growth, and they are in a hurry. However, management typically overestimates how rapidly a get-big-fast approach will bear fruit. By throwing resources at the initiative, executives create internal bureaucracy and force more complexity into the offering so that it can generate the necessary sales. Project timelines lengthen. Customers change their minds about what they want. Rather than getting to a small customer base quickly with a limited offering, the company tackles a large set of buyers slowly with a complicated product. In uncharted waters, this is a bad idea.

Celpay took eight months from that day on the chalkboard to commercial launch, about double the anticipated time. We encountered unforeseen technical and regulatory issues, and our lead customer had to obtain approvals from high in the organization to do something so radical. However, after these delays, the business took off. Based on our experience with the first customer—South African Breweries—we adjusted our processes and technical systems, and we won a slew of new accounts. Today, Celpay can profitably transact as much as 5 percent of Zambia's GDP through its systems. We had this as our ultimate vision, but the company never would have gotten to that destination without a foothold strategy that allowed for focus and fast iteration to satisfy target customers' latent needs.

───────※───────

Foothold strategies build on a paradox. Through focusing on small targets, the foothold approach enables more rapid penetration of big customer sets. Mastering this paradox requires considering why a foothold strategy is suited to a particular venture and determining which advantages of footholds are particularly important to attain. Managers then can choose a foothold to maximize those advantages. Equally, they can keep perspective about how much to invest in the foothold, given that this group of customers might seem insignificant compared with the company's ultimate aspirations. Winning in the foothold is a goal, but it is also a means to an end.

Summary

- Foothold customers are a narrow sliver of the ultimate target new market that will adopt an offering rapidly and provide critical feedback.
- Visions can be useful overarching guides to new market creation, but they need to provide teams with flexibility to find the right path to the ultimate destination via footholds.
- The virtues of foothold strategies include their speediness, scale advantages, and quick conversion of reference customers.
- The dangers of footholds include the chance of choosing an inappropriate foothold, the distractions of marquee accounts, and management impatience. By selecting footholds that provide important learnings, fast sales, and quick changes to the original strategy, firms can avoid these dangers.

Chapter | 5

PATHS TO MARKET PENETRATION

For a new venture, sales channels are like rocket fuel—extraordinarily powerful yet highly combustible. Sales channels—which are organizations such as retailers, dealers, and other distributors—can quickly propel new businesses to industry leadership. With deep relationships and vast contact networks, the right channel can help customers to shoot past the often lengthy process of evaluating new offerings, reduce the perceived risks of adopting the idea, and block out competitors from critical accounts. Conversely, an uninterested sales channel may neglect a new proposition or even actively undermine it.

It is essential for businesses in new markets to have a well-thought-through strategy on how channels will factor into the push toward market penetration. Unfortunately, many ventures approach the challenge haphazardly, as an afterthought, once a new offering has been developed. This chapter delves into these issues. It discusses

- How sales channels affected the inception of the mobile marketing industry
- Why traditional channels often dislike new markets
- How to choose between two basic strategies for market penetration: "superhighways" and "country roads"
- When firms should consider buying their channel

Mobile Marketing's Early Choices

When companies start advertising in public restrooms, no space is sacred. I had this epiphany in a London pub during the year 2000. Ads were absolutely everywhere. With emerging technologies, ads also had migrated recently into the virtual world, becoming ubiquitous on the Internet and through e-mail. Life was becoming a gigantic NASCAR race.

In 2000, people were starting to talk excitedly about blasting ads onto cell phones, and at first I found the thought horrifying. Yet the concept also made a lot of sense—cell phone ads could be targeted by personal profile, time of day, and location, and they would be almost impossible to ignore. Surely, there had to be a way to use cell phones as smart marketing tools rather than as dumb ad receptacles.

I created one of the first mobile marketing firms, Saverfone, which later became part of the mobile software development company Brainstorm. My initial goal was to let shoppers use their cell phones to browse for sales near their location—a woman in a mall is seeking shoes, and she checks what discounts are running. Only stores paying Saverfone a small fee would be listed. Other companies had different visions. A startup called Flytxt thought that people would subscribe to be part of "brand communities" to receive text messages targeted to them.

I could not grasp the appeal of Flytxt's vision until I saw one of its first campaigns. To promote the teen comedy *Get Over It*, it ran a contest on movie posters for people to text in their favorite text message dumping lines. The movie's brand community received fun information about the movie and eventually the winning line ("UR my favorite letter. A letter between W and Y"—brilliant nastiness).

Saverfone and Flytxt each had an intriguing idea. Saverfone's business model clearly had scale economies and network effects; the more ads in the system, the more compelling it was for users to search. The challenge was to gain traction in the foothold industry of chain retailers, which tended to have large headquarters, hierarchical managements, and tight relationships with ad agencies. At first, we tried selling directly to marketing departments, but we could barely get through the front door. No one within the companies we approached had responsibility for mobile marketing nor a budget for it. Nobody had an incentive to experiment with a new medium that could become associated with spam. We tried out a handful of partnerships with tech firms that said they could jumpstart our sales, but after agreeing the deals, we received very little support—the industry was just too young to merit their attention. So we tried our luck with the retailers' ad agencies.

The agencies made the retailers look positively hospitable. Agencies made their money from creative fees associated with fancy television ads and from revenues tied to ad spending. We were offering a dirt-cheap way for company merchandisers to place ads directly onto the system, with no production expense and no need for an ad agency. Next!

The idea behind Saverfone made a lot of sense in its end state (indeed, it is quite similar to the "Deals" feature that Facebook launched in 2010), but there was no easy route between our starting point and that Nirvana. Although many consumers eagerly checked the service for local promotions, we had few to list. Eventually, we got a handful of mainly tech-oriented retailers to sign on through direct sales, but it was a very rough slog. There was no simple way to make this work using either direct or channel sales.

Contrast this situation with that of Flytxt. Its business model was more labor-intensive, but its idea could be pitched to any company building a brand. Flytxt latched onto filmmakers because movies needed to create a brand overnight. There was no concern about degrading a brand built over generations and plenty of urgency to try anything inexpensive that could build buzz fast. The firm also targeted magazines and radio stations for campaigns to text in thoughts and requests. Today this is commonplace, but Flytxt was the first to do it. Media companies are constantly trying new promotions, and failed ideas can be forgotten as quickly as next month (or even as soon as tomorrow's broadcast). These customers were open to novel ideas that were easy to execute.

Not surprisingly, Flytxt quickly gained traction. The company became a sort of mobile-focused ad agency, buttressed by a team of mobile software developers. It largely avoided wasting its time on selling to ad agencies but rather competed successfully against them for a sliver of clients' overall accounts.

A year later, Saverfone turned the tables. Once it was part of the software company Brainstorm, it had the resources to develop a Web-based platform that enabled any ad agency to run its own mobile marketing campaigns without using a specialist like Flytxt. While the agencies still were not keen on mobile marketing, they increasingly saw that it was not going away, and they preferred to control their clients' full accounts rather than put up with an interloper. The platform did well, so much so that Flytxt split itself in two parts—a mobile agency selling directly to advertisers and a technology company competing with Brainstorm by selling to traditional agencies. Nearly a decade after these events, Brainstorm's and Flytxt's technology platforms are still two significant players in this space.

This tale contains several lessons about how sales strategies affect the emergence of a new market:

- Direct sales give quick feedback about the viability of markets.
- Certain types of foothold customers are much more amenable to direct sales than others are.
- Direct sales are hard to scale. While Flytxt was able to call on media accounts fairly easily from its London base, reaching a broad range of advertisers was a daunting challenge.
- Sales channels may try to sign up nascent firms with a promising story (they are salespeople, after all), but these companies are unlikely to put serious effort behind promoting a new firm until a market's potential has been proven. This is a point explored in the next section.
- Sales channels dislike having disruptive new firms impinge on their accounts, and they will seek out ways to claw back market share in their key customers.
- Industries tend to start with an integrated offering, spanning technology, sales, and service. This is the only way to bring together the offering fast enough, and it enables companies to shift approaches quickly as they learn more about the market. Eventually, industries can become modular to facilitate scaling and adaptability.[1]

Why Sales Channels Dislike New Markets

Call a salesperson with a big order on March 31, and she will move mountains to win the business—channels live to make this quarter's quota. However, if you call with a fuzzy opportunity to make huge profits in five years, prepare to wait on hold a long time. A financial analyst might estimate the net present value of the incremental sales order to be vastly less than the innovation opportunity, but this is not how most sales organizations make decisions. Salespeople are paid based on achieving short-term objectives. Channel organizations may have a business-development person looking at longer-term opportunities, but that person is often disconnected from the staff in the field, who ultimately are responsible for making sales happen.

Channels frequently dislike new markets, which take a lot of effort. Salespeople need training about the new proposition. Customers have to be made aware of the new offering, convinced that they should try it, and supported through the inevitable first hiccups. If the supplier trying to create the new offering has a quality problem, it makes the channel look bad. If the customer loves the innovation, follow-up sales are possible, but the proceeds are likely to be insignificant compared with established offerings. In short, there is certain cost, substantial risk, and little immediate reward.

There also may be issues of trust. New businesses occasionally try both direct and indirect sales at the same time. In certain situations this makes sense. As noted by David Aronoff, a leading venture capitalist at Flybridge Venture Partners, "Sometimes channels trying to push boxes will need a company's direct salesforce to help educate the customer."[2] Unfortunately, this dual-track approach requires careful balancing to get right. If the direct salesforce is seen as competing against the channel's personnel for a particular prospect, the channel may remember the episode for a long time. Firms can establish guidelines directing who will cover which accounts, yet in the quest for a hot lead, some of these rules can wind up being ignored. It is easy to say that the channel's people were present but not really serious and hard to give the channel a substantial cut of scant early sales when its salespeople have done little to earn the money.

Aronoff also points out that—despite all the challenges—sometimes there is little choice but to use a channel. "For firms in spaces like social media, the cost of customer acquisition is critical. Channels are essential. Enterprise sales are also very hard to do directly. Every company has to bring a few customers to the table through initial direct sales, and then channels will be interested in partnership."

This is a conundrum. Channels can be terrible for innovation, but they still may be essential partners. What should companies do? We can find the answer through a road trip.

Two-Channel Strategies: Superhighways versus Country Roads

Driving eight hours on a major highway is boring. The road is usually in excellent condition. There is seldom fear of running out of fuel. Restaurants are everywhere, and exits are well marked. The big highways also tend to take the shortest routes between major cities. If the mission is to drive from Boston to Washington, DC, the superhighway is the way to go.

Country roads are quite different. A map or GPS can be essential. Road conditions may vary. You never know when you will see the next filling station. Food is chancy. Yet, if the mission is to go from Washington, DC, to a small town in the Blue Ridge Mountains, country roads are absolutely the shortest route.

Channel strategy is like choosing a driving route. If a company is going to well-established destinations, selling recognized products to easily identifiable customers with a business model that makes sense to the channel, then the superhighway formed by existing channels is the right path. Channels provide a fast route to market and the full infrastructure of support services to make sales relatively straightforward. Some new markets work this way. When the American drugstore giant Walgreens wanted to use its thousands of pharmacists and nurse practitioners to provide face-to-face counseling to people with diabetes, it did not sell the service directly to the afflicted patients. Health insurers had much to gain from helping people improve their diet, exercise, and medication adherence, and many patients expected that their health needs would be covered by insurance. Walgreens also already had well-established relationships with insurers. It made sense for Walgreens to partner with UnitedHealthcare, one of America's largest insurers, to pilot the program. The offering created a new market, but the customers, stakeholders, and business model were well understood by all.

For many new markets, the ultimate shape of the industry is unclear, there is no ecosystem of firms to provide the full range of services needed, and sales channels have not yet figured out how to profit from the innovation. In these circumstances, a pioneering company has little choice but to take the country road. Flytxt did this successfully in the mobile marketing industry, creating the technology to hold automated "conversations" via text messaging, generating ideas for marketing campaigns, procuring text messages at bulk rates from cell phone networks, and selling its services directly to companies with brands to build. Because Flytxt did just about everything in this industry's nascent "value chain,"[3] it had the flexibility to adjust its strategy rapidly. As demand took off from radio stations wanting to provide their listeners with a way to text in requests, it could quickly create an interface for disk jockeys to view incoming messages. As reality television shows started asking for systems to allow viewers to vote via text message, Flytxt could do that too. The company had no critical business partners to alienate through these fast shifts, and it did not need to negotiate a host of new alliances to make the offerings possible.[4]

The Flytxt story, however, also shows how "country road strategies" can age poorly. Once an industry begins to mature, companies able to leverage channel partners can gain scale rapidly. Rather than selling direct, Brainstorm sold its system to ad agencies, and because the agencies were defending against upstarts such as Flytxt, the Brainstorm package quickly penetrated the agencies' accounts. Industries also tend to develop specialists in each link of the value chain who can focus on being the best at handling a specific task. In mobile marketing, companies like mBlox arose to aggregate the purchasing of text messaging from cell phone networks. Because it represented dozens of mobile marketing firms, mBlox could secure rock-bottom pricing for these messages, and it could invest in expensive systems capable of blasting thousands of messages in very tight time frames. (As this tale suggests, sometimes it can be more attractive to be a fast follower rather than an early mover in a new market. Chapter 6 examines this subject in depth.)

As an industry grows, companies that have followed the country road face a choice. See Table 5-1 for when to choose the superhighway or country road. One option is to focus on a small number of activities, using the superhighway to deliver the rest. Ultimately, this was Flytxt's strategy—the firm split itself in two so that a creative agency could work directly with brands and a technology company could cater to agencies and other types of buyers. This can be a difficult transition to make as formerly-core activities are wound down, the company refashions its identity, and a new set of partnerships is forged. There are also dangers of choosing the wrong link in the value chain for focus. At the dawn of the personal computer, IBM elected to outsource the microprocessor and operating system to Intel and Microsoft, respectively. Those once comparatively small firms ended up making by far the lion's share of the profits in the industry.[5]

Another option is to continue on the country road, bucking the industry trend. A firm persisting on this path must cater to a market segment valuing the highly differentiated solution that an integrated firm can supply. Apple stayed on the country road, whereas most of the PC industry drove on the superhighway—Apple had a proprietary

Table 5-1 When to Choose the Superhighway or Country Road

Circumstance Category	Favoring Superhighway	Favoring Country Road
Customer need	A specific buyer both recognizes the need and has the responsibility for meeting it.	The marketplace requires education about its need and the buyer's identity is unclear initially.
Channel incentives	Existing channels see near-term profit potential or strategic advantage in exploiting the new market.	Existing channels are unmotivated to develop the new market.
Business ecosystem	A ready-made network of firms exists to service the new market and provide complementary offerings.	Few partners exist to complement the firm in providing a full solution for the customers' needs.
Competition	Weak competition means that little advantage is gained through following the country road, or strong competitors pursuing the country road make the superhighway a potential means of differentiation.	Strong competition makes the country road a necessity in order to stand out from the crowd—unless too many competitors on the country road make the superhighway a more differentiated strategy.
Rate of market change	If the market is unlikely to change rapidly, a superhighway can allow fast scaling of a business.	If the market is likely to remain in flux, a country road can provide more flexibility in changing route.
Advantages of scale	In industries with high fixed costs and large advantages to scale, a superhighway can be the fastest route to growth.	In industries with fewer scale economies, country roads allow firms to find the right formula for success before accelerating growth.
Exit strategy	For a venture capital–backed startup or other companies seeking to sell themselves relatively quickly, superhighways can plug the company into a network of firms that might be motivated to buy the startup as a complement to existing offerings.	For companies with longer time horizons, country roads can allow the flexibility to find the right market niche and the ability to develop a range of assets (e.g., technology, salesforce, installed base, etc.) that might eventually prove interesting to buyers.

processing chip, operating system, and hardware. Eventually, it even opened its own retail stores. If Apple had tried to address the mass market in PCs, the high costs of all the insourcing along the country road would have made it uncompetitive. However, the company did fantastically well at defining a new market segment that, as the company's ads claimed, liked to "Think Different."

Hazards and Defensive Driving on the Superhighway

As noted earlier, the superhighway contains many dangers. They are particularly pronounced for companies in circumstances that favor the country road but whose corporate parents insist on using the superhighway to avoid alienating crucial business partners like distributors. For instance, financial services firms may have compelling new ideas to address the vast underconsumption of life insurance (even in a well-developed market such as the United States, 35 million households lack any form of life insurance).[6] Unfortunately, these firms seem forced to commercialize concepts through insurance agents who sell most of the company's other policies and who may have little interest in writing low-value policies that cater to typical nonconsumers in this industry.[7]

Some of the risks and related risk-mitigation strategies on the superhighway are as follows:

Market Development

Distributors may give little time to early education of a market and the creation of reference customers. The upfront investment of money and people seldom pays back in the next 12 months, much less the next quarter. To address this challenge, companies may hire market-development staff who are forbidden from selling directly. In some situations, these functions can become quite large. DePuy, a worldwide leader in orthopedic devices and a business unit of Johnson &

Johnson, has constructed a 75,000-square-foot training facility with 19 separate lab stations offering over 300 instructional programs annually. The DePuy Institute sells nothing—in the orthopedics industry, distributors rule. Rather, DePuy cultivates surgeons' understanding of advanced orthopedic procedures and the sophisticated products that make them possible. Because the fine details of these surgeries can matter immensely, surgeons are unlikely to take this newly acquired knowledge and purchase a cheaper but slightly dissimilar device from a DePuy competitor. They have been trained on DePuy products, and the distributors will reap the reward without fear that DePuy will take away their business.

Disloyal Distributors

The medical equipment firm Becton Dickinson (BD) leads the worldwide market for needles and associated equipment. As noted in Chapter 3, it recently invested heavily to create a new market for safety products that help health-care workers avoid accidental needlestick injuries that can transmit bloodborne diseases. The strategy paid off handsomely in most countries, but in some places, there were unpleasant surprises. Tom Polen, president of BD's Pre-Analytical Systems Unit, explains:

> In the early days we pushed this business in Saudi Arabia, converting people from traditional products to safety, which doubled the value of our accounts. We showed healthcare providers the impact of needlesticks and the cost of those events to a hospital, and we won some early sales. Then we saw generic copycats coming in 6 to 12 months after those efforts, and we lost accounts relatively fast. Our learning was that we cannot rely solely on distributors to develop the market. We will win ongoing loyalty through becoming intimate ourselves with the cus-

tomer. Now we have both a distribution channel plus a direct organization.[8]

Unmotivated Distributors

Farmers Insurance is trying to tackle underconsumption of life insurance through sidestepping unmotivated insurance agents. Rather than push agents specializing in life insurance to find more customers for low-value policies, it has created an offering that empowers auto and home insurance agents to easily add life insurance into the mix. Simple Term Life is a basic product with a maximum value of $150,000. It requires no bloodwork or medical exam, the paperwork is automated and can be completed quickly, and underwriting decisions are fast. The company claims that the entire process can take six minutes or less, making it an easy add-on sale when an agent is already discussing auto or home insurance with a potential customer.[9]

Shallow Ecosystem Partners

Often an early mover in an industry will partner with complementary firms to gain traction. In the mobile marketing industry, Brainstorm partnered with a wholesaler of bulk-rate text messages. We intended to introduce clients to our partner firm, and we would source services from each other as well. The two companies were clearly noncompetitive and complementary. Even so, our partnership never quite blossomed. The problem was that joint sales take a lot of coordination, and in the early days of a market, any sale can be hard won to begin with. The partnership ended up being a distraction. Instead of inking a partnership and then hoping that it will lead naturally to early sales, a company is often better off waiting for a specific prospect to have a need for the double-barreled offering. Then partners will collaborate readily, and more important, the two companies can establish personal relationships and habits that will facilitate future joint deals. For a venture pressured to do 100 things at once as it gets off the ground, it is often better to have a very small number of deep partners rather than a larger number of shallow ones.

Lack of a System-Wide View

The electric vehicle (EV) is an immensely promising technology, yet the cost of batteries has made EVs more costly than combustion engine transport in all but heavily subsidized markets. Carmakers are trying to reduce these costs through scaling up efforts, but it is a tough challenge. One issue may be that they view the problem from the perspective of their traditional position on the superhighway.

Another stakeholder could benefit enormously from EVs and may be willing to help pay car owners to go electric. Owing to environmental commitments and regulatory incentives, utilities are increasingly relying on renewable sources of energy such as solar and wind. The trouble with renewable energy is that it is unpredictable—days can be cloudy and wind patterns erratic. To compensate, utilities often keep natural gas–powered turbines running in idle mode, able to produce power very quickly as energy demand fluctuates throughout the day. These turbines are extremely expensive to buy and run in this fashion.

Siemens, the German-based engineering giant, views the problem differently than carmakers. As a leader in energy technology that recently sold off its substantial automotive equipment operations, it has a deep understanding of both industries. As explained by Professor Gernot Spiegelberg, head of Siemens' eCar program,

> A car stands still for 90 percent of its lifetime. We thought about how we can use the car's expensive battery as a resource 100 percent of the time. The business opportunity is to buy energy

from the electrical grid when it is inexpensive because renewables are producing well and to sell it back when energy is costly because renewables are not producing enough. If the utility has the option to tap into a vehicle's stored energy to meet peak power demand, then it can avoid the cost of building backup gas turbines."[10]

Siemens intends to use a superhighway strategy. It is not going into the carmaking or electric utility business. Instead, it can sell optimized equipment to each entity—including chargers, battery management systems, and grid infrastructure. Rather than being caught in the currently slow-moving traffic on the EV superhighway, the company has identified an opportunity to connect formerly disjointed industries in a way that benefits all.

Managing Breakdowns on the Country Road

The challenges of a country road strategy are readily apparent. It is expensive and time-consuming for a new venture to create a direct sales capability as well as a set of complementary offerings. Sales leads need cultivation from scratch. Overcoming these obstacles requires keen attention to both the sales process and whatever routes are open to make the pioneer the preferred vendor for risk-averse buyers, who predominate in new markets.[11] At a more strategic level, companies may face several issues.

Channel Conflict

Companies can get into deep trouble with their existing sales channels by pursuing direct sales in new markets. The networking giant Cisco, for example, used to sell over $2 billion of equipment through

IBM and Hewlett-Packard (HP), but when it started selling a new type of product direct to customers—in competition with IBM and HP's own gear—it rapidly lost market share in categories where those firms had substantial influence.[12] For companies whose growth prospects are constricted by their channels but feel unable to abandon them, a superior approach can be to hollow out channel partners, gradually moving into direct sales by starting with customers that the channel does not like to serve. Those customers may be low value, or they may require types of service that the channel is ill suited to provide. Once a company has started selling directly to the customers that the channel loves to hate, it can gradually move into extending its relationships to more customer types.

Buying the Channel

Another option for firms constrained by channels is to buy a distributor. Occasionally, this makes a great deal of sense. The luxury goods maker Coach recently bought its distributor in China, a market where it will invest heavily over the coming years to build its brand. Coach needed its distributor to work closely in concert with its other channels, including in-store boutiques and Coach retail stores, in the delicate work of building a high-end brand.[13] Buying a distributor holds many dangers. Distribution requires a skill set completely distinct from creating products. If distributors must offer products from a range of companies in order to interest customers, the new owner has to allay these other firms' fears of neglect while also devoting substantial time to managing sales of products that are ultimately unstrategic. Finally, competitive distributors may quickly drop the company's product line. The strategy can make sense in Coach's circumstances—a company with one principal distributor that needs to be aligned in an intricate operation to build a growth market—but this is an unusual situation.

Switching to the Country Road from the Superhighway

It is a courageous, and sometimes foolish, move to exit a traffic jam on the superhighway and instead try your luck on the country road. A company will lose its channel sales quickly and may have to create a whole new set of competencies. Yet this is precisely how Vanguard Group became one of the world's largest asset managers. In 1977, the company disposed of its traditional broker-dealer distribution network and established the mutual fund industry's first "no load" funds, where there was no sales charge for customers moving into the funds—and therefore no money to pay sales commissions. Direct sales also were the best way to market low-cost index funds, a category that Vanguard pioneered in 1976. The company escaped the highly competitive structure of a fund industry selling through brokers who pocketed big fees and instead raced through open space, growing quickly as a result.[14] Vanguard was able to make the switch because it had little choice; it was losing money otherwise. It also had an idea that catered to a readily identifiable market segment—individual investors who took an active role in managing their funds—and an easy means of reaching those customers through advertisements in publications targeted at them.

Emergence of Superhighway Competitors

As the Flytxt story demonstrated, industries often start on the country road only to see competitors zooming up on the superhighway once other firms see the opportunity. Companies that wish to persist on the country road can exploit the fact that the first superhighway deals may go poorly. Channels may not understand how to sell into the new market, disconnects between partners may lead to communications issues and missed opportunities, and new competitors likely will make mistakes as they learn about how a new market works. At the same time, potential customers will remain risk averse (customers are usually risk averse, but this is particularly true when a market is new and scarcely proven). Country road firms can use their integration to offer buyers security and then lock in customers using means such as technical standards, long-term contracts, and pricing schemes. This is not a route to hypergrowth because new customers may be wary of lock-in, but it buys time for the firm to double-down on a focused niche where a country road strategy may continue to win.

Great ideas can struggle in the marketplace. Without a well-conceived commercialization strategy, ventures will find that any route to market penetration leads steeply uphill. Conversely, a clear strategy can speed early sales, help a venture to scale up, and point the way through the foggy conditions that can set in as a new market starts to mature. Commercialization is never easy, but its progression can be made predictable.

Summary

- The emergence of the mobile marketing industry shows how new markets often start through early movers integrating a set of offerings and selling directly to customers, only to have the industry disaggregate into specialists and sales channels as the market matures.
- Sales channels often dislike new markets, yet eventually they can be critical to making the market big. The process of moving from direct to channel sales holds many perils.

- A company's choice of commercialization strategy can be likened to deciding between driving on a superhighway or country road, and a firm's circumstances can point the way to the best route.
- Both the superhighway and the country road contain many dangers for early movers in a market, but the risks can be mitigated on either path.

Chapter | 6

ENTERING AT THE RIGHT TIME

"The pioneers are the ones with arrows in their backs." This business saying captures the feeling of many toward new markets: They generate immense value, but not for the people who create them. Building a market can take more money and time than pioneers bargain for. Once these firms have laid the groundwork for an industry's growth, well-funded companies can swoop in to scale up and capture most of the profits. Yet there are endless counterexamples to this hard-bitten sentiment, including more than 450 startups that have grown to the point of becoming publicly traded companies in the past decade in the United States alone.[1]

We can learn from a huge range of case studies. VisiCalc, Friendster, and Diners Club each helped to create their respective industries yet faded away, sometimes swiftly, as their industries matured. Yet, in many instances, businesses that were early entrants became long-term winners; Zipcar today looks unassailable as the leader in car-sharing services. What explains the difference in outcomes? What do those findings imply about timing when a company should enter a particular market?[2]

This chapter focuses on these questions, addressing the advantages and drawbacks of being an early mover (as opposed to being a first mover). While *first-mover advantage* has become a common business term, it can be hard to define who is actually first; there is ample debate, for instance, about who can claim to have invented the automobile. Companies also may not know in advance if they will be first to market because competitors' initiatives are often opaque to the outside world until they are nearly ready to launch. Usually what matters is not so much being the very first as being early.

Xerox invented many major technologies, such as the Ethernet and the personal computer, but these programs were so disconnected from the company's commercial business that they stood little chance of making the company any money. This is a different issue from the one discussed here. We will look at markets that can become real businesses sometime soon and moreover will focus on new markets that are likely to be in flux for some time owing to the pace of technological and consumer change.[3] While there are many instances of new markets that have grown over the long term at a linear pace—think of the trash compactor—contemporary business has far more exponential growth curves and discontinuities than in years past.

In this chapter you will read about

- The lessons of Atari's spectacular growth and disintegration
- The conditions that determine when a company should be early, a *fast follower* once the market has been established, or a *late follower* once the market is starting to mature
- How key strategies differ for early movers, fast followers, and late followers

- How one of America's largest health insurers entered on multiple fronts to win in a new segment of its industry

Atari Creates an Industry, Then Vanishes

Nolan Bushnell knew he had a hit when he heard about the trouble at Andy Capp's Tavern. The founder of Atari had created only one prototype machine of the company's first video game, Pong, and it had stopped working after just two weeks. The problem was that the can for collecting coins was getting overstuffed. The bar's owner said that on some mornings there was a line outside before the doors opened; people came just to play the game.[4]

These are the kinds of problems we all should have. In 1972, Bushnell's Pong became the first commercially viable video game, and it churned out money. Yet it followed a string of failures. Bushnell himself had created perhaps the first video arcade game, Computer Space; it was so complex that its instruction manual ran to several pages. That flopped. Magnavox had launched a Pong system for home use at the same time that Atari targeted arcades, but it was sold only through Magnavox dealers, who were most interested in selling televisions. That failed as well. Atari's Pong overcame earlier entrants' shortcomings. It was simple. The arcade setting allowed for new users to easily observe others' play and to try the system out for just a few cents. Arcades were motivated to get people to try the game. By overcoming barriers to trial and adoption, it created a runaway success.

Atari's win in the arcade seeded the market for a home system. The company's home version of Pong sold 150,000 units, but Bushnell had his sights on building a system that could play a range of games through inserting cartridges into a machine. He could not raise funds adequate to that task, so in 1976 he sold the company to Warner Communications for the seemingly princely sum of $28 million.

Six years later, Atari's revenues were over $2 billion. It had become the fastest-growing company in U.S. history. Atari introduced video games to millions of consumers, and its 2600 system console defined the category, with over 15 million units being sold. Atari had a market share of 75 percent and seemed utterly dominant.

Then it collapsed. Atari's revenue halved in just one year. The company was sold off in 1984 and, despite a few comeback attempts, never recovered.

Why?

As often happens in promising new markets, a host of competitors entered. Mattel, Coleco, and others launched sophisticated systems, whereas Warner held off investing in a follow-on platform. Personal computers attacked from a completely different angle, being able to run simple word-processing and other programs as well as games; one PC manufacturer advertised its product as "a real computer for the price of a toy."[5]

Another problem was the company's strategy toward games. Atari made most of its money from selling game cartridges, not the console, but it did not control the supply of games. The company could not hold onto its most talented programmers—a cadre that included two youngsters named Steve Jobs and Steve Wozniak, who figured they might do better by cofounding Apple Computer. Other programmers created rival games publishers such as Activision. Many more competitors emerged from nowhere, often with low-quality games that degraded the overall experience.

Of course, the industry later rejuvenated. Nintendo launched a highly successful, more complex system, only to encounter tough competition from Sega, Sony, and Microsoft. These companies built progressively more advanced and expensive systems catering mainly to hard-core gamers, until Nintendo reinvented the category again with its groundbreaking Wii, a console so straightforward that it is found at many senior centers.

There are several take-aways from Atari's story:

- Atari did not need to be the first home videogame system, and in fact, it was not. But it was critical for a startup like Atari to be early. Well-funded companies such as Sony and Microsoft could take more time, although eventually there was room left only for competitors to attack from a completely different direction (Zynga is one such firm, building an estimated market value of over $5 billion just three years after its founding in 2007 by amassing huge numbers of players through Facebook and other browser-based environments).[6]

- In environments of rapid flux in technology and customer preferences, there may be many competitors entering, each with slightly different assumptions about what formula will win. Early winners such as Atari can do very well through reaping quick profits or selling themselves to bigger companies. Under conditions explored later in this chapter, some early movers may become long-term winners. Even runners-up can succeed if they watch their expenses; Mattel and Coleco each sold more than 2 million video game consoles before withdrawing from the market.

- When a company leads a burgeoning market, by all means it should fight to stay there. Warner Communications looked at the large investment needed to create newer systems and thought it could squeeze further profits from the Atari 2600 before plunging forward. Meanwhile, Mattel and Coleco brought out competitive products that performed better and eroded Atari's status as the clear leader. By the time Atari launched its successor systems, the competitive landscape had changed fundamentally.

- An industry's business model profoundly affects the fate of early versus late movers. Atari had a razors-and-blades business model that sold the console at a small profit and aimed to make more money on the cartridges containing its games. Unfortunately, it ended up making worse games than its competitors.[7] If Atari could have limited games to only select titles, as later games systems have done, it could have ensured a better-quality experience and made greater profits. The imperative would have been to clobber its target market segment with terrific games that made it unattractive for consumers to switch systems. Alternatively, Atari could have focused on creating ever-improving premium-priced consoles with backward compatibility to play older games, thereby making its system the de facto industry standard. It did neither.

Timing the Market

Companies that have a basic thesis about the advantages and disadvantages of their market timing should be able to avoid many of Atari's missteps. The thesis is straightforward—it is better to be early when a company can

- Preserve an early market lead stemming from barriers that later entrants will face.
- Build resources and competencies that larger firms eventually could imitate but which they will prefer to acquire.
- Avoid becoming locked in to inappropriate technologies or business models before the market is deeply understood.
- Avoid incurring large upfront costs because it is early to market.

If a company cannot meet at least two or three of these conditions, then it may be better off as a fast follower that learns from others' mistakes. Fast followers have their own set of strategies, a topic we will turn to in a few pages.

Below we will look quickly at three very different enterprises and then examine how they met these conditions[8]:

- *Zipcar.* This company rose from an idle coffee shop discussion in 1999 to become a giant in car-sharing services, renting cars by the hour from locations distributed around urban centers. In the decade since that fateful café encounter, it has become a $140 million firm with an estimated 80 percent market share in North America and promising operations in Europe. Zipcar has over 400,000 members paying fees to reserve cars online and access them from more than 4,400 locations.

- *Bosch Healthcare.* The market leader in technologies to remotely monitor chronically ill patients in their homes, the core of Bosch Healthcare used to be a startup called Health Hero Network before it was purchased by Bosch, the $45 billion leader in sensor technologies. Bosch is betting that remote patient monitoring can become a giant industry that improves patient care while offloading work from overstretched physicians and nurses.

- *The Wiggles.* Branching out from bands such as Bang Shang a Lang and The Cockroaches, a quartet of talented Australians redefined the rock scene when they created The Wiggles, far and away the world's biggest band catering to children. With the ability to make tunes like *Toot Toot, Chugga Chugga, Big Red Car* into real toe-tappers, The Wiggles play at Madison Square Garden, record with superstars such as John Fogerty and Kylie Minogue, produce their own TV show, and have millions of young (and older!) fans who understand each of their characters in detail. The long road from their beginnings as outdoor buskers in 1991 has paid off; the Wiggles are pulling in $45 million a year.[9]

Condition 1: Raise Barriers to Competitors' Entry

Imagine Hertz's task in trying to knock off Zipcar's concept with its new business called Connect by Hertz. First, people will use such terms as *knock-off* because another company has completely defined the category in consumers' minds. Then Hertz has to replicate its competitor's density of locations in urban areas to offer similar levels of flexibility while facing a chicken-and-egg conundrum of whether to establish these locations in advance of having people register for the service. It also has to create technology to allow an individual subscriber's key card to unlock a car he just booked online, wirelessly track the car's mileage and hours of use, and do many other important and complex tasks. A further challenge is that the most attractive customers in a city already may belong to Zipcar, and it is unclear how Hertz will pry these customers away short of engaging in a price war.

Bosch is responsible for around half the remote monitoring patients in the world. With an early start, the firm that Bosch acquired had received 63 patents, completed a raft of clinical studies, and made its technology recognizable to many hospitals and physicians. The remote monitoring field is currently packed with startups, including ventures by big names such as General Electric (GE) and Intel. However, these firms lack Bosch's many advantages and have to try to compete by offering expensive services at low prices—not a typical formula for success.

If you think that Hertz and remote monitoring startups face an uphill battle, then pity Eric Herman. One reviewer called his album, *Monkey Business*, "the best kids' record ever."[10] However, if a child goes to school singing a Herman tune, her friends will have no idea what she is doing. Children are going to follow only so many bands, and they are not looking for fresh hits. Moreover, Herman lacks a TV show, major concert tour, merchandising, and a cast of well-known characters—he is a musician, not a parallel universe. When The Wiggles started out, they had little competition in their genre, but it is now very tough for others to gain the attention of children.

Condition 2: Build Resources and Competencies that Are Easier to Acquire than to Imitate

With thousands of engineers specializing in sensor technology, Bosch easily could have created a bevy of remote monitoring devices. Yet it would have needed to invent around or license a large number of Health Hero patents, and it would have had to invest in sometimes lengthy clinical studies. The company had no background in health care and would have needed to build up expertise in an arcane industry while cultivating opinion leaders who could persuade physicians to consider this unfamiliar company. Alternatively, it could buy the market leader. It is easy to understand Bosch's choice.

Had it remained independent, Health Hero may have struggled against the dozens of competitors eyeing this field. Eventually, those competitors would have chipped away at the company's market share through sheer persistence in selling and desperation in pricing. There also were other challenges. Like many startups, Health Hero lacked a large salesforce and deep pockets for marketing. Some customers may have worried about trusting patient care to a relatively new firm. The Bosch acquisition dealt with both firms' shortcomings at a single stroke through combining the advantages of a large, technology-oriented company with those of a small, health-care-oriented early leader.

In many industries, it is hard to envision a startup withstanding the eventual onslaught of giants. If a relative minnow thrives in a new niche, like the cloud-computing specialist 3PAR did in storage technology, sooner or later big companies with broad product lines and vast sales resources are going to look to the niche for expansion. 3PAR found itself as the target of a bidding war between Hewlett-

Packard (HP) and Dell, and the company likely viewed this to be a happy outcome. The same dynamic often occurs in life sciences, where startups can create promising new drugs but typically sell out to or partner with big firms to get those drugs commercialized. The startups reap big gains from being an early mover even if their lead cannot be sustained over the long term.

Condition 3: Avoid Lock-in

A potential disadvantage of starting early is the risk of lock-in to a technology or business model that proves inappropriate to the new market. Zipcar mitigated this risk through extensive piloting. For instance, when it first ventured outside the United States, it aimed for the relatively straightforward market of Toronto, where it could work through basic issues of global expansion such as differences in auto insurance requirements. For the U.K. market, it opted to buy a small local firm, and it also has taken a large stake in a Spanish company. The company seems to recognize that each country has its nuances, and it proceeds without hubris.

Yet many companies succumb to this danger. CompuServe took great pride in being the first Internet service provider (ISP), founded in 1969. Its interfaces were awkward, and members had lengthy numbers rather than names as their e-mail addresses. The anachronisms were endearing but impractical. As AOL covered the United States with CDs of its software and provided Internet newbies with a simple introduction to the Web, CompuServe clung to its model. It was acquired by AOL in 1998.

Another form of lock-in is the *innovator's dilemma*, which was first described by Clayton Christensen in his 1997 book with that title. The dilemma arises as companies target their biggest, most profitable customers as the focus of their innovation efforts, creating ever-fancier products at ever-higher prices. This makes good business sense, except when discontinuities arise in the market that lead to new waves of growth coming from different business models or new categories of customers. Cable and satellite television companies seem to be in the midst of this dilemma now as they try to get customers to pay for blisteringly fast bandwidth and picture quality even while many are content with the selection and price advantages of streaming videos over the Web. As a result, the incumbents have been ceding ground to relative newcomers such as Netflix.

Condition 4: Avoid Large Upfront Costs

Another hazard of being an early mover is the potential expense of investing in a product that proves poorly suited to the market's eventual direction. I learned about this problem personally in 2000 when my startup, Saverfone, invested over £100,000 in one of the very first Wireless Application Protocol (WAP)–based services, which the company started creating before there were any WAP handsets on the market. Alas, WAP proved to be less than it was hyped up to be—connections were slow and easily dropped. The winning platform in those days was text messaging, and we had to abandon our earlier investment to shift the business. Later entrants could learn from those mistakes.

However, the danger of upfront costs can be addressed through careful management. Zipcar has managed its risks through expanding city by city, creating a critical mass of members and local sites in each area it targets. Bosch managed to get a large health-care provider, the U.S. Veteran's Administration, to conduct several key clinical studies with its equipment, thereby minimizing the company's outlays.

Upfront expenses are unavoidable in some industries, so the question is whether these might escalate rapidly if a company delays action. Celtel had to pay good money for its cellular licenses throughout Africa in the late 1990s, but as the value of cellular spectrum became better understood, the auctions for these licenses became dramatically more expensive. Because Celtel had moved early to secure large amounts of spectrum at relatively good prices, it had an advantaged position.

Table 6-1 lays out several of the factors that can make each of these conditions apply, as well as how they relate to Zipcar, Bosch, and The Wiggles.

Strategies for Early Movers

If the viability of an early mover position is determined by the factors in Table 6-1, a company fitting these criteria should milk its advantages for all they are worth. For instance, if part of Zipcar's appeal versus Hertz is that it has a critical mass of both users and cars in key cities, then it should focus on attaining those scale advantages in the most important cities rather than establishing subscale outposts in a large number of second-tier geographies.

Beyond this imperative, early movers should look closely at the business model of their industry to see how their position creates advantages and vulnerabilities. Clayton Christensen, Charles Stabell, and Øystein Fjeldstad have suggested that there are three general types of business models: solution shops that create customized offerings, value-chain businesses that produce standardized outputs, and facilitated networks that enable interactions.[11] There are, of course, infinite shades of gray within this framework, but the overarching categories are useful in charting potential strategies.

Solution shops often dominate at the early stage of an industry. An ecosystem of suppliers has yet to coalesce, customers are not yet certain about what they want, and firms are flexible in adapting their offerings as they learn more about the market. In the language of Chapter 5, solution-shop companies are following a "country road" approach. When an industry is fated to remain a solution shop because its value lies in customization or its customers are inherently

Table 6-1 When to Be an Early Mover

Raise Barriers to Entry	Become Acquisition Target	Avoid Lock-in	Avoid Upfront Costs
Become completely associated with the category (Zipcar, Wiggles)	Establish advantages replicable only with long lead times (Bosch)	Able to shift technology or business model with modest costs (Bosch)	Able to pilot at modest cost (Zipcar, Bosch, Wiggles)
Create customer preference through helping users define their tastes (Wiggles)	Create desirable brand (Zipcar)	Able to catch changing technologies or customer preferences quickly (Zipcar, Bosch, Wiggles)	Scale-up costs are roughly linear with income potential (Zipcar, Wiggles)
Lock up distribution channels (Bosch, Wiggles)	Establish strong customer relationships (Bosch)	Able to make decisions rapidly (Zipcar, Bosch, Wiggles)	Generate income quickly because of fast customer adoption (Zipcar, Wiggles)
Lock up physical infrastructure (Zipcar)	Create costs for customers to switch solutions (Bosch)		
Accumulate learning (Zipcar, Bosch)			
Develop a broad product line (Wiggles)			
Benefit from economies of scale (Zipcar, Bosch)			
Breadth of users creates more useful network (Zipcar, Wiggles)			
Own intellectual property (Zipcar, Bosch)			

heterogeneous, early movers can do quite well. Customers frequently buy solution-shop outputs based on the supplier's reputation because there are few other ways of judging the quality of a highly customized offering. Early movers in the market can create a reputation that others will have a hard time matching—think of a high-end consulting or law firm. However, if an industry looks set to standardize—perhaps because this will lower costs or bring about a broader product line—leadership in the solution-shop phase may translate poorly to the next stage of industry development. The Altair 8800 was the first personal computer, but it catered to the sort of hobbyists who read electronics magazines. They were quite different from the people who bought the first Microsoft and Intel-based PCs; the hobbyists sought out the technical challenges that mainstream users decried. As the PC industry transitioned toward the mass market, the Altair was left behind.[12]

Value-chain business models organize companies into a chain in which the outputs of one step become the inputs of another. These systems put a premium on efficiency, consistency, market power, and sales channel access. Microsoft capitalized on its work with the Altair to become a value-chain business catering to PC manufacturers, especially IBM. IBM had leverage with suppliers, software developers, resellers, and others to create an ecosystem of firms that made the PC take off. In a value-chain business, it is not essential to be early—the iPod was far from the first portable music player. However, it is important to be early in creating the ecosystem. Once Apple established its ecosystem around iTunes, the company had a big advantage over potential rivals in that market.

In some value-chain businesses, the early movers may collaborate to set standards, such as for software interfaces and data exchange. When this occurs, companies tacitly agree that their real battles lie not against each other but in generating overall market demand. Standards help to decrease the risk and increase the utility of adopting new solutions.

However, standards also can make it easier for new companies to enter the industry because the incumbents' installed base becomes less of a competitive advantage. Standard-setting strategies are usually most relevant to high-tech businesses, and a full discussion of the complexities of standards would go well beyond the scope of this book.[13] The basic point to make is that a company in a value-chain business will have to work smoothly with partners, and standard setting can facilitate that task unless one company has overwhelming market power or there is a large risk of destructive competition between standards. If standards are set, then companies should plan to compete on other factors, such as price, quality of service, or salesforce strength.

Facilitated-network businesses reap their competitive advantage from the size of their network. This is why eBay is so dominant in online auctions or Facebook in social media. With the network business model, it is critical to be early. A firm need not be first—Friendster's fate is discussed in an upcoming example—but it should quickly earn a strong position in a foothold it can own and that can serve as a launching pad to penetrating the broader market while the industry is still nascent.[14]

The Challenges for Fast Followers

Followers need the discipline to hold back and then to move quickly before an industry's competitive order becomes set in stone. But there is a critical caveat: *For many companies, it is impossible to be a fast follower. By the time they get to market in a significant way, they will be late.* Because of factors such as decision-making time frames, product-development cycles, and the length of the sales process, a company's eventual entry into a quickly moving market may be so delayed as to be irrelevant. Hertz' experience versus Zipcar may be instructive; although Hertz probably has some cost advantages in its bulk purchasing of cars, it has few trump cards that can make its position viable.

There are some circumstances, however, in which being a fast follower makes sense.[15] If a company has strong local market power, such as a grocery or newspaper, it can learn from experiments happening in other territories and then copy the winning formulas. Firms also can win if they have such strong sales capabilities that they can overcome the lead of early movers; companies like IBM and Pfizer have executed this move many times, although as information flows improve because of technology, the power of brute sales strength may be eroding. Companies also should proceed cautiously if there is simply too much unknown about the eventual market to justify costly upfront bets—a current example may be vehicle-to-grid (V2G) power, in which electric vehicles will discharge their batteries into the electric grid at times of peak power consumption. V2G is theoretically intriguing but is highly dependent on uncertainties such as consumer behavior, smart grid systems, charging infrastructure in parking lots, utilities' evolving business models, and regulations. A firm entering V2G now may gain valuable learning and expertise, but it should not expect to build the dominant system during such early days.

Fast followers can try to exploit some of the advantages of early movers through the strategy University of California Berkeley Professor Henry Chesbrough has termed *open innovation*. By developing a network of contacts that are pursuing early stage ventures and inventions, large companies may have first crack at scaling up the most promising ideas. The early tinkerers in a category—working in startups, academia, or their own garages—can affiliate with large enterprises due to modest investments of money, time, and strategic advice. Johnson & Johnson's (J&J's) Corporate Office of Science and Technology (COSAT) has had many successes in pursuing this strategy since 1978. Alongside J&J's huge budgets for internal research and development (R&D), COSAT is currently looking to invest in fields as diverse as molecular diagnostics, cell therapies, nutritionals, medical devices, health-care informatics platforms, and bioartificial organs.

A related strategy is to invest in startups much like a venture capitalist would. J&J does this as well, investing in outside companies since 1973 through its Johnson & Johnson Development Corporation.[16]

When being a fast follower means completely missing out on key early mover advantages, there are still options available. Japan's Sharp Corporation illustrates what can be done.[17] As a world leader in display technology, Sharp has doubtless studied the potential of tablet computers for years, as have many other consumer electronics firms. The category eventually may be worth over $10 billion, and it has been open for pioneers to lay a claim. Yet these companies waited until Apple moved first with its iPad. Now that Apple has created a runaway success, Sharp, Acer, Toshiba, Dell, and many others are pouring in. How do they distinguish their offerings from those of the clear market leader?

The irony for these firms is that they would love to be in Apple's current position, but it was not feasible for them. Lacking Apple's millions of loyal fans, strong brand, retail outlets, and ecosystem of software developers, their launch of a tablet may have been widely ignored. Only a firm with Apple's strengths could have created this category quickly.

Sharp now has three options. It could choose a niche to pursue vigorously, seeking to be known quickly as the dominant player for that particular market need. Relatedly, it could focus on a geographic territory where it is comparatively strong. A second route would be to ride a different horse into the market, perhaps subsuming its brand under that of strong sales channels that can do the heavy lifting of seizing market share. A third option would be leverage Sharp's other advantages as a leader in displays.

Sharp has opted for all three approaches. It is emphasizing Asian character handling and is concentrating heavily on its home turf of Japan. Outside Asia, the company is partnering with wireless carriers such as Verizon to provide them with tablets sold exclusively through their channels. It is also using a new Sharp display to be the first tablet offering glasses-free 3D capabilities for pictures, videos, and games.

Examples of Fast Followers that Won and Late Followers that Lost

STRATEGY: TIGHT FOCUS ON A POORLY-SERVED MARKET

Example: Friendster (early mover), Facebook (fast follower), Orkut (late follower)

Friendster took an early lead in the emerging industry of social networking, but it clung to an inflexible and slow interface that alienated users. Facebook provided a simple and fast alternative that rapidly gained strength. Rather than take on Friendster directly, it focused at first on a handful of college campuses where it could gain critical mass. Friendster is now using the same strategy, concentrating overwhelmingly on Asia, where it has over 100 million registered users. Google launched its rival social network, Orkut, but struggled to compete where Facebook and Friendster were already strong. Close to 70 percent of Orkut's traffic comes from India and Brazil, where it has won nearly as many users as Friendster.

STRATEGY: RIDE A DIFFERENT HORSE

Example: VisiCalc (early mover), Excel (fast follower), StarOffice (late follower)

The VisiCalc spreadsheet program is regarded as the first "killer application" for the PC, leading thousands of companies to introduce the PC into the workplace. However, the product improved slowly, and it was soon supplanted by competitors such as Lotus 1-2-3. Microsoft was the first to bring its program, Excel, to the emerging Windows operating system, and as Windows gained strength, it pushed the rivals aside. Had Microsoft needed to beat its competitors on a toe-to-toe comparison of features, the familiarity of leading spreadsheet users with earlier programs would have made this a tough challenge. A later competitor, StarOffice, has offered a free program based on open-source software, but with Excel having a huge network of users already accustomed to its interface, it has been tough for StarOffice (now called OpenOffice) to gain much traction.

STRATEGY: LEVERAGE THE NETWORK

Example: Diners Club (early mover), BankAmericard (fast follower), Discover (late follower)

Diners Club was the world's first independent credit card company, founded in 1950. Bank of America launched its competitor, BankAmeri-Card, in 1958, and it used its large presence throughout California to build a strong market share in that state. However, the industry was very competitive until Bank of America hit on a masterstroke in 1965—it would license the program to other banks. Collectively, the licensees could create a critical mass of cards and card-accepting merchants, and in 1975, they renamed their program Visa. Visa continues to be the market leader to this day. The department store Sears introduced the Discover Card in 1985 in an effort to compete and offered more generous terms to both cardholders and merchants than Visa or its smaller rivals MasterCard and American Express. Yet the incumbent firms had a strong lead in the size of their networks, and Discover has remained a distant follower in the market.

When Can Late Followers Succeed?

In quick-moving industries, by the time followers get around to taking action, they may well be late. Sometimes, however, the late movers have done well. Motorola invented the cell phone, whereas Nokia and

Ericsson were fast followers and early market leaders, particularly in Europe. Yet, today, Korea's LG and Samsung are global giants in the industry despite having entered the category relatively late.[18] When can late followers win?

- *Exploiting missteps.* LG and Samsung grew rapidly in part because of missteps by the market leaders. The Korean companies created fashionable designs and mastered the intricacies of executing rapid design cycles. Similarly, Nintendo and Sega reaped the benefits of Atari's reluctance to invest in follow-ons to its megahit 2600 console.

- *Leveraging channels.* LG and Samsung also benefited from the fact that many people buy their handsets through cellular carriers that subsidize the devices. Carriers will put only so many handsets into their lineup, and the limited selection forced consumers to consider these new brands. Similarly, Microsoft hopes that its search engine Bing can leverage the company's presence on the desktop to get users to try the service. Channels put these firms on a more level playing field versus incumbents, allowing them to compete toe to toe on whose products offer the best features.

- *Using the network.* The large businesses that both LG and Samsung have in display technologies and other cell phone components create advantages for these firms. They can be first to market with innovative features such as large and stunningly clear screens. For its part, Nintendo could draw on its arcade game hits to build share for its home console, displacing Mattel and Coleco as rivals to Atari.

- *Low-end disruption.* The Koreans and Chinese were very late entrants to the car market, yet they have won a respectable share. While some of the first cars launched by these firms earned the moniker, "You get what you pay for" (I had one whose back door fell off one day), they took advantage of the innovator's dilemma facing the major automakers and won customers in a part of the market that was broadly ignored. They have improved steadily to the point that some of these companies are now moving credibly into the luxury market.

- *Redefine the category.* If LG and Samsung arrived once the cell phone party was in full swing, Apple seemed to enter once guests were already starting to leave. Yet, as noted in Chapter 1, the iPhone captures over 30 percent of the profits in the entire handset industry. Apple achieved this feat partly because the iPhone is a mobile Internet device as much as it is a phone. In a similar vein, Nintendo exploded (again) onto the home gaming scene through reconceiving the market with its intuitive and addictive Wii console.

Entering on Multiple Fronts

When a radically new type of health insurance plan gained traction in the United States shortly after 2000, UnitedHealthcare played the role of both early mover and fast follower. UnitedHealthcare is one of America's largest health insurers, with 78,000 employees serving over 70 million people. It has a broad product line that caters to all sizes of customers, from large companies to single individuals. The company has industry-leading information technology operations and a vast sales capability. However, around 2002, it saw small insurance startups winning business from major employers, and it realized the ground was starting to shift.

The startups were offering consumer-directed health-care plans, a product that upended traditional assumptions about how health insurance should be structured. In these plans, employers provide consumers with a lump sum that they can use to pay their health expenses, in addition to insurance for catastrophic events. People who do not spend their full lump sum in a year can keep the balance or roll it over to use in future years. Because consumers pay directly for care, they tend to become more cost conscious as well as more involved in choices affecting their health. The plans can cost employers less to provide than traditional insurance while also giving consumers substantial choice in the physicians they see.

The company started offering its own consumer-directed plan in 2002, yet it remained an uncharacteristically small player in this fast-growing market. According to Meredith Baratz, UnitedHealthcare's vice president for market solutions, "We hadn't grasped early on that there was a philosophy here that people adhered to. It was about personal responsibility and the need to better prepare and engage consumers to make decisions through information and coaching. It wasn't just about benefit design. The startups had built more into their model than we had."[18]

The firm moved on several fronts. It acquired a small company that offered members discounts on health-related services not typically covered by an insurance plan, including fitness equipment and massage therapy. It built services to coach consumers through treatment options, such as the various ways of addressing lower back pain. Most radically, it obtained a banking license so that it could link consumer-directed plans with savings accounts without needing to involve an outside financial institution as an intermediary.

The company's early presence in consumer-directed health care gave it an understanding of the market that some competitors lacked. Baratz says, "We made a series of small bets that got us very attuned to the marketplace and able to act rapidly when the landscape started to shift."

By 2004, consumer-directed health care was gaining significant momentum in the marketplace, and it was time for the bold stroke of a fast follower. UnitedHealthcare acquired a startup called Definity

Health that had created a strong reputation in this field, and it maintained the Definity brand as a way of illustrating the difference in philosophy and approach. The company then scaled up the business using its sales resources and national presence. With the industry offering few advantages to companies entering later than UnitedHealthcare, the firm remains a leader in this market today.

For UnitedHealthcare, there were benefits to being both an early mover and a fast follower. Its small initial steps provided essential learning and also helped to orient company management to the opportunity. When the market started to grow fast, the firm understood the business enough to make an informed choice about whether to acquire and whom it should buy. It then exploited its advantages as a large player to reap the benefits of a well-timed fast follower strategy.

———◦◦◦◦———

The right timing makes a huge difference to the success of a new venture. For both startups and established companies, reasonably reliable principles suggest when and how to enter. Through careful attention to these principles, companies can improve their chances of winning in the scrambled competition that frequently characterizes new markets.

Summary

- Atari's sudden success and failure demonstrate the potential and peril of being an early mover, whereas Nintendo's first and second waves of growth show how both fast and late followers can flourish.

- Early movers can triumph under four conditions: rising barriers to entry, compelling reasons to be acquired, flexibility to shift approach, and modest upfront costs.
- The business model of an industry—solution shop, value chain, or facilitated network—affects the right strategy for early movers to pursue.
- Fast followers can succeed under a different set of conditions that include tightly focusing on a market, riding a different horse, and leveraging a distinct network.
- Late followers also may win through exploiting missteps, leveraging channels, using their networks, and re-defining the category. However, they often start at a disadvantage to early movers and fast followers.
- UnitedHealthcare shows how it is possible to pursue several of these strategies at once—learning about a market as an early mover and then pouncing on an attractive acquisition candidate as a fast follower.

Chapter | 7

FULFILLING THE POTENTIAL OF EMERGING MARKETS

Developing countries contain some of the most enticing new markets. With 80 percent of the world's population, they already account for 48 percent of the world's economy. The International Monetary Fund (IMF) predicts that they will generate two-thirds of global economic growth from 2011 to 2016. Companies seeking growth would be foolish to ignore the opportunity.[1]

The potential of emerging markets is widespread. Many people would think first of the $4.4 trillion expansion of China's gross domestic product (GDP) over the past 30 years—a sum that constitutes over 7 percent of today's global economy.[2] The nation's tremendous growth has led it to become the world's largest consumer of construction equipment, automobiles, and much else. As impressive as China's growth has been, though, it presents just one facet of the story. Take a look at sub-Saharan Africa. More often associated with development aid than high-growth industry, the region nevertheless has seen an explosion in the field of cellular technology. Mobile communications is now a huge, multi-billion-dollar business throughout the continent. In another industry, developing-country retailers such as India's Pantaloon, Brazil's Pão de Açúcar, and South Africa's Shoprite have become giant enterprises.

Despite all this opportunity, emerging markets are still a sideshow for most large companies. Among the Standard & Poor's (S&P) 500, developing countries represent only around 8 percent of revenues.[3] Even for a company highly focused on the opportunity, such as GE Healthcare, emerging markets bring in only about one-third of sales. There is a huge upside for growth.

So why has it not happened?

A big impediment to aggressively targeting these countries has been the pesky issue of profits. For many companies, emerging markets historically have been a black hole of investment. Customers can be keenly sensitive to price, and local competitors may be ferocious. Given the big money that some firms spend to begin operations in these countries, the prospect of enduringly bleak returns makes many companies remarkably consistent about when they will consider a serious move—next year.

Yet an alternative scenario is quite plausible. When my former company, Celtel, started in 1998 with a vision of becoming the AT&T of Africa, it had to turn to government-backed financial institutions to raise much of its capital. Despite investors' initial hesitations, the company grew very quickly, with 98 percent of subscribers being lower-income prepaid customers. It was sold seven years later for $3.4 billion, creating enormous returns for those courageous first backers and making the company founder a billionaire. Along the way, the firm made major contributions to economic growth in the countries it served.[4]

This chapter does not offer a road map for success in emerging markets. Oceans of ink have been spilled on that subject, and the full complexity of market entry can fill several volumes. Even at that length, it would not be realistic to speak in generalities about 5.7 billion consumers. The rich Brazilian in Rio's Copacabana has little in common with a rice farmer in Vietnam. There is, of course, no substitute for rigorous analysis of local dynamics. Still, companies can be quickly overwhelmed by the complexity and diversity of emerging markets, and it is useful to take a basic strategic lens to the opportunity. The successes and failures of firms that have pursued new markets in these environments hold many lessons.

The chapter focuses on a handful of major strategic issues that frequently make the difference between success and failure. It covers

- How a small firm in an unlikely place challenged one of the developing world's most sophisticated banking industries and what its story tells about patterns of success
- What levers firms can pull to change their business models in emerging markets
- How to build scale in efforts targeting emerging markets

Lessons from an Unlikely Revolutionary

In the majestic Winelands outside South Africa's Cape Town, the farming community of Stellenbosch seems an implausible setting for revolution. Quiet lanes through rolling vineyards lead to houses that frequently evoke the architecture of the Dutch settlers who came to the area over 300 years ago. Yet, amid the tranquility of the region, there is frequent poverty and great unmet need. At the turn of the millennium, this is where Riaan Stassen saw opportunity.

As an experienced banker and former operations director of a nearby wine and spirits firm, Stassen knew that South Africa's formal banking sector—proud of its sparkling branches and first-world infrastructure—catered poorly to rank-and-file workers. The alternative providers were mainly in the informal sector; money might be saved through buying livestock or other readily sold assets, and lending came via township-based moneylenders charging astronomical interest rates.

Rather than try to strip cost out of a mainstream bank's business model, Stassen built a new firm—Capitec—from a blank slate. A first step was to bring in experienced marketers from Stassen's former beverages business. As Capitec's Chairman Michiel Le Roux puts it, "The fact that our people came in from another industry has been an advantage. It may be an advantage to grow up in an industry, but there is also a danger that you can't see the wood for the trees."[5]

Looking at the existing high-cost banking system built for South Africa's elite, Stassen said that his team found it "complex, cumbersome, and inconvenient for the average customer." Capitec focused on households earning between $1,500 and $10,000—not the poorest of the poor by any means but also far from wealthy. The company defined a tight set of services for this market that it could deliver through a low-cost business model.

Money handling would have to be part of Capitec's business because most small transactions in an economy such as South Africa's occur in cash. However, the bank could eliminate complexity in the process. The only cash in Capitec bank branches lies in that day's deposits, and these are placed immediately into drop safes accessible solely to staff in armored vehicles. If customers want to withdraw cash, they must go to an ATM or a partner retailer. Because this model nearly eliminates cash handling at branches, it both reduces the threat of robbery and abolishes many back-office functions. In fact, all staff at a Capitec branch are front-line, customer-facing people. A relatively small hub of employees located in a central location near Cape Town handles the back-office processes. Because branch staff can focus on customer service rather than on transaction processing, they have the time to explain unfamiliar financial services to their target customers. The company narrowly defines what it offers, so all employees in a branch are qualified to sell every service. Furthermore, with branches being almost cashless, no one is standing behind bullet-proof glass, and staff can interact with customers in a personal way that traditional bank tellers cannot duplicate.

There are no forms in a Capitec branch—the office is entirely paperless. Rather than directing customers to fill out paperwork, staff ask questions of customers and input answers into PCs. In addition to making the environment more human-centered, the paperless approach also enables rapid processing of loan applications, which is tightly valued by customers with erratic incomes and unpredictable financial emergencies. Capitec combines computerization with biometric identification via cameras and fingerprints, so customers can enter a branch and within 15 minutes walk out with a loan credited to their account.

In a market dominated by moneylenders, Capitec has positioned its brand on savings and transactions. The company offers very high interest rates on small savings deposits, as well as some of the lowest fees on cash withdrawals and debit-card transactions. The catch is that these fees increase quickly if customers make a lot of withdrawals, but this is quite transparent—Capitec is highly focused on customers who can be served simply and at low cost. Through these mechanisms, the company develops a detailed understanding of the savings and transaction behavior of a customer, and that is invaluable in a country with few credit-rating institutions. It then can pick with laser precision which customers should receive unsecured loans.

Capitec started at the middle of the market but is moving upward. The company has begun to open branches in affluent locations, and it is also taking tentative steps into banking for small businesses. Had the company leapt straight into these markets, it would have had few advantages over well-established rivals. By starting in the middle, the firm has established a branch network, brand name, and customer data that can serve it well as it reaches out to wealthier customers.

The bank has yet to move concertedly into serving the poorest tiers of society. This is a very different environment, often served via a completely different business model, such as lending to small, self-organized groups that collectively shoulder the burden of repayment. Some banks elsewhere have done extremely well with this approach. In India, for example, SKS Microfinance is a for-profit institution that has grown exponentially by honing its approaches for this market and using technology to lower operating costs.

Capitec and SKS both make healthy profits. Even through the recent financial crisis, their return on equity, a standard measure of bank profitability, has been well above standard benchmarks in the West.[6] Capitec's market capitalization has surged over 150 times above the value at which its shares were first traded publicly. The companies have expanded quickly by tapping into the new market, and there is still much room for growth. In South Africa, approximately 50 percent of adults are still unbanked, and they are estimated to have stashed nearly $2 billion in mattresses and elsewhere. In India, 41 percent of adults (which means 300 million people) are unbanked, and there is far more cash socked away under the floorboards.

There are three morals to this story. First, the business model for addressing new customers in emerging markets needs to be built from the ground up. Western companies often struggle in emerging markets because they simply cannot abandon the approaches that have served them so well elsewhere. They enter through serving the top end of the market, and then they cannot move into lower-income tiers because of their model's high costs and presumptions about how products should be sold.

Second, the lower-income tiers in emerging markets offer great potential for growth. In India, for example, 70 percent of the country live in households projected to earn between roughly $2,000 to $12,000 per year by 2015.[7] Some observers point to spending power further up the pyramid, and undoubtedly there is much growth there as well. However, these richer levels of society are often not new markets with new dynamics, so they can be fiercely competitive. While growing ranks of people are becoming well-off, the markets can be already well served, and this makes entry quite challenging. Capitec and SKS created strong businesses where others were not already competing. Other firms have followed, but the early movers created formidable advantages around customer data, distribution systems, and other factors.

The third moral relates to the bottom of the pyramid, where abject poverty creates immense need. Certainly, many companies have illustrated the potential in this market, which is addressed at length in work by the late C. K. Prahalad and others.[8] But if the strain of reimagining a business model for middle-income levels is hard, it is immensely difficult to remake a model to serve the destitute. SKS has pulled off the feat, but Capitec has not prioritized it. Even for these local companies steeped in the nuances of their markets, it has been tough to center a business model on consumers with highly unstable lives and very little disposable income. Readers in the West seeking profits through jumping first to new markets among the world's most deprived consumers likely will find success to be extremely hard won. It can be a better strategy to get to know a market through serving its middle and then to imagine how to move downward into addressing the poorest before competition there becomes too intense. SKS rivals ICICI Bank and State Bank of India have done this effectively. The neediest are ill-served by fitful efforts that ultimately fail and frighten off other potential investors. They will benefit from firms that understand a market intimately and use the clear profit potential to justify a long-term focus on addressing the poor.

Levers for Remaking Business Models

As discussed in Chapter 3, a business model centers on what a company is offering for a target group of consumers. Competitive strategy, partnerships and sales channels, financial models, and corporate competencies should support the delivery of this offering (too often the reverse occurs, with companies taking these four parameters as fixed and then casting about for new offerings that will fit within their static model). For emerging markets, each lever merits close examination.

Rethinking the Offering

The Yachana Foundation is based on Ecuador's Napo River, a wide brown torrent coursing through dense rainforest on its way to joining the Amazon. Headed by Douglas McMeekin, a Kentucky businessman who relocated to this scarcely developed region in 1982, it provides education to indigenous tribespeople and employment in the local ecological tourism industry. A hallmark project is a boarding school providing one of the only options for secondary education in the region. With classrooms abutting the jungle, it educates dozens of promising students every year.

But Yachana had a problem. Computers are essential to a modern education, yet standard PCs quickly fall prey to high humidity and insects persistently looking for new homes. Finding skilled local service for the machines was out of the question. Moreover, the facility runs as much as possible on solar-powered electricity, and the low wattage generated by its system is insufficient to run traditional power-gulping computers.

So Yachana sought out Aleutia, a startup in London with a radically different approach. Because the company's computers have no fans, they offer little access to insects. Their operating system is based on inexpensive, ultrareliable Linux, and there are very few moving parts to break down. Aleutia has designed the machines from the ground up to consume just 15 percent of the electricity of a traditional desktop, so they can be powered by common solar cells.

Because Aleutia's products are engineered for remote locations in developing countries, for customers such as Yachana, they sell themselves. The company would have had a hard time breaking into the ranks of the mainstream PC industry by fighting entrenched rivals, but by targeting the millions of potential locations such as Yachana's, it has a strong position in a niche with high potential for growth. The four-year-old company has already sold its machines in 62 countries.

Aleutia illustrates how firms need to think carefully through the jobs that target customers are trying to get done and then engineer a solution tightly tailored to their needs. The company's Web site states

> Our take on the market is that large computer manufacturers overshoot the needs of most customers. We prefer to think of computers as appliances—simple devices with a minimal learning curve that people can use to get something done. Unless you're editing videos or playing advanced 3D games, you don't need the processing power of a modern desktop. Most people just want to write documents, create spreadsheets, send e-mails, and browse the Web. We provide PCs that do that well, and whose minimal power requirements can be met by small, inexpensive solar panels and 12-V batteries.[9]

Note that the company says nothing about low prices. While its machines are inexpensive, they are not dramatically cheaper than rivals. Many firms automatically think of emerging markets as places demanding rock-bottom prices, but often there are several other unmet needs that customers will gladly pay to address.

Competitive Strategy

Traditional competitive strategy involves beating rivals on key selling points that matter deeply to a company's most important customers. This approach can lead firms to provide ever fancier, more complex offerings to a thin slice of demanding customers who supply the greatest profits—It brings us sport utility vehicles (SUVs) from Cadillac. This is a solid approach for established markets because those Cadillac SUVs make good money. However, it can utterly fail in tackling new markets, especially in developing countries. In such settings, direct competitors often do not exist, and success comes from addressing barriers to market development rather than beating out other firms.[10]

It is hard to observe something that has not yet happened. On the other hand, competitors are easy to spot, and it is persistently tempting to focus on what is readily seen. Resist this urge. Competitors may be your allies initially in generating demand. Rigorously charting barriers to consumption and your strategy for surmounting them will help to keep the focus where it belongs.

Competitive weaknesses, of course, should be exploited. In some emerging markets, and especially in the world's smaller economies, the cozy, cartel-like nature of competition among a small number of firms creates ample opportunity to undercut prices. If an upstart is targeting customers who are relatively unimportant for existing firms, the incumbents often will hold back from lowering their prices to match the entrant. The new company may fail for any number of reasons, and it would be difficult both economically and politically for the established firms to raise prices back to their former level. While it enjoys a price advantage, the new firm can hone a low-cost business model and build a formidable market position before the incumbents start to counterattack.

Partnerships and Sales Channels

Success in emerging markets often hinges on one variable: distribution. Take, for example, the soft drink industry. The developing world generally can be divided up between red and blue countries, where either Coca-Cola or Pepsi dominates. Each company's market position has little to do with local tastes but rather results from an ironclad control of distribution networks. It is amazing how in a village miles from the nearest road, with no power lines and little clean water, there can be a stand selling soft drinks. The sophistication of these networks is truly remarkable. The networks frequently are proprietary, and if a merchant were to start stocking a rival's products, he could find himself quickly cut off from supply of the dominant brand. Worse, his refrigerator could be repossessed by the bottling company. With few ways to win a foothold market and scale economies being a critical factor in distribution, it is very hard for a soft drink upstart to gain traction in a new territory.

Even if traditional resellers wish to stock a new product category, they may lack the skill to sell and service it. This was Lotus Energy's experience. The Katmandu company had a vision of providing solar electricity to countless Nepalese villages underserved by existing systems, but it ended up having to do everything. The company designs systems, sells and installs them, trains users, and provides service. It was not easy to create each of these competencies, but over the years, these abilities have led Lotus to become an industry leader, with over 120 employees in 20 branch offices throughout the country.[11]

Local partnerships also matter in another sense. Agriculture may be civilization's oldest market, but contemporary networks of growers and high-tech processors make possible many new markets within this giant industry. Billionaire investor George Soros apparently has come to this conclusion, making a large investment in the Argentine-Brazilian food company Adecoagro. A major emphasis of the firm is growing sugarcane for ethanol production, an industry in which Brazil is the world's largest exporter. Given Brazil's state-of-the-art technologies for sugarcane refinement and ethanol processing, the country makes possible innumerable new uses for this age-old product.[12]

Financial Model

Aleutia demonstrates that successful solutions for emerging markets need not be the lowest in price. Similarly, Nokia has created a huge business in emerging markets without supplying the cheapest handsets. However, it certainly helps to be price competitive when selling to poorer consumers, as well as to the family-owned businesses that predominate in developing countries. These buyers are looking for good value.

To make money while keeping prices low, companies can focus on a few key moves:

- *Minimize capital expenditures.* While profit margins may be thin, the return on the capital employed by businesses may be high. Developing countries can supply low-cost labor, so capital-intensive automation is not necessarily wise. In addition, keeping a business relatively labor intensive can enable the firm to grow its costs commensurately with its revenue, reducing the investment risks assumed in these sometimes unstable environments.
- *Narrowly target the market.* Capitec demonstrates the power of engineering a solution for a well-defined market. Because it has rigorously defined who it wishes to service with what sorts of

offerings, the bank can have both lower costs and better service than many of its competitors.

- *Remember that affordable is different from inexpensive.* Leasing or pay-as-you-go solutions can reduce the upfront expense of purchases, putting them in reach of people with scant savings. Use of Celtel's airtime took off once the company started topping up subscribers' prepaid accounts with credits of just $1. Even though prices were not falling dramatically, many more people had the ability to scrape together $1 to purchase airtime rather than the $5 needed previously.

- *Master the challenge of getting paid.* A big impediment to the extension of electricity and water supply in developing countries is that it is very difficult to collect payment. Mail systems function poorly, credit ratings can be nonexistent, and the dearth of bank accounts makes it difficult to create direct-debit orders.[13] While many firms are focused on creating the lowest-cost, most efficient technologies in fields such as solar cells, there may be abundant returns available to companies that crack the challenge of collecting payment for these systems, such as through rolling out inexpensive and reliable prepaid meters. Payment is also a challenge for other types of companies, given that distributors often have little working capital to fund inventories and push for credit terms from their suppliers.

Competencies

Companies seeking new markets in developing countries need to think carefully through the competencies that really matter in this context. For example, the skill and responsiveness of front-line staff can make a big difference in winning trust from hesitant customers and overcoming reluctance to try something new. Our most significant advantage at Celpay Zambia was not the technology system, company parentage, or relationship with regulators. Rather, the people whom our customers dealt with day to day were superb, recruited for their initiative and quick thinking more than for ticking the right boxes on their résumés. To overgeneralize, staff in many emerging markets often are managed in an extremely hierarchical manner that does not emphasize proactive customer service; when a company can offer the opposite experience, it stands out.

Building Scale in Emerging Markets

Emerging markets can lack a voice in Western corporations because they are small contributors to revenue. Unfortunately, this becomes a self-perpetuating situation because efforts in these markets do not receive sustained attention and so continually languish. The reverse scenario is equally grim—high-profile, aggressive investment in key emerging markets before they are deeply understood, leading to equally high-profile losses.

What is a company to do? One answer can be to develop scale in a handful of key countries that serve as learning laboratories and bellwethers of opportunity. This sort of effort can be managed without continual intervention by senior management, and it allows for the kind of focus essential to creating profitable businesses. Venture capitalists, after all, are not asking their startups to tackle the entirety of new markets all at once but rather to demonstrate viability in a foothold first.

One dangerous tendency of companies is to choose a very large emerging market for an initial foray to the exclusion of any others. India and China often top the list of prospects. While the allure of these countries is clear, they can be difficult places to work, especially for inexperienced Western firms. Regulations are complex, local firms are difficult to displace, and labor laws can be challenging. Of 183 countries, the World Bank ranks China seventh-ninth and India one-hundred and thirty-fourth on an index of ease of doing business.[14] Their scores do not even factor in how the countries' vastness can require serious investment for creating ventures with any kind of market power. By contrast, the World Bank rankings—which include industrialized countries—list Hong Kong second and Georgia twelfth. Midsized countries ranking well include Thailand (nineteenth), Malaysia (twenty-first), South Africa (thirty-fourth), and Colombia (thirty-ninth). Of course, many factors need to go into choosing a target market, including economic growth, corruption, and openness to foreign investment. The point is that it can be far easier to establish a reasonable business in a handful of midsized markets than to do the same thing in a single gigantic market. Moreover, the variation between these markets helps to mitigate risks associated with any given country and can enhance the amount learned through these efforts.

Once firms understand how to succeed in these markets, they can leverage that knowledge in their expansion. Shoprite, a South African grocer with nearly $10 billion in revenue, generates 10 percent of that sum from 16 other African countries where it has expanded over the past 15 years. In many of those countries, it is the dominant player. Expertise gained by several consumer products companies in Mexico has aided their efforts worldwide. India and China certainly are important places to be, but companies may struggle to find success there if they cannot make things work in simpler places.

This is not to say that companies should be absent from India and China. Even some of the most insular industries are being affected by emerging competitors from these nations, and in some businesses, the countries' roles are fundamental. IBM now employs more people in India than in the United States and has become India's second-largest private sector employer. If there is potential for a Western firm in these countries, there is likely at least as much opportunity for an indigenous company to attack attractive Western markets. Local presence can be essential to comprehending the future competitive landscape, as well as to building the market understanding and relationships that will enable a push for business among billions of consumers. Companies simply should anticipate major struggles in India and China— even well-managed global giants such as Ford and Vodafone have had big difficulties—and they should have a portfolio of emerging-market investments, some less risky than others.

With developing countries being so diverse, firms need to map out what advantages translate effectively between national markets. After all, customers in Uruguay are not going to care all that much about a company's leading position in Bangladesh. Advantages that can transfer across countries may include

- *Brand.* The allure of global brands is somewhat overstated, given that in consumer products they tend to concentrate in sexy industries such as sport and fashion that have worldwide stars. However, in business-to-business (B2B) markets, there can be more potential. It is challenging to cost-effectively create a B2B brand with the power to pull in potential customers, but creating case studies of success in relevant environments is more feasible. Software companies, for example, make good use of implementation case studies to illustrate their impact.

- *Specialized skills.* For Celtel, a key competitive advantage lay in a small cadre of technical specialists who could support the rollout of new telecom infrastructure, billing systems, and other critical but arcane elements of the business. These people were very difficult to find in sub-Saharan Africa. However, the picture is changing quickly. Today, telecom equipment companies such as Ericsson are diversifying into support services, and in many emerging markets intermediaries are developing to fill previous voids.

- *Economies in research and development (R&D) and production.* A few years ago, analysts were projecting that Nokia would lose out in China to local, low-cost upstarts such as Ningbo Bird. It has not happened. Nokia and other global manufacturers have exploited their scale economies to provide relatively advanced handsets to even the bottom tiers of the market.

- *Technology pipeline.* Western market leaders can have abundant in-house expertise and technology to create cost-effective offerings for emerging economies. The challenge may lie in fighting ingrained impulses to engineer expensive solutions that lose sight of real market needs. When company leadership pushes staff to stay customer-centric in their thinking, technology pipelines from developed nations can convey real advantages.

While developing countries hold clear potential, they are easy to deprioritize; it is simpler to exploit other sources of growth. But catching up is expensive. The drug company Abbott is spending $3.7 billion to jumpstart its business in India through acquiring a market leader. The food company Kraft bought Britain's Cadbury for $19 billion largely for its strong position in key emerging markets. Had these firms devoted more energy in previous years to growing organically in these countries, they might not have had to take such drastic actions.

A key theme of this chapter is that efforts in emerging markets should not be costly. There are ways to learn inexpensively about these territories even while building viable businesses. A company then will be in far better shape to expand at a pace commensurate with the opportunity.

Summary

- Developing countries are a critical new market, yet they win scant attention from most large companies.
- Businesses can win in these environments by creating ventures from a blank slate, targeting lower-income tiers, and not over-stretching all aspects of their business model at once.
- Key levers to pull in remaking the business model include taking a broad look at which customer needs to address, asymmetrically attacking competitors, securing distributors that are hungry for new markets, emphasizing new financial formulas, and developing staff competencies suited for these environments.
- Some of the biggest emerging markets are tough places to do business, and it is important to pursue a portfolio of emerging-market investments that can provide local scale as well as springboards for expansion.

Chapter | 8

ENABLING THE
CORPORATION

Sony Corporation became a titan of the consumer electronics industry through pioneering new markets: the transistor radio, the Walkman, the camcorder, and much else. The company's cofounder and long-time chairman, Akio Morita, was legendary for his close observation of consumer habits and brilliant insights about potential new-product categories. His retirement in 1994 was a tragedy for the company—since then, Sony's stock price has been essentially unchanged.

How can firms create a corporate competency around finding and exploiting new markets? This book has stressed that the dynamics in new markets require a perspective distinct from the one that wins in established industries. As this chapter will explain, in some situations it is sufficient to have a handful of exceptional individuals guiding the way into these new sources of growth. For many companies, however, there needs to be a broader and more institutional competency around new markets.

Organizations often look for a transformative "silver bullet." They create an incubator, do some scenario planning, or build a corporate venture-capital unit. Sometimes they invest in the trappings of innovation—makers of beanbag furniture love these programs. Yet, if creating a competency around new sources of growth were so easy, these markets would be much more competitive and have less transformative potential. Becoming sustainably successful in new markets is hard work involving careful balancing of priorities and tailoring of approaches to a company's particular circumstances.

One decision to make early on is how widespread these new competencies need to be. While innovation programs can be broadly based, targeting both new ventures and better execution of existing businesses, new-market programs may be more focused. They may be walled-off efforts that draw minimally on the organization's core but nonetheless derive some advantage from that legacy. A software company, for example, can task a few developers and marketers to create a new product, leveraging their understanding of customers, the computing environment, and product distribution. Alternatively, a company may require extensive collaboration from existing business units, such as when a retailer or bank tries to use its current physical locations to provide new services. The software firm can focus its new-market efforts around a small, high-octane group, whereas the bank has to think through political mandates, widespread training, human resources (HR) systems, and many other variables.

This chapter applies to both these circumstances. It is organized in three parts. The chapter starts with an overall perspective on how to plan a new-markets program—whatever a firm's size or industry. It proceeds to a section addressing organizational transformation, which will be of most interest to larger companies that have to commercialize new ventures alongside their core business units. The chapter concludes with a section offering several lessons and watch-outs from firms that have successfully created units devoted to new markets. The chapter details

- How venture capital provides a better model for pursuing new markets than traditional corporate planning processes
- How culture and management systems work hand in hand to create organizational change
- How some firms have created a discipline around repeatedly finding growth in new markets

Why Are Venture Capitalists So Successful?

The success of the venture capital industry is staggering. Despite financing just one-sixth of 1 percent of the new businesses in the United States, VC firms (VCs) back a full 60 percent of the companies that grow to the point of an initial public offering (IPO). Year after year, VC returns exceed public market comparables—one study found that the average VC fund has outperformed publicly traded stocks by 25 percent.[1] Especially for new markets, the VC model is tremendous.

Why? We can boil the distinctness of the VC approach down to four major elements.

Blank-Slate Strategy

Most large companies devote substantial resources to strategic planning, so it may seem odd to say that VCs succeed in part because of strategic clarity. The distinction is that corporate planning typically is focused on maximizing the potential of an existing business, so it sees the world from the perspective of a company seeking to push more units of whatever the firm sells. The plan revolves around such variables as how much to invest in marketing and research and development (R&D) and how aggressively to price. Frequently, the strategic plan is really a financial plan with a thin veneer of competitive analysis on top. There is little fresh thinking about industry change, or about how an entrepreneur would approach the industry if he had a blank slate. As Clayton Christensen has chronicled very well, this is how companies end up in strategic dead ends—Digital Equipment kept on making better and better minicomputers, but owners of PCs simply did not care.

A VC uses a totally different lens. The firm is constantly scanning the world for new markets that seem on the cusp of taking off. The firm develops a clear point of view about how these markets might evolve and what sorts of bets might work out. Then, sometimes, the firm waits. As explained by David Aronoff of the leading early-stage investor Flybridge Ventures,

> We take the crocodile approach. We identify trends that we have a passion for, we find out enough about them, and then we lie in the relevant pools waiting for interesting things to float by, from entrepreneurs, academia or companies that have been bootstrapped.[2]

Other VCs will seek to run a strategic play again and again. Versant Ventures, a major health-care VC firm, invests across a wide array of medical specialties and technologies. However, it looks for some common features in its portfolio companies. As explained by Versant's Charles Warden,

> We like to pursue breakthrough solutions for patients that also reduce the total cost of care to the healthcare system. A less invasive technology might solve an important clinical problem that can't otherwise be addressed. In addition, it might move the site of care from an expensive and centralized setting to one that is more

cost-effective and accessible. We also try to be first to market with a strong intellectual property position and an ability to generate better clinical data about medical outcomes than competitors. Sometimes we will follow if a technology is clearly superior to current options. But we typically avoid the middle ground, where there are multiple players in a nascent market and we are trying to pick which of several unproven technologies will win.[3]

VCs succeed because they are strategic opportunists. They follow a strategy suited to the moment, not to yesteryear when an established company first entered a market. They focus resources on what has high growth potential today, not on sustaining businesses that already may have passed their peak. Because the canvas for VCs is so broad and open, they have to be very clear about what they are seeking. When the opportunity presents itself, the crocodile can move lightening fast.

Portfolio Planning

Consider your retirement plan. It likely has a mix of assets—stocks and bonds, domestic and foreign holdings, and perhaps precious metals and real estate. In some years, conservative investments will do well. Other times are more favorable to riskier assets. While any particular holding might have a great or terrible year total performance balances out over time.

Now consider the typical company's portfolio of investments in new markets, when these investments exist. There may be a very small handful of ventures—not nearly enough to provide year-to-year stability. Because sallying into new markets is so distinct from most companies' norms, approval for these investments may come all the way from "Mount Olympus." The "gods" in their plush offices decreed that they liked an idea. The C-suite does not deal in small figures, so plenty of money supports the few ventures approved. Failure therefore would be crushingly expensive—financially and for a few peoples' careers—so the venture may play "small ball"—going for easy wins that may not be market-shaping moves. Or, if the going gets really bleak, the venture may try to double-down on its wagers by investing in a massive push to snatch victory from the jaws of defeat.[4] Either way, many of the investments fail to meet expectations. They sputter forward, or they flame out.

In other words, the corporate portfolio lacks asset diversity. It owns Treasury bills and a couple of wild and risky bets. This is not really what the gods wanted, but their lack of a portfolio plan allowed the peculiar calculus of company politics to create a mix of holdings that no right-minded investment advisor would dream of recommending.[5]

A VC looks at the world in a completely different way. The firm knows that six of ten VC investments will be a total loss. Another two or three will pay back the investment but make little positive return. Hopefully, the remaining one or two will be huge wins. The VC can make this formula work by rigorously limiting amounts invested until companies prove their potential, spreading its wagers over several investment theses and ensuring that the inevitable failures are quick and inexpensive. The firm looks askance at portfolios where every investment works out. As the auto-racing great Mario Andretti once said, "If everything seems under control, you're just not going fast enough."

A portfolio plan provides courage to kill new ventures. For a large company, this can be terribly hard. Ending a venture sometimes means effectively terminating a career, so the natural tendency in most big firms is to struggle forward. With a portfolio plan, it is easier to kill two of five investments if the plan allows for only three to move forward. The plan provides cover for people associated with the losing ventures, allowing them to save face by blaming the strictness of the process; it can make the career stakes less life and death.

Additionally, the plan allows for better budgeting of resources. Many new-markets programs start with backing multiple ideas. As the concepts grow to become real businesses, the needs increase for money and skilled staff. New projects also keep coming in; there is often no shortage of interesting ideas or their champions, and it is hard to deny support to potential internal allies of the new-markets program. Thus the firm tries to stretch its resources, leading to longer time lines for building the ventures. Ultimately, the situation reaches a breaking point, and many projects are cut all at once. Critical decisions get made very quickly about what stays and what goes. A VC avoids this trap by knowing at the outset how many financial and human resources likely will be required at what time. The firm does not spread its resources too thinly, and it can provide appropriate support to ventures as they grow.

Few companies are more rigorous than Royal Dutch Shell. In a business where billions of dollars are invested on the basis of geologic probabilities, Shell puts great emphasis on detailed analysis and minimizing its number of failed explorations. Yet in its Gamechanger program, which emulates VC practices, the company has a totally different approach. Gamechanger aims for three to five big wins per year. To get there, the program estimates that it needs at least 200 ideas, with 50 active projects at any one time, of which 15 percent get to proof-of-concept. In some years, just 35 percent of those are deployed. By expecting such a high rate of failure, Shell can pay appropriate attention to sourcing the requisite number of ideas while preserving resources for its most promising ventures.[6]

Expectation of Variabiity

For a well-established business, spreadsheets rule. The potential profitability of investments determines where the money flows. Because the company understands its business deeply, it can require managers to submit detailed budgets for coming years and hold them to their word.

New markets should be treated differently, but often they are not. When I was building a mobile commerce business in Africa, a very senior executive at our corporate parent—one of the continent's largest cell phone networks—closely examined the two-year budget I had just passed to him. He leaned over his desk, looked me keenly in the eye, and said, "This is a *contract*. Do you understand?" Unfortunately, I did, and I was terrified. We had just set up our systems, had no customers, and did not even have regulatory approval to operate. The revenue figures were an overall guess. I had a rough idea of the total market size but huge uncertainty about how quickly customers would sign on. One might think that a totally new industry in a place such as Zambia would be given some leeway to find its path, but no. The company's budgeting process needed my figures to create an overall revenue estimate for noncore businesses. The consequence was that my speculations were placed on an equal footing with rock-solid estimates from well-known holdings that the company had owned for years.

Now listen to how a VC approaches this task. David Aronoff at Flybridge Ventures explains,

> The VC approach to financials for new startups has nothing to do with what I learned in business school. I want to ensure that expected expenses are reasonable, and we do some sensitivity analysis around that. This tells us how much money we need to raise. We look at the business plan's revenue picture, and then we throw it out the window. This is at best a dream.

The VC method reflects how an asset manager would evaluate high-risk holdings. She has a plan for how much will be allocated to these assets every year and a targeted rate of return on those investments. However, she knows that any one investment likely will deviate significantly from that target. The secret is to have enough investments so that the variability is neutralized.

Because a VC does not budget based on fictional revenues but instead focuses on real costs, it does not overfund ventures. The firm asks how much is needed to finance the company until its next funding round, which typically is associated with a major milestone in the company's development, such as its first customer. This approach concentrates the company on that milestone, avoiding distraction from the countless other things that the company eventually will need to do but which matter little in terms of reaching that immediate goal. The VC thereby keeps its investments manageably small, enabling it to spread its bets.[7]

Sequencing Risks

The VC not only sets focused goals for reaching the next milestone but also ties those criteria to the most important risks facing the venture. The firm is not looking to build an institution for the ages—there will be time for that later. At the moment, the VC wants to know that the institution is worth building.

For instance, if a company is trying to sell something online, the VC may not look for the company to build a sophisticated information technology and order-fulfillment system. In the near term, that can be borrowed from another company, or some manual processing can handle the few sales the business will chalk up in its early days. While the company eventually will need such a system, there is little doubt that it can be created. A much bigger risk is whether customers actually want to buy whatever the company is selling.

For all their sometimes cumbersome bureaucracy, established companies can lack patience. Even if senior executives expect new-market ventures to iterate their way toward success, the managers of those businesses may feel differently. They are frequently high-potential staff on a brief stopover in the venture to build their credentials. They do not have years to show results. Because they are A-list players seeking an unbroken string of successes in their careers, they push to build the business fast. Often they will be in another position before the potential flaws in this strategy become apparent, and it will be easy to escape blame. By contrast, a VC fund typically has a 10-year duration, and venture capitalists receive much of their compensation on the back end of that time frame as investment returns become clear. They have few incentives to game the system by tackling too much too soon.

Creating Organizational Competencies

Some industries operate as a series of half-connected markets, where the distinctions between customer types make it straightforward to create separate business units dedicated to their service. Retailers and life-science companies both need to use complex databases, but the configuration of those products, their interoperability with other systems, and much else are totally distinct. The enterprise software firm Oracle thus could grow into a giant by combining a deep competency in databases with an organization highly oriented around the uniqueness of customers' industries. If Oracle aims for a new market, as it did with software managing clinical trials for pharmaceuticals, it does not need to change approaches in other business units. Oracle has little reason to alter organizational competencies but rather a need to create a stellar team that is highly focused on a given opportunity.

Other companies may build walls between new ventures and the core business because the new market threatens the old one. Kodak delayed development of a digital camera for years because the new technology was so threatening to film.[8] Fortunately, new markets that cannibalize old ones often have few interdependencies with the core business. Digital cameras used a different technology marketed through a different channel with a different business model. Eventually, Kodak set up a separate organization to pursue the market.

Sometimes an industry's interdependencies require more internal collaboration. When Lufthansa entered the air taxi business—chartering private jets on an as-needed basis—it made little sense to wall the venture off from the rest of the company. The whole reason why travelers would choose a Lufthansa private jet is that the firm is renowned for its outstanding aircraft maintenance, consistent in-flight service, and tightly integrated route network. Lufthansa's competitive advantage in this new market lay in coupling its offering with its core business. Figure 8-1 lays out how to think about these variables in the context of both competitive advantage and risk.

Figure 8-1 Separation versus integration of a new-markets program.

	Low — Impact of Failure on the Core Business — High	
Intangibles, such as employee knowledge or brand	Carve out venture development and execution into a largely distinct group	Carve out venture development and execution into a group with tight governance by senior leaders from the core business
Source of Competitive Advantage		
Tangibles, such as physical infrastructure or front-line staff	Develop ventures separately but integrate them early; govern program through a board of senior leaders from the core business	Consider seeding venture efforts within the core business, with success metrics including the extent of growth from new markets

A huge distinction between the VC approach and corporate venturing is the need in many firms to pursue new markets through collaborating with existing business units. This is tough to execute well, requiring attention both to the "soft," cultural aspects of organizations in addition to the "hard" variables of management systems. We now turn to those issues.

A Culture of Innovation and the "Soft" Side of Change

Google lists 900,000 links for the phrase *culture of innovation*. Rarely has a term been used so much with so little agreement about what it means (in fairness, *business model* has 14.8 million links). People know an innovative workplace when they are in one; there is a can-do spirit and a willingness to listen to any idea. They also know that some innovative companies work in nontraditional offices—this is where the beanbag chairs come in. People want their workplaces to be more like those firms.

The problem is that culture is a lagging variable, not a leading one. Changing a company's competencies by beginning with its culture is a nonstarter. Culture exists because a firm's organization, processes, and leadership favor certain behaviors. If a company's structure is a complex matrix, with ample input sought on decisions, it is very unlikely to act quickly and risk boldly. A wall-sized poster of a square-jawed sailing team battling the fiercest of seas is a beautiful thing—but it will not change the culture.

Although it lags other changes in management systems, culture can be a very real impediment to pursuing new markets. It provides the guiding compass for the hundreds of daily decisions that management will never explicitly make. Culture affects how aggressively a firm might partner, whether it will accept launching a quick-and-dirty Web site, how it will deal with dissatisfied initial customers, and countless other variables affecting how a company approaches new sources of growth. How can companies address such a significant but slow-to-change barrier?

Progress begins by defining the exact nature of the problem. It is too easy to ascribe organizational deficiencies to "culture" rather than to more specific variables such as performance metrics or governance processes. Interviews and employee surveys are tried-and-true means of making the problem concrete. The challenge is to drive from vague frustrations to detailed statements that spell out an issue to be tackled—not "we never make decisions" but rather "marketing can change project mandates even after engineering spends months working out how to create what they originally requested."

Chip and Dan Heath, brothers who work at Stanford and Duke universities, have put forth a theory of how behaviors change.[9] One of their findings is that even when institutions face deeply entrenched problems, there are almost always "bright spots" where specific challenges have been conquered. By finding what works in the bright spots, organizations can replicate those successes and also make those solutions feel homegrown. What can gain the most eager reception is not a solution suggested in some book (perish the thought) but rather the thoughtful shaping of an already successful approach into something that can be broadly rolled out. While external benchmarks can help to guide that shaping exercise, behavior ultimately shifts when people believe that change can be readily achieved by individuals much like themselves.

As examples build of how the right behaviors are occurring, organizations can trumpet them. The key is to go beyond a headline ("We Sold $50 Million in China Last Month") to a story that registers with people on a visceral level ("Sheila lived in a Chinese village for a week and learned that our price can't exceed the cost of an egg"). It is hard to see how to match the headline in day-to-day behavior but easier to inculcate the story into everyday actions.

Because culture lags, these stories will go nowhere if they are not accompanied by a simultaneous change in management systems. People need to see that new behaviors are swimming with the tide. While this push for culture change never can supplant attention to systems, it can help to ensure that the other efforts yield lasting impact.

Management Systems and the "Hard" Variables that Build Competency

Firms on a quest for new-market competencies sometimes mimic innovation powerhouses. Google, Apple, Philips, and Facebook are often seen as important benchmarks. The problem is that these companies are *completely* different. Their management styles, approaches to partnering, and internal processes bear no resemblance to each other. It is little wonder that firms embarking on benchmarking exercises can wind up confused.

Before copying another company's management systems, an organization should have a good idea of its archetype. This is like surgery. Transfusions can be an excellent idea, but they really need to be of the same blood type. Table 8-1 lays out four distinct archetypes for how firms can approach new markets.[10]

Large companies frequently fall within the systematic innovation archetype. Their size reflects the fact that they deal across multiple markets, and over time, they develop a competitive advantage through mastering a complex business model with many organizational interdependencies. While a big, long-established firm could create a totally distinct unit focused on new markets, that approach may not leverage the assets that give the company an advantage over entrepreneurial rivals. A better outcome might be to navigate the challenging path of commercializing new ventures alongside existing businesses. An incubator may be a means of providing new ventures sufficient attention while linking their development to other business units in the company. Seven issues are often encountered when following this road:

Table 8-1: Company Archetypes

	Description	Strategic Environment	Governance and Process	Human Resources
Marketplace of ideas (Google)	Set employees free to create own ideas and build internal support, then seek executive buy-in for ramp-up and commercialization	Diffuse opportunities and threats, ability to rapidly prototype at low cost without extensive internal coordination	Clear strategy providing cohesion, fast-moving seed funding, systems facilitating collaboration	Staff provided portion of their time for experiments, awards for outputs, no penalty for early failure
Visionary leader (Apple)	Key executive who conceives future growth platforms and avoids dilution of the vision through committees	Growth comes from a small number of big potential markets, few dependencies on outside entities	Excellent market intelligence, plan that creates detailed links between vision and execution	Staff rewarded for collaboration and success of overall company
Systematic innovation (Philips)	Rigorous management of new-markets exploration, widespread toolkit for assessing new-market opportunities	Complex businesses with large sets of offerings and/or high interdependence between business units	Structured means of gaining cross-functional support and resources, portfolio approach	Minimal expectation of "night job" experiments, rotations to dedicated projects, awards for collective achievement
Collaborative innovation (Facebook)	Rapid-fire partnerships that quickly trial new offerings and invest in what succeeds	Ability to plug-and-play with strategic partners, company owns an audience or asset where it is easy to try new things	Delegated responsibility for partnerships, simple process for partners, clear metrics for assessing experiments	Staff incented on success of enterprise and effectiveness of process rather than their individual ideas

1. Mandate

Before a company decides on the inputs required to create its next growth engine, it should determine the outputs. How large a contribution to revenue and/or profit should the new businesses collectively make, and by when? What types of ventures are clearly out of bounds—for example, things that could disrupt the core business or damage its reputation? What kinds of new markets are most strategic for the corporation, such as through creating a new source of growth while entrenching the core business with its customers? How important will it be to create partnerships? Coupling these considerations with a portfolio plan will help the company to estimate how many projects it will need during different time frames, immediately prune initiatives that are off-strategy, bring aboard people with the right competencies, and inoculate the effort against the pet projects that executives inevitably will direct its way.

2. Process

Entrepreneurial activities can be stifled by large binders of processes, but it is equally hazardous to have little process at all. A well-understood process gives staff a clear way to gain a hearing for their ideas, a means of funneling the typical cascade of ideas to a manageable number of opportunities, and a mechanism to seek broad-based input without undergoing endless rounds of internal meetings.

The process should make it very easy for anyone to gain an initial hearing. At Shell, even junior staff can request a quick meeting with the firm's Gamechanger program to discuss an idea, with no numbers. Eventually, there will be a time for more detailed explorations of an idea and thorough financial analysis, but Shell follows the approach of venture capitalists, who give short meetings to a wide array of entrepreneurs.

Process is a necessary analogue to having a portfolio plan. With a clear way of reviewing ventures at a handful of milestones, executives can whittle down their list of initiatives on a regular basis and avoid the messy axe swinging needed to chop large chunks out of an unwieldy project list.

An effective process for new markets needs to be flexible. In traditional lines of business, there may be a set sequence of hurdles to be addressed at any one stage—first customer demand, then product design, preselling, and so forth. New markets may be quite distinct from each other. Process steps should focus on first addressing the most important variables that are the easiest to assess. If the key issue is whether a technology works and a prototype can be built inexpensively, do it! If instead the big concern is pricing, run a quick study to understand the value that a new offering creates for customers. The process should facilitate projects taking many potential routes to their ultimate goal depending on the timing and outcome of potential events that are somewhat outside the company's control.

The company's process should extend to what happens after a venture is terminated. Too often the aftermath of a failed effort is a combination of forgetting and scapegoating. This is a waste. Just like people, companies can learn much more from failure than from success. The U.S. military has created a ubiquitous process of after-action reviews (AARs) that are performed after almost any event to assess what happened, why it happened, and how things might have been done better. An AAR is not a postmortem but rather has a tight focus on a handful of issues related to key objectives. It concentrates on the participants' role rather than on what nonparticipants should have done. AAR participants may be at the platoon level or top brass; it is a universal approach to learning that aids immensely in making a giant organization responsive to fast-changing conditions.[11]

3. Governance

New markets are inherently cross-functional. While a function such as marketing or R&D might take the lead on exploring new markets in particular industries, it is typically impossible to commercialize a venture without involving a wide assortment of functions from across the firm. Therefore, programs devoted to new markets face a choice:

Option A: Avoid political bottlenecks and horse trading by keeping ventures housed entirely in one function, and later try to bring other functions on board through the utterly compelling nature of the business plan.

Option B: Recognize that internal dissent can create huge problems for ventures in the late stages of commercialization, so short-circuit that issue by creating a cross-functional governing board that is in charge from the get-go.

If there is any ability to pursue option B, do so. A cross-functional board can surface tensions early, hugely facilitate handoffs from an incubator to established lines of business, and provide useful diversity in assessing ventures from all sides. Do not tack governance meetings onto the ends of other meetings when these people get together because the tone may be wrong (potshot-taking instead of business-building), and minds may be wandering someplace else. Rather, create a regular rhythm of relatively brief meetings of these leaders in which they will review ideas in a range of development stages. The gatherings will begin to develop their own tenor distinct from more everyday happenings. I have seen many times how senior leaders look forward to these events as a kind of mental refreshment.

4. Metrics

Given that the ultimate output of a new-markets program might be in the medium to long term, how can management assess progress early on? The key is to create a mix of metrics[12] for

- Inputs such as ideas, partnerships, broad-based participation, and experiments
- Processes such as speed of concept development and fit with the portfolio plan
- Outputs such as results of company-wide competitions, market tests, and major learnings

Any one metric may bias what is inevitably a multidimensional endeavor. It is important to assess upfront what unhealthy behaviors might result from a metric. For instance, an emphasis on patents might limit external collaborations and yield technically interesting ideas that lack an ecosystem of firms supporting the venture.

Firms also benefit from mapping metrics as closely as possible to corporate strategies. A young company in a rapidly changing, fragmented industry will measure success quite differently than a long-established firm trying to reignite growth in a commoditized field. The former company may prize reference customers and market share, whereas the latter may value price premiums and the growth of particular buyers' accounts.

5. People
For a VC, one of a startup's most essential strengths is its people. A great idea backed by a mediocre team is unlikely to receive funding. The same principle applies to corporations sallying into new markets—a small cadre of outstanding people makes all the difference. Who are they?

They have passion. Entering a new market is hard, often thankless work. There is constant frustration and redirection. While the highs are tremendous, the lows are terrible. Hopefully, the participants' passion is not around a specific idea (which eventually may get shelved) but rather around taking initiative and creating something new. Staff also should be adept at handling the sorts of situations they are likely to encounter in the venture, such as forming outside partnerships and selling to potential customers.

Often their résumés will only hint at these strengths because the company has not valued "young Turk" behavior in the past. They may display such traits in other ways, such as chairing a group at their child's school or starting a small nonprofit organization. They also may be at the periphery of the company, leading an operating unit in an emerging market where there are few resources and a highly fluid environment.

Who should be avoided? Be wary of rising stars who are constantly networking in the company—they will have internal alliances that facilitate getting things done, but they may avoid pushing forward with unpopular ideas. Also watch out for senior leaders who may need to tend to many other responsibilities; startup CEOs have only one full-time job. Finally, try to avoid overly rapid turnover in leadership. New businesses can take time to develop, and pressure to rush things before the next staffing rotation can lead to unhealthy overinvestment in a small handful of ideas. Staffing changes also can lead to strategic redirection at the wrong times.

As Professors Vijay Govindrajan and Chris Trimble of Dartmouth's Tuck School of Business have investigated in depth,[13] teams supporting new ventures should include both dedicated staff and people in the core organization who eventually may be responsible for scaling up the business. These "ball catchers" may need to devote only a small portion of their time to the effort, but they should feel as though they have shared ownership of the program.

Sometimes the people involved with a corporate venture will argue for entrepreneur-like financial incentives. This is hazardous. These rewards can create tension between people on successful teams and those on failed efforts, as well as an unhelpful bandwagon effect for the clear winners that makes team size unmanageable. Financial incentives also can lead to neglect of exploratory projects that are highly unlikely to produce a big business soon. Awards, in contrast to rewards, can provide the necessary motivation, foster less ill will, and generate positive buzz throughout the company. Awards should go not just to the obvious winners but also to learning efforts and even to failed ventures that produced important findings. For example, the Mayo Clinic gives a "Queasy Eagle" award to teams that fail for good reasons.[14]

6. Mechanisms

The myth of lone genius makes for great movies. Picture Russell Crowe as the mathematical economist John Nash, scrawling equations with chalk on Princeton's windows in *A Beautiful Mind*. The notion is terrifically entertaining—but usually dead wrong.

In the modern era, the vast majority of major innovations have been collective endeavors, often stemming from the intersection of disciplines and the novel application of established technologies.[15] I may have led many teams on revolutionary ventures, but I would have been completely useless acting alone. Progress comes from teams concentrating wide diversity in expertise and perspectives.

Software systems are one way of pulling together communities of interest from throughout a corporation. Engineers in China can collaborate with marketers in California and regulatory specialists in Brussels to create truly novel ideas. Companies also can benefit from training people in the basics of approaching new markets so that there is a common language for staff to use in framing their perspectives. As with other aspects of new-markets programs, beware of silver bullets. One large technology firm invested heavily in a high-profile online ideation event. The most popular suggestion was that the company should give more money away to charitable causes—a nice concept but not exactly what the sponsors had in mind.

7. Getting Started

The person tasked with moving a company into new markets is on the receiving end of a firehose. The onslaught of ideas, internal meetings, external partnerships, interviews, and other immediate imperatives can feel never-ending. Where to begin?

The answer, of course, depends on circumstances. If the CEO is strongly behind a particular idea, by all means look into it. In the ideal world, though, the program leader should strike a balance between deep dives into a handful of priority areas and broad-based efforts that get the rest of the company involved in the program. These two thrusts yield both near-term opportunities and organizational enthusiasm that will be helpful down the road.

The deep dives need to be linked to strategy, and they should be reviewed at regular checkpoints with senior management. Whirlpool Corporation once picked a select team of 25 from throughout the company and sequestered them for months in the Italian Alps to dream up a totally new concept. They were given complete creative freedom. The result? An idea for people racing stationary bikes against each other over the Internet![16] That gem has yet to see the light of day.

If the quest for new markets is to be coupled with a push to make the core organization more innovative, the program can choose among several approaches to outreach. It is important to anchor people in strategic intent and provide them with a simple, stripped-down toolkit for reframing long-established markets. Companies then can deploy

- Internal program ambassadors who have been trained in the patterns of new markets and can jumpstart initiatives throughout the firm as they are called on by their peers.
- Events that get individuals to form their own teams and create ideas in a very short-period of time. Often called "hackathons," these efforts yield rough sketches and half-formed ideas, which

lead to energizing give-and-take discussions with management rather than the usual buttoned-up business-plan reviews. "Hackathons" are different from brainstorming sessions because they focus teams on creating a single concept with enough detail to understand how it would really work in practice.[17]

- Competitions for teams throughout the company to submit business plans. Note that competitions can be better suited for industries such as software that have discrete product lines rather than for fields such as health insurance where offerings have more interdependencies among corporate functions. Competitions also create losers, which may undermine efforts to build enthusiasm and momentum.[18]

- Efforts at "crowdsourcing" to generate ideas from customers. Because people tend to suggest modest enhancements on what they already purchase, and because new markets can hinge on the details of ideas, many firms find it most fruitful to have in-depth discussions with a small number of customers about unmet needs and then to look carefully together at potential opportunity areas.[19]

Inevitably, efforts to engage the rest of the organization or the outside world take a lot of time. Program leaders are often wise to generate some quick wins through first pursuing a small handful of tightly focused opportunities. This builds momentum and interest from the rest of the company, which helps considerably in making outreach more impactful.

The most important imperative is to get moving fast. The process of developing a new-markets program could be endless. Do what you can over a period not longer than four months; then make it real by pursuing a few projects quickly. The actual path taken by the program will set key precedents that matter much more than abstract design.

Avoid hype. One company I worked with launched its program at an event where a midlevel executive dressed as a superhero. I asked him who he was. "Innovation Man." It was a lot of fun but immediately created cynicism. It also proved that some men just should not wear tights.[20]

The Pathologies of Incubators

Why do incubator programs often begin with such fanfare, only to die quietly a few years later? One study of 300 programs found that only 47 percent met their strategic objectives, and only 24 percent met their financial goals.[21] If he or she is being honest, the head of almost any successful corporate incubator will admit that the unit has had a tough slog—the work is uncertain, builds few internal allies, and requires new corporate competencies. Yet success is critical to a company's future, so it is imperative to persevere. By diagnosing the root cause of incubator struggles, firms can take straightforward steps to improve outcomes quickly (see Table 8-2).

Case Studies of Success

Clearly, it is difficult to create the new while executing on the old. This section looks at two companies that have taken a highly deliberate approach to the mission. Both firms are over 150 years old and are based in namesake cities in the northeastern United States. The similarities end there.

Corning

Once a leader in making glass lightbulbs—by hand—Corning has come a long way from its nineteenth-century origins. This nearly $6 billion firm invented heat-resistant glass for baking (Pyrex), shatter-

Table 8-2 Diagnosing Incubators' Illnesses

Problem	Underlying Issue	Remedy
Too little output	Too many projects and too few resources create backlogs; people try to do too many things at once; attention gets divided and time lines lengthen.	Use a portfolio plan to prune projects and budget resources appropriately.
		Focus project teams on the one or two key risks facing a venture at any one time.
		Concentrate internal meetings into set events, minimizing the bilateral discussions that can consume so much staff time.
Irrelevant outputs	Companies have big expectations of incubators, but the resulting ventures look small and nonstrategic.	Define upfront the realistic outputs expected—how many businesses of what range in size?
		Set clear strategic parameters for ventures, and use these throughout milestone reviews.
		Assess whether the incubator is making big ideas small because it is overly risk averse.
		Compare, if possible, the incubator's output to VC-backed firms in the industry and determine how the VC portfolio looks different from the company's.
Outputs too risky	The portfolio becomes concentrated in a very small number of high-stakes ventures.	Compare, if possible, the success rate needed from the current portfolio to VCs' success rates in the relevant industry. What do the numbers say about the risk taken on?
		Use a portfolio plan to ensure that there is a balance of quick wins and more speculative investments.
		Diversify risks by balancing across technical, market, regulatory, and other risk types.

(continued)

Table 8-2 Diagnosing Incubators' Illnesses *(continued)*

Problem	Underlying Issue	Remedy
Failure in commercialization	Good ideas get neglected by the core organization once they "graduate" from the incubator.	Involve "ball catchers" early on—these are the people who will have day-to-day responsibility for commercialization.
		Involve the heads of ball-catching business units in the governance process.
		Help defray the costs of "graduated" businesses for a period of time after they transfer over, recognizing that established business units may have little budget flexibility to support ventures that are still in their early stages.
Victim of cost cutting	The company is supportive but needs to find money fast, and other budgets have nearer-term returns on investment.	Avoid overfunding. If ventures are focused on one or two risks at any one time, their budget requirements should be modest.
		Develop robust success metrics that assess progress even before the first ventures launch in the marketplace.
		Compare return on investing in new markets versus creating line extensions in existing markets. If internal numbers are unavailable for new ventures, use VC benchmarks.
		Calculate the company's gap between likely growth from line extensions and its overall financial targets for growth over the next five years. Assess the likelihood that other approaches will hit those objectives.

resistant containers (Corningware), and the first process for mass producing cathode-ray tubes for the nascent television market. It made the window glass on America's first space capsules, dominated the market for automobile catalytic converters, and pioneered optical fiber. The company is constantly inventing new markets. In 1984, it commercialized liquid-crystal display (LCD) glass and today supplies more than half the glass screens for the world's electronics. Today, around 70 percent of the company's revenue comes from products that did not exist five years ago.[22]

The firm's evolution is due in part to its willingness to shed businesses that have lost their growth potential. Corning is no longer the firm that makes Pyrex, Corningware, or many other products that it created. The money generated from these asset sales has funded a continuous quest for new markets.

Yet this inspiring tale of reinvention almost ended in tragedy. Corning was a huge winner in the Internet boom of the 1990s, dominating a highly profitable fiberoptic industry that was growing at lightning speed. It made major investments in research and production capacity to stay at the crest of the wave. Then the dot-com bubble imploded and nearly took the company down with it. Almost 50 percent of employees were let go. The stock lost 98 percent of its value.

In 2002, during the worst of the company's troubles, Corning invested to create still more new markets. The firm built an Exploratory Markets and Technologies Group reporting to the chief technology officer. Early on, the group organized a workshop bringing together more than 150 of its scientists and commercial people. For one and a half days, it listened to 14 external speakers ranging from academics to industry and government experts in fields such as communications technology, health, automotive, and energy. The speakers did not try to predict the future or ask for specific products but rather described the major challenges they were facing in their work. Corning's staff then split into 11 groups that over a half day shared what surprised them, what big shifts were creating new markets, and how Corning's competencies in materials science could play a role. They sought problems, not solutions.

Through this event, Corning identified several growth fields. One was the hybrid electric powertrain, the first really new powertrain technology in decades. The company studied the needs of hybrid vehicles in detail, and it identified an opportunity area in the power surges caused by both acceleration and braking. The capacitors then in use were not ideal for the job, so Corning started to define what an "ultracapacitor" might do. It identified applications extending beyond hybrid vehicles to a range of equipment including garbage trucks and earthmovers. The firm looked not just at the size of the market and its needs but also at its receptivity to new technology, the process by which new technologies had been adopted, the value that would be created for the customer, the full system into which the products would be inserted, and the range of traditional and new competitors it might encounter.

Exploratory Markets, a part of Corning's Strategic Growth unit, took on the challenge. The group is comanaged by a Ph.D. in materials science as well as a marketing expert, and its 14 staff members have a broad range of backgrounds. It seeks people who have worked in at least a couple different industries with several technologies so that they can recognize patterns of new-market development. These individuals manage a diverse portfolio based on metrics such as time frame, impact on existing versus new businesses, return on investment, and risk. They also measure the quality of processes such as project churn, making decisions quickly, and the number and depth of assessments. There are no financial metrics at projects' early stages and no expected value calculated for the portfolio.

Corning has found it best to continue building new ventures within the Strategic Growth group rather than transitioning them to existing lines of business that might not fully exploit the opportunity. As

Exploratory Markets' cohead Daniel Ricoult explains, "The downside is that late-stage projects take a lot of resources, but we have to be disciplined about keeping focus upstream as well." Projects in their later stages often leverage external resources, so the group is able to keep its balance of incubation versus business-building.

Governance of Strategic Growth's projects is split. For early stage explorations, the CTO chairs a Corporate Technology Council that draws on technical resources from throughout the company. Later stage efforts are governed by a Growth and Strategy Council, which is chaired by Corning's CEO.

The company has high hopes for ultracapacitors, but it has many other initiatives under way as well. A full 50 percent of Corning's R&D budget is devoted to projects outside existing businesses. The company's 155-year evolution is set to continue in exciting new directions.[23]

The Hartford

A five-hour drive away from Corning, The Hartford works in an environment that seems like a different planet. With $25 billion in revenues, it is a leader in the investment industry and both the life and property and casualty insurance markets. The company's storied history includes selling insurance policies to both Abraham Lincoln and Robert E. Lee. In the wealth management and insurance industries, product sales traditionally are done by agents and brokers, so The Hartford often lacks the direct customer contact that aids Corning in creating new businesses and communicating new ideas. In the United States, the company is regulated through a patchwork of state and federal institutions. New products in fields such as commercial general liability insurance may remain on a company's books for decades, even if the firm decides never to scale up its small experiments. If the company misjudges risk in an area, its losses could be significant. This is a tough setting for creating new markets.

The Hartford picked an outsider for the task. Jacqueline LeSage Krause had been a global management consultant, CEO of a digital media startup, and chief financial officer of a college prep school. Her responsibilities at The Hartford include both the company's strategic VC group and its incubator for new business concepts. Combining an entrepreneur's scrappy perspective and an understanding of how big companies work, she has created a unit that is working hard to churn out innovations. One result so far for this relatively new group is a program created with customer feedback. Called FleetAhead, it helps commercial fleet managers to improve driving safety through the use of advanced telematic technology.

Krause set up a governance structure that balances between the needs for flexibility and integration. She explains,

> We are very connected to the businesses but not directly part of the businesses. We have our own budget, and we "contract" with senior leadership, not an individual leader. With decisions being distributed among the members of the Innovation Investment Council that governs us, we don't reflect just one person's view of strategy or risk. Also, we're not a shared service that is billed out to business units, and that's very important. This way, the business unit leader isn't making a choice between today and tomorrow. The corporation has made that decision.

Conscious of the pitfalls in transitioning ventures between incubation and commercialization, Krause has tried to build buy-in from business units in several ways.

> The people and money for taking something from idea to scale-up happens within our group, but we partner with the business units from the get-go. Approval for starting an exploration of a new venture in a particular segment requires signatures from the

head of the business unit and its head of strategy. The business then has to commit a point person in usually a 5 percent time allocation who can help coordinate with others in the business and brainstorm with us. During some phases of development, like market testing, this person may be intensively involved, along with other individuals and groups such as a call center or field sales. So we benefit from the deep expertise of the business without needing to follow their processes or use their management tools.

A financial services company tends to manage by the numbers. Yet Krause's group works on ventures that will not be commercialized for at least two years or are in areas that are outside the core business. The group has input metrics, but it also needed an appropriate measure of output. It created "Return on Knowledge," a compendium of learnings from every project that are relevant to the core business, even if a project fails. The return on knowledge is summarized in an annual report for the firm's senior leadership team.

Krause tried to learn from others in similar roles, but there were still surprises. For her, one stood out:

Execution for us is so different than it is in the core. It's not just about thinking differently but how you run your processes. Our world is so nonlinear and full of uncertainty. We need to adapt constantly. You can't assess projects like that with red/yellow/ green indicators. How do you do that when you're not certain of the destination? We have our own methods—they are rigorous and transparent, so leaders are comfortable with that. But they reflect our world. You just cannot manage uncertainty in a linear way.[24]

The great challenge of new markets is often not the idea—exciting and sometimes even obvious. Instead, companies struggle with creating the new while executing faithfully on the old. There are no magic tactics to make this happen seamlessly. Instead, sophisticated managers use disciplined techniques, balance between competing objectives, and think carefully about how their goals mesh with corporate and business-unit strategies. While ventures must be highly adaptable, a program to create these businesses needs upfront planning about its mission, portfolio, governance, and a host of other factors. It is all too easy to succumb to expediency, making small but continuous compromises that lead to where so many have gone before—failure. This chapter has shown that there is another way, which is difficult and sometimes uncomfortable—but ultimately a far surer path to success.

Summary

- Venture capitalists are role models for how companies should attack new markets. They combine blank-slate strategy with portfolio planning, a tailored approach to financial analysis, and a deliberate sequencing of risks.

- In some environments it is possible for companies to enter new markets by creating dedicated business units, but in other industries, this makes little strategic sense. Balancing separation and integration is a delicate act requiring substantial forethought. Although companies need to be flexible in how they address the external world, internally they need to lay out clear rules of the road for internal audiences about how they will organize their efforts around new markets.

- Culture can be a major impediment to creating new ventures. It can be addressed through attention to examples and role models, but it will not fundamentally change without simultaneous efforts to alter management systems.

- Management systems comprise several dimensions that need to be aligned if companies are to tackle new-market opportunities effectively and avoid the afflictions common to corporate incubators.

- Corning and The Hartford provide two quite dissimilar case studies about how companies can organize their efforts around pursuing new markets.

Chapter | 9

A CATALYTIC ROLE
FOR GOVERNMENT

The Chinese government is investing $1.5 billion in a genome institute that will have 100 times more processing capacity than the rest of the world has previously had combined.[1] It has moved assertively to become a global leader in high-speed train technology. China is also spending over $700 million to create a Solar Valley that already employs 800,000 people across 100 companies in what a prescient red banner at the city claims will be "The Biggest Solar Energy Production Base in the Whole World."[2] China understands the power of new markets.

Nascent industries are an obvious way to create economic growth and good jobs, and they can be a long-term antidote to underlying ills in health care, energy, and many other fields. Even in the polarized political climate now present in so many countries, leaders seem to agree that embracing new markets is an essential component of sustained national success.

Yet government's record in this area is spotty. Examples abound of national industrial policy pushing companies to chase the wrong targets and crowding out private-sector initiatives. Many new markets have suffered from nonsensical and outdated regulation. Billions of dollars have been spent on initiatives with few useful outcomes. To be sure, government can point to clear successes—the Internet, railroads, aviation, and many others—but there is much room to improve.

Several recommendations for how government can support the creation of new markets are fairly standard. Education needs to get better, particularly in math and the sciences. Cities or universities can develop "innovation clusters" that make them world leaders in a growth field; for instance, San Diego has become the locus for health-care solutions employing wireless technologies. Government needs to support basic research that creates inventions with little immediate value but great long-term potential. Businesses should be easy to establish and contracts simple to enforce.

Beyond these basic moves, things get trickier. Some observers have called for massive national investment programs in relatively new industries such as electric vehicles.[3] Undoubtedly, these efforts would have an impact, but in most developed economies the odds of those happening today are virtually nil. The money simply is not there, and voters have little appetite to borrow from the future to invest those funds now, particularly in light of heavy deficits and austerity programs that many governments face following the "great recession." There are exceptions—the Emirate of Abu Dhabi has made huge investments to make itself an innovation hub for industries such as health care and alternative energy. China, Singapore, and a handful of economies with good strategic investment track-records are finding the money to build these industries. As China's Solar Valley shows, these governments are not shy about their ambitions. However, the circumstances surrounding these unusual cases are quite different from those prevailing in Washington, London, Tokyo, and most other developed-country capitals. Fortunately, there are some relatively straightforward and inexpensive actions that governments can take.

This chapter focuses on those ideas. It does not look at government policies to create leadership in an industry, such as being the lowest-cost producer of solar modules. Such efforts involve the maturation of an industry rather than its inception, and they can be both costly and futile. Rather, this chapter concentrates on how to get new markets started inexpensively.

The chapter covers

- Why it is so difficult for government to support new markets effectively
- How government can play a critical and cost-effective role in fostering four essential elements of new markets
- How different governments played helpful and harmful roles in the early days of the mobile phone industry and what lessons emerge about how governments can enable new fields to flourish

The Challenges that Public Programs Face

"Democracy is the worst form of government, except all the others." When he made this remark, Winston Churchill could have been talking about government's role as a catalyst for new markets. Democratic institutions hobble the potential of government as a venture capitalist, but their legitimacy and transparency create opportunity to lay essential groundwork for the growth of new markets. Let us look first at democracy's limits[4]:

- *Sizzle.* Politicians love to be associated with gee-whiz technologies. What's more failsafe than kissing an electric car? Yet, impactful ideas are often numbingly complex (e.g., health-care information exchange) or exceptionally boring (e.g., energy-efficient windows). Politicians often attack funding for niche applications of unfamiliar technologies, yet new markets often get their start in obscure crannies of the economy that few people understand. These highly-technical fields may be a couple steps in the value chain behind the end product that voters can observe. As a result, government sometimes focuses on sexy fields that likely already receive substantial private investment, and it may neglect cash-starved areas that really could use the attention. Big automotive companies have finally focused in earnest on electric vehicles, but the chemistry and materials science needed to make leaps in battery performance 10 years from now could probably use extra financing. Moreover, such investments in platform technologies could result in totally unexpected new markets as well.

- *Flexibility.* The entrepreneur's lore is that the average successful startup changes its business plan four times. New markets can evolve very quickly. Unfortunately, government programs do not. By the time an idea makes it through a legislative committee, is enacted into law, and becomes implemented by a government agency, the world might have moved on. An alternative approach would provide a substantial amount of loosely circumscribed funds to a quasi-public body authorized to invest it wisely. This is what Singapore does. However, the approach runs counter to the governance philosophy of many democratic countries. New England town meetings have voters deciding on whether to upgrade the sewage treatment plant, and we are going to delegate billions to these investment institutions?

- *Concentration of benefits.* While new markets create untold benefits for consumers (i.e., voters), these gains tend to be hypothetical before the markets blossom. Moreover, consumers' benefits can be diffuse and easily ignored within a vast economy. The gains for a few companies can be more readily noticed, and these firms may lobby aggressively for government programs. Often, however, the best-suited firms to build new markets are not dispersed evenly across congressional districts. Silicon Valley, Boston, and other technological clusters tend to benefit disproportionately. Neglected districts dislike this arrangement, so programs may have mandates to spread their largesse around. This approach makes for good politics but bad business because the expertise to build a particular industry is usually found in small pockets of a country.

- *Consistency.* Companies may bemoan their lack of patience, but the average corporate officer does not have to contend with the 24-hour news cycle. With legislative priorities changing even faster than the cast of legislators, it is no wonder that few governments provide reliable multiyear support to projects that may be long in gestation. Not only does inconsistent funding make such programs difficult to plan, but fear of having money yanked also may make administrators wary of trying risky things. In theory, the public sector should be supporting the uncertain long-term projects that the private sector will not prioritize, so the result is perverse.

Where Can Government Succeed?

The problems just listed are most acute for government programs that spend money on grants and subsidies. These initiatives are often expensive, and they provide attractive targets for special interests and legislative meddling. Other, less costly types of initiatives can be more immune to these ill effects.

New markets share many characteristics with other fields where government has a much-needed role. For instance, few would dispute that government is essential to road safety. It is well suited to performing crash tests, making traffic laws, and building roads. In other words, it publicizes important data, coordinates action, and lays critical infrastructure. Sometimes it also lays out mandates without specifying methods of compliance—for example, it sets vehicle emission standards but does not dictate how automakers meet those goals.

Government also puts a price on public goods such as the environment. We can debate the right level at which to set the cost of pollution, but there is little doubt that this function rightly sits in the public domain.

Government is also a large buyer from the private sector, and it makes sense for public officials to think broadly about how their purchasing can encourage desirable behaviors. For instance, government pays over half the medical costs in the United States, so it makes sense for government to offer performance incentives to physicians for adopting health-care information technology (IT) systems that can improve the quality of care while lowering long-run expenses. The public sector's behavior in this regard is not very distinct from how other big purchasers try to shape the actions of their vendors.

So how do these functions relate to supporting new markets? Let us look back at what makes new markets grow. In Chapter 2 we examined what triggers the formation of new markets, and in Chapter 3 we looked at what factors lead to rapid growth. Those indicators are summarized very briefly in Table 9-1.

One topic discussed in Chapter 2 was regulation. Government's role in regulation is obvious and not the subject of this chapter. My presumption is that regulations exist to bring about some greater social good and not primarily to create growing businesses in new markets for pollution-control equipment, data-protection software, or whatever the field may be. Perhaps this is the wishful thinking of an author whose first graduate degree was in public policy.

Table 9-1 Indicators of New Markets

Market Formation	Rapid Market Growth
New platform technologies	Physical infrastructure
New business systems	Business infrastructure
Changing customer capabilities	Decision makers
Changing customer behavior	Need and performance
Changing business partner incentives	Little behavior change
Regulations' upside	Speedy sales and use
	Low switching cost
	Low cost of failure

Beyond regulation, we can abstract from Table 9-1 four cornerstones of new markets in which government can play a key role. Underlying each is a theme of openness.

Open Information

Information undergirds a huge number of new markets ranging from geophysical analysis to hedge funds. The availability of data allows specialists to emerge in assessing and acting on that information. The result is better decision making, more efficient resource allocation, and higher-quality products.

Todd Park understands this. As the chief technology officer for the U.S. Department of Health and Human Services (HHS), he comes across a bit differently than the stereotypical federal bureaucrat. Park cofounded the health-care IT company Athenahealth in 1997 while he was in his mid-20s, and he helped guide it to become a firm valued at over $1 billion. He breaks molds.

Park has embarked on a revolutionary campaign that he calls "Data Liberación!" HHS has oceans of information about health—health status, quality of care, public health indicators, and so forth. This information has been locked away previously, not because of privacy concerns (the information is anonymous) but because HHS has not known what to do with it. Park sees vast potential for new uses of this information; for instance, Microsoft's Bing is integrating the data into search results for hospitals. Park's inspiration comes from an unlikely place—the weather. Public weather information underlies a huge number of private-sector services, including online weather forecasts and the travel industry.

Park wants the government to be a "data sugar daddy that creates a self-propelled ecosystem of health data supply and use."[5] Aside from putting community health data online, Park is enabling the U.S. Medicare program's 47 million beneficiaries to securely download their health records to their PCs through a single "Blue Button" on its Web site. The federal government has tried to jumpstart the use of electronic medical records in many ways, and Park figures that providing an army of senior citizens with their records might be a good way of persuading physicians to start using these systems meaningfully.

In addition to sharing data, government helps to set standards for how information is presented and used. HHS is creating a Nationwide Health Information Network to enable secure health data exchange over the Internet. This sort of activity may be mundane, but it is essential to creating new markets that use health-care data in productive new ways.

These initiatives are dirt cheap and apolitical. They were easy for government to do but would have been nearly impossible for the private sector to execute. Looking at how the outputs of Data Liberación correlate with Table 9-1, the results include new business systems, changing customer capabilities, new behaviors and incentives, a business infrastructure for new industries, faster decision making, speedier learning, and reduced costs of switching systems. This straightforward campaign turbocharges new markets.

Open Platforms

Chapter 2 delves into how open platforms create a basis for new markets. These platforms might stack on top of each other—integrated circuit, cell phone, Android Operating System, and so forth—to enable uses that the originators of the underlying platforms scarcely could imagine.

Many of these platforms are commercially attractive and need no government support. However, some initiatives are not viable as businesses but are important and well handled by a trusted intermediary such government. For instance, the U.S. National Cancer Institute holds a tumor repository that can provide medical researchers with innumerable types of cells to understand the dynamics of cancer. The U.S. National Science Foundation (NSF) provides another example. With an annual budget of about $7 billion, NSF provides roughly 10,000 grants per year to support basic research at universities and elsewhere in fields such as mathematics, computer science, and physics. It also funds platforms for research, including bases in Antarctica, ocean vessels, and very high-end computing facilities. NSF-funded researchers have won 180 Nobel Prizes, so this organization is clearly doing something right.

Other types of platforms can be relatively inexpensive to support. India's Council on Scientific and Industrial Research is spending just $38 million to create an initiative called "Open Source Drug Discovery" (OSDD). Focusing on tuberculosis, malaria, and other neglected diseases, OSDD provides a means for academics and other researchers to share information about biology and genetics related to these ailments. The British Standards Organization codifies quality metrics in industries ranging from information security to food safety, enabling a huge number of private-sector firms to compete on well-understood criteria.

Government also affects platforms through its laws on intellectual property. While innovations often stem from collaboration and cross-fertilization of ideas,[6] the patent system can lead researchers to keep their work secret for as long as possible. The remedies are complex and well beyond the scope of this book, but it is time for policymakers to take a hard look at the negative economic consequences that have accumulated as the result of seemingly arcane legal decisions in this field.[7]

Open Experimentation

The barriers to new markets' success frequently lie not so much in creating new solutions as in getting them broadly adopted. To take perhaps the most dramatic example, during the eighteenth century the British Navy lost more men to scurvy than to the enemy. It was a tremendous boon to the Navy once ships started including citrus in sailors' diets in the 1790s; indeed, this breakthrough was partly responsible for Britain's victory in the Napoleonic Wars. Alas, the solution had first been published—by no less than the surgeon general of the East India Company—in 1614.[8]

Fortunately, we have learned a bit since those days. In some areas, public programs have played a huge role in enabling new markets. The Philippines' Bureau of Plant Industry (BPI) has contributed extensively to improving farmers' knowledge about developments in areas such as seeds and agricultural techniques. BPI can experiment with new approaches, demonstrate their success, and then promote these to farms throughout the archipelago, removing the risk and communication barriers that hinder the adoption of new solutions.

Where solutions are well proven elsewhere, government can create incentives for their quick implementation in a new territory. In Haiti, for instance, the U.S. Agency for International Development created a competition among mobile networks to be the first to market with a cell phone–based wallet that addresses the needs of the unbanked. The first network to launch this solution, which had to meet certain criteria, was eligible to receive $2.5 million. This money is miniscule in relation to development aid for Haiti, and through bringing about a new market, it has substantial potential to improve the lives of the poor.

Openness to People

People—entrepreneurs, corporate venturers, skilled professionals, and other critical actors—are not mentioned in Table 9-1, but they underlie most of the factors within it. This is a book about business strategy, not about what kinds of individuals start new industries.[9] Yet the fact is that people are utterly fundamental to shaping new markets. Individuals have played essential roles in new markets from the days of Andrew Carnegie and Levi Strauss through to Max Factor and Andrew Grove.

What does the government have to do with this? Everything. It is a truism that education is fundamental to creating great innovators. It is apparently not a truism to suggest that we should welcome them with open arms when they show up at our door, as those four individuals did early in their lives. Consider two policy options for the U.S. government:

1. Recruit the best and brightest from around the world, teach them at the country's finest universities about leading-edge technologies, and encourage them to stay in America to build great companies and create untold numbers of excellent jobs.

2. Make it exceedingly hard for an outstanding student from abroad to study in this country. If he does manage to get a student visa, erect major barriers to his staying after graduation and urge him to return home, where he can build enterprises to compete against American firms.

The United States has selected option 2. We give a brilliant Chinese computer scientist a Ph.D. from the Massachusetts Institute of Technology and then send her packing. Indeed, the policy goes even further. For highly qualified people who have received all their education overseas, often at other governments' expense, America will make it still more difficult to enter the country and create new industries. The United States acts as though these immigrants are stealing American jobs while simultaneously preaching that math and science skills are necessary to create growth. This is bizarre.

It is a sad but true fact that American students often have an inferior education in math and science than counterparts elsewhere. For example, the Indian education system—which certainly has its difficulties in other respects—churns out huge numbers of world-class engineers. It is no coincidence that over a quarter of Silicon Valley startups have Indian founders.[10] As universities and technological clusters improve in other nations, America should stop taking this magnificent influx of talent for granted.[11]

Government's Effectiveness and Dysfunction— in the Same Industry

Why was Europe five years ahead of the United States in broadly adopting cell phones? Differences in public policy between Europe and the United States played a large role.

Europe switched on its first mobile networks at about the same time as the United States—in the early 1980s. The first, analog-based generation of technology saw several different standards deployed among European countries, and this lack of harmonization prevented most travelers from roaming outside their home nations. To ensure better European integration and also economies of scale in equipment supply, regulators developed a second, digital standard they called Global System for Mobile Communications (GSM) that all European countries would implement across identical blocs of frequencies. Beyond enabling simple calls, the standard contained some interesting features. A data channel called Short Message Service (SMS) was established, although people were not really sure how it would be used. GSM also enabled subscribers to switch handsets easily and to keep their saved phone numbers by moving a tiny Subscriber Identity Module (SIM) card. The standard was well documented and open for any vendor to use.

GSM was a massive success. Countries allocated their frequencies on a national basis, meaning that people could travel from Paris to Cannes without changing networks. Because the same frequencies were used throughout Europe, subscribers also could easily roam across countries. As people started to use SMS in totally unanticipated ways, it was easy to enable subscribers on one network to send text messages to friends on other networks. SIM cards allowed for super-simple upgrading of mobile phones. Proliferating infrastructure and handset vendors ensured that prices would continually decline. Even today, 20 years after the first GSM commercial service, successors to this standard hold a 90 percent share of the global market.[12]

The American government took a more hands-off approach. The inability to use U.S. analog phones outside the country was not the major issue that it was in Europe, so there was less urgency in upgrading networks to a digital standard such as GSM. No major transition in standards was mandated. The United States also allowed different standards to be used. In 1989, an American company called Qualcomm released a digital standard called Code Division Multiple

Access (CDMA) that had some technical superiorities to GSM. The American networks splintered, with some embracing CDMA, some GSM, and some a GSM derivative.

Qualcomm tightly controlled the CDMA standard and boasts of owning 13,000 patents. Partly as a result, CDMA devices tended to be more expensive than GSM equipment. The differing standards hindered subscribers' ability to migrate between networks, and initially their phone books could not be moved easily from handset to handset. Even after SMS took off in Europe, the lack of a single standard in the United States was partly to blame for a delay of several years before Americans could send text messages from one network to another.

The United States also decided that it should mimic the approach it took with radio and television stations and allocate spectrum by metropolitan area, not nationwide.[13] Therefore, different cities had distinct networks, and subscribers' ability to roam, as well as the price of roaming service, could be uncertain. Given that some of the earliest adopters of mobile phones would be people who were highly *mobile*, this scheme retarded the industry's growth. Indeed, American networks referred to their tortuous acquisition of licenses across the country as "putting Humpty Dumpty back together again."[14]

This story shows the importance of creating open systems based on common standards wherever possible. These standards should allow for multiple vendors, simplify initial adoption of a solution, reduce customers' fears of being locked into any given supplier, and facilitate customers' upgrading to newer systems.

There is a downside to standards: The long process of building consensus means that standards such as GSM often will be outdated even before they are published. However, early adopters of new solutions are frequently not trying to push the limits of the latest technologies, and they may not be too bothered by the fact that theoretically higher-performing systems could be available.[15] Rather, they want to reduce their confusion and risk, so they appreciate standards.

There is, of course, a range of situations, and policies need to be tailored to the matter at hand. Governments need to regulate the quality of surgical instruments, but they do not need to standardize them. Doctors will choose the instruments that work best for them, and they do not share those instruments across hospitals (we hope). Similarly, it may be unwise to set a standard at the earliest stages of an industry when much is unknown about the nature of customer demand. The goal for policymakers should not be standardization per se, but rather open systems, multiple vendors, easy adoption, and fast upgrading to improved solutions.

Business is an intensely pragmatic field, so it is fascinating to see how discussion around government's role in enabling new markets can tend toward extremes. On one side, observers see China's headlong pursuit of a few select markets as proof that national industrial policy can equip countries to compete in decades ahead. They can neglect abundant examples of failed efforts. New markets are highly fluid, and it is difficult for inflexible government programs to plot out their evolution years in advance. But the other side also can be unreasonable. While entrepreneurs can be zealous advocates of free markets, the fact is that government is an essential actor in many new fields. The government really *did* create the Internet,[16] and the public sector provides the information, coordination, and infrastructure for innumerable industries. A nonideological view of new markets shows that government's role can be apolitical and inexpensive yet highly impactful.

Summary

- While a few unusual economies and sovereign wealth funds can invest aggressively in establishing new industries, this option is not available to the cash-strapped governments of most developed nations.
- Government has a very mixed track record in supporting new industries. The political process can favor trendy, inflexible, and inconsistent programs that spread cash broadly. New markets need just the opposite approach.
- Public policy should have an important role to play in ensuring openness in four key areas: information, platforms, experimentation, and flows of skilled labor. This role costs little and involves no political ideology.
- The history of mobile communications shows how government can catalyze open systems with multiple vendors that surmount barriers to initial adoption and enable rapid upgrading of solutions.

AFTERWORD

Cornelius Vander Starr was one of the first Westerners to sell insurance policies to the Chinese. Starting in Shanghai in 1919, Starr captured a new market and thrived in this difficult environment. His company, eventually called American International Group (AIG), went on to become one of the world's largest businesses, generating $110 billion in annual revenues in 2007. It succeeded through pioneering a long succession of new markets—from offshore wind farm insurance to global insurance policies for huge multinational clients. AIG was a serial innovator that ran some of the most successful insurance businesses in the world.

Then came disaster. AIG's Financial Products Division had minted money for a decade by lending securities and insuring against defaults, but the financial crisis of 2008 led to an intersection of improbable events that created a giant need for cash, fast. The U.S. government had to step in, effectively nationalizing the firm. In most industries, a fruitless effort in a new market means that the business has lost the money it invested in the venture, but in insurance failure can be catastrophic.

Did AIG subsequently turn its back on new markets? Absolutely not. Its restructured and rebranded property and casualty business, Chartis, has set up an incubator for targeting emerging markets, and it has pushed into carbon markets through its Lexington Insurance subsidiary. Lexington's chief innovation officer, Karen O'Reilly, puts it this way, "We've moved toward a more collaborative approach and a higher level of communication, so we have heightened transparency about our business. Yet we've never changed the way we function in the marketplace—innovation is part of our culture."[1]

If an organization such as AIG can live through that scale of crisis and come back as committed as ever to capturing new markets, what should less-troubled companies do? Oddly, the most reluctance to pursue new markets can come not from companies with their backs against the wall but rather from firms at their peak. Things are great—why change? The trouble is that industries can evolve at sometimes breathtaking speed, and success formulas can wear out quickly. Business history holds innumerable examples of formerly great firms being left behind as someone disrupts the placid hierarchy of an industry or creates an immense enterprise in an adjacent field overlooked by the traditional leaders. Just ask Coca-Cola, Disney, Microsoft, or Motorola.

There are two overarching reasons why successful companies ignore new markets. First, the return on their investment in new markets is initially unknowable. Firms may try to fool themselves by creating fancy spreadsheets forecasting a new unit's growth, but good venture capitalists (VCs) will scoff at these plans. There are far too many factors affecting a new business in an unfamiliar field to plan revenues with certainty (expenses are another matter). If companies can create a portfolio of ventures, then some of the vicissitudes of new markets will balance out, but many firms can summon the will to try for only one venture at a time. Unfortunately, they cannot ask advice from VCs who have tried this approach because those VCs have not survived.

A second obstacle is that the competencies making companies great in their core business can act as deadweights on new ventures. Meticulous planning, highly organized salesforces, and extreme attention to detail are great assets in established businesses, but new markets may call for rapid prototyping and iteration. Established firms have many advantages over entrepreneurs—capital, brand, technology, distribution, and more—but they can lose out to startups because of inflexibility.

The Distinctiveness of New Markets

Flexibility and dynamism are two themes permeating this book. If companies can adjust their approaches rapidly in the early days of a market, they can capture the upside of fast change. There are organizational methods that help to retain this flexibility within a large corporation (see Chapter 8).

Beyond the need for quickly evolving their strategies, managers tackling new markets should keep in mind the many ways in which new markets are distinct from established ones. This book has explored dozens of these differences, but there are 10 major ones that can be abstracted from the preceding chapters.

1. Define Markets Broadly

As the management scholar Peter Drucker put it back in 1964,

> That the bowling equipment makers were first in realizing the potential and growth of the discretionary-time market, first to promote a new family activity, explains their tremendous success in the fifties. That they, apparently, defined competition as other bowling equipment makers rather than as all suppliers of activity-satisfactions is in large part responsible for the abrupt decline of their fortunes in the sixties.[2]

It is remarkable that a fact so clear to Drucker almost 50 years ago can remain so opaque in business today. Defining a market according to the jobs that people are trying to get done rather than as a product they are trying to buy invariably opens up new routes to rescope the competitive landscape and serve latent needs.[3] This discipline also protects firms from asymmetric competitive threats such as the ones that beset bowling. A six-step process can accomplish this objective: Map the jobs to be done, current activities and pain points, range of alternatives, performance criteria, consumption impediments, and value at stake (see Chapter 2). While this process can create insight in any industry, in new markets it is especially impactful owing to the fact that customers will readily consider new solutions or vendors. A firm that attacks the market by better addressing jobs to be done can attain quick advantages even when facing seemingly formidable competitors.

2. Create Demand Before Vanquishing Competitors

Competitors can be valuable allies in creating demand (see Chapter 3). They are educating customers and validating that a new industry should be taken seriously. The struggle in a new market is not to eliminate the competition (yet) but rather to convert sales prospects into paying customers. Collaborative initiatives such as industry associations, trade shows, newsletters, and other tactics can gain traction for a new industry. In 2000, for example, I banded together with several other mobile marketing CEOs and launched the Wireless Marketing Association (now called the Mobile Marketing Association) to set standards for the industry, promote awareness about its offerings, and bring the largest mobile networks into a collective discussion about how to grow this new advertising medium. It was one of the most successful initiatives that any of us undertook at the time.

A related imperative is the need to prioritize customer types who will adopt a new solution readily, even if there may be a gaggle of competitors vying to serve these accounts. Eight factors indicate whether a market will rapidly adopt something new; these can be grouped into the headings of having few dependencies, relative advantage, and low perceived risk (see Chapter 3). Discussions of business strategy usually revolve around competitive advantage, but frequently with new markets these advantages can be built later. The priority is to get early customers fast because they provide critical learnings and can endorse the company.

3. Leverage the Power of Platforms

When others have invested time and money in creating subsystems that enable innovations—from Wi-Fi networks to deep fryers—we would be foolish to try to invent the whole shebang ourselves. But this is exactly what many companies attempt to do. When my team at Psion sought to create the world's first smartphone, we had a proprietary processor, operating system, applications, and much else. The system was truly elegant, but it was unnecessary. Our battles did not lie with Nokia and other vendors in this space but rather with creating the market in the first place. Had we pursued a more mundane first smartphone, our costs would have been lower, the project would have been less risky, and buyers may have been less wary of adopting so many new technologies at once. Platforms may reduce differentiation, but that is not the priority in a market's early days. Indeed, differentiation can be harmful if it complicates the buying decision and reduces the perceived safety of a purchase (Chapter 2 discusses platforms, and Chapters 3 and 9 deal with impediments to adoption).

Platform vendors also can do well. If a company can create a platform catering to the firms rushing into a new space, it can thrive even while other pioneers struggle. Levi Strauss followed this strategy in the California Gold Rush. He targeted an acute need—prospectors needing durable pants—and his invention of jeans proved more valuable than the nuggets the miners were trying so hard to find.

4. Keep Pricing Flexible

While it is essential for a new venture to gain customers' trust, the business should try to avoid being too transparent about its pricing. A company's first customers will teach it a lot about the value inherent in its solution (see Chapter 2). Also, the firm probably will have to adjust what exactly it is selling. Published prices are very hard to push upward, and downward moves can create tensions with early customers who paid more. There are many ways to keep pricing fuzzy—contingent payments, limited trials, customization, and so forth. Given that early customers may demand very steep discounts, it pays to use these approaches to avoid creating unsustainable precedents.

5. Invest in Scenarios, Not Plans

Big companies sometimes ask their new ventures to submit strategic plans in the parent's format. I have even seen one Fortune 50 enterprise insist on using a standard 10-slide format for a new business in a totally unfamiliar field, with 3 of the 10 slides containing only financial estimates. This is dysfunctional nonsense.

If the ultimate destination is unclear, it is impossible to create a detailed plan for arriving there. Rather, firms should think carefully through the major decision points in their journey and how those bear on the range of potential outcomes. Then they can assess both what prior learnings will be needed to inform a decision and the time line for resolving uncertainties after the decision has been taken (see Chapter 3).

For instance, a company investing in a new medical device does not know in advance how effective it will be or whether regulators will approve it. However, it does know that it will face a critical decision in how to structure the clinical trial that will seek to justify regulatory approval. The company can think through what information it will need in order to decide what are the most valuable and feasible outcomes to prove in that trial. The firm also can estimate when the trial will have its results and how much additional time might be necessary from that point until the company undertakes the full-scale launch. This plan therefore affects both immediate actions (data gathering to make big decisions about the trial) and long-term resource needs.

6. Keep Fixed Costs Low

Shortly after we got married, my wife and I bought a really nice couch. It worked perfectly in our apartment in Boston, and we figured that we should invest in something that we will use for 20 years. Unfortunately, it proved to be too big for our flat in London and too small for our house in Zambia. We also got a cat who thought it was an ideal instrument for sharpening his claws. Then we had yogurt-spilling children. After a few years, our smart long-term investment had become an expensive short-term purchase (but it had stopped *looking* expensive). We would have done better if we had bought a couple less costly pieces that would have gotten us through some major lifestyle changes prior to things becoming a bit more predictable.

When they are starting out in a new area, companies should buy fewer nice couches and more cheap futons. Financial analysts can point to the long-run savings of buying something once or of building a system in-house.[4] But if you accept the entrepreneur's maxim that a successful startup changes business model four times, you would do well to minimize fixed costs and increase variable costs instead. It is not only cheaper, but it also preserves flexibility (see Chapters 4 and 8).

7. Focus on Small Footholds

Traditional business strategy advocates pursuing the biggest, highest-spending customer segments. This makes a lot of sense—one day.

Unfortunately, as a market gets going, these segments may be slow to buy, impose innumerable demands, and negotiate mercilessly on price. It is far better to gain quick traction in a foothold customer segment that has all the indicators of rapid adoption (see Chapter 4). Footholds speed a company's development, focus its efforts, and provide reference customers for other buyers.[5] Take it from someone who once ignored an eager Maltese telecom customer to focus instead on a laborious, two-year, and ultimately successful effort to sell a fancy solution to the world's largest mobile network—take that trip to Malta.

8. Consider Country Roads as Well as the Superhighway

There are two basic approaches to market penetration (see Chapter 5). Established markets look like a superhighway, with lots of traffic moving in the same direction along well-marked roads offering many roadside services. New markets can be better accessed via country roads that meander and lack a support network but which also allow travelers to move at their own pace to destinations off the beaten path. Companies following a country road have to stitch together a solution to customers' problems without relying on an extensive network of partners, particularly sales channels. This keeps them flexible. As an industry matures, the superhighways will form. While it may be challenging, it is certainly feasible to manage the transition between these two business models.[6]

9. Base Strategy on Timing

In a new market, a company's strategy depends heavily on its timing. Several factors affect the viability of early movers, fast followers, and late followers in an industry (see Chapter 6). Companies such as eBay, Visa, and Samsung have done well in each of these positions, but they have needed to take account of the virtues and drawbacks associated with how early or late they entered their markets. Firms also can choose to follow several paths, entering early at a small scale in order to learn and then acquiring a leader to benefit from a fast follower's advantages.

10. Sequence Risks

A good venture capitalist stages his investments and focuses his portfolio companies on mitigating a few key risks at a time (see Chapters 4 and 8). He is not trying to build the business in miniature but rather to verify that the company has a reasonable shot at success. This approach keeps investments modest and allows the venture capitalist to fail frequently but inexpensively. It also concentrates managers' attention on what really matters for the company's success.[7]

Putting the Pieces Together

Pressure can tempt a busy manager to ignore the principles just listed. After all, the whole point of these principles is that they diverge from usual practice. It is easy to minimize internal resistance by reverting to well-trodden paths, but sad results follow.

The best way to make these principles stick is to establish a rigor around them. If there are management systems that facilitate behaving in a new way, people will do so.

Philips illustrates the power of innovation-centric management systems. For a company with a 120-year heritage, it places remarkable importance on new markets, with new ventures including

- Shapeways (three-dimensional printing services for consumers)
- CareServant (an automated attendant and entertainment system at a patient's hospital bedside)

- Lumalive (textile-based LED lighting)
- Aerasense (continuous monitoring for pollution from ultrafine particles)
- uWand (gesture interpretation for controlling electronic devices)

These initiatives result from conscious strategy. Philips has an explicit portfolio plan by business sector, allocating resources across business stage (declining through emerging) and type of innovation (improvement through new to world). Business units have mandates for how aggressively they will reach for breakthrough innovations, and incubators at the corporate level foster new growth ventures.

Teams throughout Philips share a common methodology for creating new concepts.[8] Value Proposition House is a proprietary approach to ensuring that teams start with the customer, think carefully about the job to be done, and only then define the product and user experience. For example, a team addressing sleep apnea in China will first develop detailed personas for target customers such as businesspeople and students. It will think through issues such as whether a businessman bunks with colleagues while traveling and how he feels about keeping others awake. Then it will address what job to address; for instance, is the customer looking to address sleep apnea (in a culture where snoring is seen as a sign of good health), or is he trying to get better-quality sleep? Subsequently, the process leads to creating a solution designed within a business system. In the case of apnea, the team would ask questions including how Philips could create sleep-analysis labs where they do not exist.[9]

Other companies have their own systems for capturing new markets. Procter & Gamble brings teams to an off-site facility called Clay Street where they can draw insights from field research and create bold new concepts using a well-structured approach. Samsung can sequester engineers for weeks at a time at its Value Innovation Program Center near Seoul, forcing teams to work across functions and hammer out differences using rigorous innovation methodologies. SABMiller has clear strategies for growing strongly in emerging markets while using sophisticated information technology platforms to facilitate worldwide idea sharing around new products.

Getting Started

New markets can be huge, amorphous, and rapidly moving. Where do you start?

As with other recommendations in this book, your strategy should depend on your circumstances. Top executives have the authority to set a strategy and portfolio plan for the corporation. They should be wary of dictating a new-market concept in too much detail because it is tough for the staff down at the coalface to rapidly adjust approaches on a dictate that comes from the pinnacle of a company. Rather, executives can articulate how much growth they expect from what types of new markets (new geographies, customer types, product types, and so on). They can also kick off an effort to bolster the firm's capabilities in these endeavors through rigorous methods.

Many of this book's readers will not be top executives of large corporations. Lower-level managers in big companies can make a general argument upward about the power of new markets, but that thesis becomes more compelling if it is linked to a specific opportunity.[10] Perhaps a project has languished because it has been wrongly directed toward established rather than new markets. Possibly there is a promising customer group that the company has not cracked. A new technology might be emerging that could affect the industry in poorly understood ways. These questions help to make the urgency of new markets clear and their potential concrete.

Entrepreneurs target new markets because they have to—this is where they stand a fighting chance against big incumbents. Their priority is usually around how to focus very limited time and money. Startups need a thorough profile of the latent need they are targeting, a clear idea of their foothold market, and a sequenced plan of risk mitigation. Other imperatives are important but often secondary.

Whatever your circumstance, you may think that this is a poor time to tackle new markets. Business is too good, too weak, too concentrated, too diffuse—delay is easy to justify. But the world is not waiting. New platforms, emerging consumers, and proliferating discontinuities are opening up countless new markets even as they threaten more established ones. The pace of change will not slow down. This is the time to act.

NOTES

Preface

1. For more on the engine that Hero (also called Heron) designed, see Peter James and Nick Thorpe, *Ancient Inventions* (New York: Ballantine Books, 1995). This book also sets Hero's engine in its historical context and notes that the Romans' use of slave labor inhibited demand for this type of labor-saving device. The Greeks had already invented a primitive, slave-powered railroad that ran a distance of nearly four miles close to Corinth.

2. To improve readability, the terms *new market* and *new industry* are used interchangeably in this book. Strictly speaking, *new market* refers to the demand for a new solution, whereas *new industry* refers to the supply of that solution. The two concepts are tightly linked because customer demand enables suppliers to exist, and without suppliers, that demand is only hypothetical. Therefore, in practice, we can speak of new markets and new industries arising together. Some writers have suggested that in the case of radically new technologies, industries can arise prior to markets forming (a phenomenon sometimes called *supply-push innovation*), but in practice, this is unusual. If a technology has no customers, it may advance in academia but will draw little capital to fund commercialization. Of course, there have been speculative bubbles such as with the Internet boom, but thankfully, this is not the norm— venture capitalists tend to be realists more motivated by making money within three to five years than by wild dreams of future customers. Moreover, services constitute the bulk of developed economies and, by definition, are consumed at the same time they are produced. Chapter 6 addresses what circumstances affect when it is best to enter new markets.

3. Based on the 2010 Fortune 500 list. The seven firms in the Fortune 50 that were not counted as reliant on new markets are Bank of America, Berkshire Hathaway, Citigroup, CVS Caremark, Goldman Sachs, JP Morgan Chase, US Bancorp, and Wells Fargo. It is debatable whether the financial services

underpinning many of these firms have been new markets. Split-second quantitative trading generates an abundant share of some of these companies' profits, and this is certainly a new market that has contributed to vast increases in trading volumes and an explosion in the types of securities to be traded. Credit and debit cards, electronic funds transfer, and many other important financial services also have been new markets. However, other banking activities are almost as old as civilization. In the same vein, the Caremark half of CVS Caremark provides pharmacy benefit management services that have arisen only in the past few decades. Yet the majority of the company's revenues are from its retail operations.

4. An interesting blog post on this topic can be found at http://bob.wyman.us/main/2008/06/newspaper-class.html The author links newspapers' failings to other industries missing opportunities and also provides a link to a piece he published in 1996 advising newspapers to seize the opportunity of online classified advertising.

5. S. Davies, P. Geroski, M. Lund, and A. Vlassopoulos, "The Dynamics of Market Leadership in UK Manufacturing Industry, 1979-1986." Centre for Business Strategy, London Business School Working Paper No. 93, 1991, as referenced in Constantinos C. Markides, *Game-Changing Strategies: How to Create New Market Space in Established Industries by Breaking the Rules* (San Francisco: Jossey-Bass, 2008).

6. This book builds on a literature of others' research into new markets. One of the first key articles appeared in *Harvard Business Review* in 1991, written by the London Business School's Gary Hamel and the late C. K. Prahalad. Titled, "Corporate Imagination and Expeditionary Marketing," the article showed how firms such as Motorola and Fidelity Investments created vast new growth through redefining their industries and how companies must organize fast, low-cost experiments to quickly build an understanding of these spaces. Harvard Business School's Clayton Christensen's extensive series of articles and books have been enormously influential. Beginning with a 1995 article in *Harvard Business Review* coauthored with Joseph Bower and titled, "Disruptive Technologies: Catching the Wave," his publications have laid out how new markets can form through targeting an industry's worst customers and providing them with offerings that radically alter traditional definitions of performance. Among his many contributions to the literature, Christensen also has outlined how firms can compete asymmetrically against incumbents, organize to pursue disruptive strategies, and employ alternative financial tools that give a true picture of new markets' potential. Some of Christensen's thinking has been translated into a useful toolkit by my former Innosight colleague Scott Anthony and his coauthors in the 2008 book, *The Innovator's Guide to Growth: Putting Disruptive Innovation to Work* (Boston:

Harvard Business School Press, 2008). In a different vein, Geoffrey Moore has argued in his 1991 book, *Crossing the Chasm: Marketing and Selling Technology Products to Mainstream Customers* (New York: HarperCollins, 1991), and several subsequent works that the earliest adopters of a new offering can be quite distinct from mainstream customers and that companies must develop a strategy in a market's first days that may vary substantially from how they would pursue more established industries. Dartmouth's Vijay Govindarajan also has influenced my thinking through works such as his 2005 book with Chris Trimble, *10 Rules for Strategic Innovators: From Idea to Execution* (Boston: Harvard Business School Press, 2005), and several conversations. Govindarajan and Trimble are especially powerful in explaining how companies often must forget some of the attributes that once made them great in order to build new competencies to attack opportunities, and in looking at how firms must change to succeed in emerging markets. Additionally, London Business School's Constantinos Markides has published many times on this topic in books such as 2005's *Fast Second: How Smart Companies Bypass Radical Innovation to Enter and Dominate New Markets* (San Francisco: Jossey-Bass, 2005) and 2008's *Game-Changing Strategies: How to Create New Market Space in Established Industries by Breaking the Rules* (San Francisco: Jossey-Bass, 2008). Markides illustrates the challenges that established companies have in pioneering new markets and shows how acquiring early trailblazers and innovating business models also can lead to great success in these emerging industries.

Chapter 1

1. Prince Philip had the British government devote an entire nationwide frequency to his line, and this was not a scalable solution. See http://en.wikipedia.org/wiki/History_of_mobile_phones.
2. The historic Motorola press release can be found at www.motorola.com/staticfiles/Business/Corporate/US-EN/docs/history-motorola-demonstrates-portable-telephone-605kb-3.pdf.
3. Early phone data are drawn from http://cellphones.techfresh.net/motorola-dynatac-8000x-the-first-portable-cellphone/.
4. Cellular data are from www.zdnet.com/blog/itfacts/global-wireless-subscriber-numbers-china-398-mln-usa-202-mln-russia-115-mln-japan-95-mln/9060.
5. Data from http://en.wikipedia.org/wiki/List_of_countries_by_number_of_mobile_phones_in_use.
6. Ira Brodsky, *The History of Wireless* (St. Louis, MO: Telescope Books, 2008).
7. Data from www.ctia.org/advocacy/research/index.cfm/AID/10323.

8. Author's experience as Managing Director of Celpay Zambia and 2010 correspondence with current Managing Director. Celpay is used as a case study in Chapter 4.

9. Data from U.S. Department of Commerce, Economic Census and Bureau of Economic Analysis.

10. Data from www.bio.org/speeches/pubs/er/statistics.asp.

11. Data from U.S. Department of Commerce, Economic Census, 2007. This Census is performed every five years

12. Data from Smith Travel Research, 2006, and "Hotels Hope Extended Stays Extend Revenue," USA Today, February 24, 2009.

13. Data from General Electric 2010 Securities and Exchange Commission (SEC) Form 10-K, note 27.

14. Data from U.S. Department of Commerce, Econonic Census, 2007.

15. In some of the markets listed, the companies in Table 1-1 were not the very first. Procter & Gamble, for example, was not the first with disposable diapers. As explored in Chapter 6, sometimes it is sufficient to be early, not first. The point of Table 1-1 is not order of entry but rather that the markets were still new when these companies made their forays.

16. Data from http://en.wikipedia.org/wiki/History_of_Google.

17. W. R. Hambrecht quoted at www.innosight.com/our_approach/innosight_labs.html.

18. Nielsen NetRatings for December 1, 1998, via search engine Watch.

19. Data from http://investor.google.com/financial/tables.html.

20. Google's mission statement can be found at www.google.com/corporate/.

21. Figures for July 9, 2010. Percentage of market capitalization comes from www.trefis.com.

22. See http://en.wikipedia.org/wiki/Apple_II_series.

23. See http://en.wikipedia.org/wiki/LaserWriter.

24. See http://en.wikipedia.org/wiki/Rio_PMP300.

25. Data from http://digitaldaily.allthingsd.com/20090804/iphone-claims-32-percent-of-handset-industry-operating-profits/.

26. Data from http://phx.corporate-ir.net/External.File?item=UGFyZW50SUQ9Mjc1Mzd8Q2hpbGRJRD0tMXxUeXBlPTM=&t=1.

27. Data from www.booz.com/media/uploads/Innovation_1000-2009.pdf.

28. www.associatedcontent.com/article/2863160/netflix_and_blockbuster_video_on_demand.html?cat=15.

29. Data from Blockbuster 2004 SEC Form 10-K.

30. See www.fundinguniverse.com/company-histories/Netflix-Inc-Company-History.html.

31. See http://seekingalpha.com/article/21558-a-virtual-happy-meal-mcdonald-s-redbox-a-smashing-success.

32. See http://en.wikipedia.org/wiki/Redbox.

33. See www.cbsnews.com/stories/2005/02/18/entertainment/main675086.shtml. In 1999, the only year in which it provided the data, Blockbuster made 15.5 percent of its revenue from late fees. The company had only a 3 percent operating profit margin, so these fees were essential to the company's business model. 1999 SEC Form 10-K.

34. See http://en.wikipedia.org/wiki/Blockbuster_Inc.

35. Dell's low prices and configurable machines undoubtedly helped to expand consumption, but it is an example of a new market only in the broader context of the overall growth of PCs.

36. This line of thinking originated in a 1960 *Harvard Business Review* article by Professor Theodore Levitt entitled, "Marketing Myopia." Levitt argued that firms could grow by redefining their industries; for example, railroad companies could become transportation firms. His piece, referencing many of the biggest industries 50 years ago, seems remarkably prescient when thinking about the relative decline of those industries alongside the creation of new markets in adjacent fields.

37. Data from *Beverage Digest*, 2009 datasheet.

38. Data from the market research firm Mintel 2008. See http://www.mintel.com/press-centre/press-releases/268/energy-drink-explosion-hits-food

39. Data from www3.interscience.wiley.com/journal/123397541/abstract?CRETRY=1&SRETRY=0 and Nielsen via SeekingAlpha.

40. Hertz CEO, conference call with stock analysts, April 26, 2010.

41. Thanks go to Monitor Innovation for researching the data behind this figure as part of my *Monitor Perspectives* article with Geoff Tuff entitled, "Beacons for Business Model Innovation," December 2010; available at www.monitor.com.

42. See www.philips.com/about/company/history/ourheritage/index.page. While cassette tapes clearly created new consumption opportunities, for example, in-car audio systems and boom boxes, it is arguable whether CDs and DVDs similarly created new markets or transformed existing ones. These technologies did make possible new industries, such as the rental-by-mail system represented by Netflix. However, they may have cannibalized existing consumption of vinyl records and tapes more than they grew total demand by creating new kinds of consumption.

43. See www.directlife.philips.com/.

44. See www.fundinguniverse.com/company-histories/Fidelity-Investments-Inc-Company-History.html.

45. See www.bizjournals.com/pittsburgh/stories/2010/05/10/daily34.html.

46. See www.medtronic.com/about-medtronic/our-story/index.htm.

47. See www.jnj.com/connect/about-jnj/company-history/healthcare-inno vations?&pageNo=1.

48. Data from my coauthored article: Clayton M. Christensen, Stephen Wunker, and Hari Nair, "Innovation vs. Poverty," *Forbes*, October 13, 2008.

49. This example is explored in depth in Steven Johnson's book, *Where Good Ideas Come From: The Natural History of Innovation.* New York: Riverhead Books, 2010. As framed by Harvard Business School historian Richard Tedlow, "The business history of [the] twentieth century in the United States was the history of the introduction of new products." From *Giants of Enterprise: Seven Business Innovators and the Empires They Built* (New York: HarperCollins, 2001), p. 99.

Chapter 2

1. Material on George Eastman and Kodak in this chapter is drawn from Harvard Business School Professor Richard's Tedlow's detailed chapter on Eastman in his 2001 book, *Giants of Enterprise: Seven Business Innovators and the Empires They Built* (New York: HarperCollins, 2001), as well as from www.kodak.com/global/en/corp/historyOfKodak/eastmanTheMan.jhtml and Bernard Weisberger, "You Press the Button, We Do the Rest," *American Heritage Magazine*, October 1972.

2. See http://en.wikipedia.org/wiki/History_of_photography.

3. Weisberger, "You Press the Button."

4. Price data from *Historical Statistics of the United States* and Bureau of Labor Statistics.

5. Testimony of George Eastman, *Goodwin Film & Camera v. Eastman Kodak Company,* Transcript of Record, Vol. 1, p. 353, quoted in Reese V. Jenkins, *Images and Enterprise: Technology and the American Photographic Industry, 1839–1925* (Baltimore, MD: Johns Hopkins University Press, 1987).

6. This point is explored in depth in Chapter 2 of Clayton M. Christensen, Jerome H. Grossman, and Jason Hwang, *The Innovator's Prescription: A Disruptive Solution for Health Care* (New York: McGraw-Hill, 2009).

7. See A. G. Lafley and Ram Charan, *The Game-Changer: How You Can Drive Revenue and Profit Growth with Innovation* (New York: Crown Business, 2008). This book is an excellent resource for new market pioneers. In Chap-

ter 3, Lafley, who is the former CEO of Procter & Gamble, recounts how reorienting P&G's market research to scout for latent needs has opened up billions of dollars of new markets for the consumer goods company.

8. This framework was first put forth in Chapter 3 of Clayton Christensen and Michael Raynor, *The Innovator's Solution: Creating and Sustaining Successful Growth* (Boston: Harvard Business School Press, 2003).

9. See www.businessweek.com/magazine/content/04_14/b3877075_mz054. htm.

10. See www.ft.com/cms/s/0/71cc5562-770c-11df-ba79-00144feabdc0.html.

11. See http://news.cnet.com/8301-17938_105-10450354-1.html.

12. For more detail on this approach, see Clayton M. Christensen, Scott D. Anthony, Gerald Berstell, and Denise Nitterhouse, "Finding the Right Job for your Product," *MIT Sloan Management Review*, Spring 2007.

13. See http://history1900s.about.com/od/1900s/p/brownie.htm and www. brownie-camera.com/posters/pages/002_1900.shtml.

14. See www.gizmodiva.com/other_stuff/love_mode_ginger_is_a_pink_fizzy_ drink.php.

15. For more on the use of performance criteria, see Anthony Ulwick, *What Customers Want: Using Outcome-Driven Innovation to Create Breakthrough Products and Services* (New York: McGraw-Hill, 2005). Ulwick suggests framing criteria in terms of maximization and minimization wherever possible.

16. See Dan Ariely, *Predictably Irrational: The Hidden Forces That Shape Our Decisions* (New York: Harper Perennial, 2010) for a good overview. An excellent, if older, collection of articles was published in Daniel Kahneman, Paul Slovic, and Amos Tversky *Judgment under Uncertainty: Heuristics and Biases.* (Cambridge, England: Cambridge University Press, 1982). Kahneman and Tversky went on to share the Nobel Prize in economics for their work on these topics.

17. A categorization of some of these barriers is presented in Chapter 2 of a book by my former Innosight colleague, Scott Anthony and his coauthors, *The Innovator's Guide to Growth: Putting Disruptive Innovation to Work.* (Boston: Harvard Business Press, 2008).

18. A reader interested in a much more detailed discussion of pricing new offerings should refer to Thomas Nagle, John Hogan, and Joseph Zale, *The Strategy and Tactics of Pricing: A Guide to Growing More Profitably*, 5th ed. (Englewood Cliffs, NJ: Prentice-Hall, 2010).

19. See, for example, Clayton M. Christensen, *The Innovator's Dilemma: When New Technologies Cause Great Firms to Fail* (Boston: Harvard Business School Press, 1997).

20. Data from Colgate Q1 2010 Earnings Report, April 29, 2010.

21. Data from U.S. Economic Census, 2007.

22. See www.loc.gov/rr/scitech/mysteries/tooth.html.

23. An interesting discourse on this topic has been published by Ray Kurzweil at www.kurzweilai.net/articles/art0134.html?printable=1.

24. See www.gillette.com/en/us/mens-style/gillette-science.aspx.

25. I had the dubious distinction of launching one of the first WAP services, Saverfone, on British Telecom's Genie portal and so grappled with these issues firsthand.

26. See www.sunpowerafrique.org/About.html.

27. Data from *CIA World Factbook 2009* and http://makanaka.wordpress.com/2010/04/08/what-they-spend-their-rupee-on/.

28. Data from http://tech2.in.com/india/news/mobile-phones/nokia-sees-sales-growth-in-india-despite-drought/83332/0.

29. Data from www.business-standard.com/india/news/nokia-revenues-dip-huawei-crosses-rs-10k-cr-in-2009-10-study/97528/on.

30. See www.nokia.co.in/services-and-apps/nokia-life-tools/services#agriculture.

31. For a focused discussion on the dynamics of new markets in developing countries, see Clayton M. Christensen, Stephen Wunker, and Hari Nair, "Innovation vs. Poverty," *Forbes*, October 13, 2008. Despite the title, this article is not just about how to serve the poor in emerging markets but the overall approach that firms, particularly multinationals, can take in these nations.

32. See www.prnewswire.co.uk/cgi/news/release?id=86630.

33. I launched many of these services for media outlets such as Britain's Great Western Radio. I still think friend-finder services are a ghastly concept.

34. See http://latimesblogs.latimes.com/technology/2010/04/foursquare-tops-silicon-valleys-most-wanted-list.html.

35. See www.healthcareitnews.com/news/big-growth-projected-his-market.

36. Data from www.worldcoal.org/coal/uses-of-coal/coal-electricity/ sourcing IEA 2008.

37. See http://web.mit.edu/coal/The_Future_of_Coal_Summary_Report.pdf.

38. See www.statoil.com/annualreport2008/en/sustainability/climate/pages/5-3-2-3_sleipnerccs.aspx.

39. See www.statoil.com/en/technologyinnovation/newenergy/co2management/pages/sleipnervest.aspx.

40. See http://web.mit.edu/coal/The_Future_of_Coal_Summary_Report.pdf.

41. See www.statoil.com/en/TechnologyInnovation/NewEnergy/Co2Management/pages/carboncapture.aspx.

Chapter 3

1. As noted in Chapter 1, DVDs probably do not qualify as a new market, and flat-screen televisions (at least the big kind that I was testing) do not fit the criteria either. The point being made in this section is that customers can struggle to see the value in new solutions whether or not those products constitute a new market.

2. Criteria may be tailored according to patterns of success in an industry. For good examples of how this can be done in an early first screen, see the piece by my former Innosight colleagues, Scott D. Anthony and Matthew Eyring, along with Bell Canada's Lib Gibson, "Mapping Your Innovation Strategy," *Harvard Business Review*, May 2006. This was expanded on in Scott D. Anthony, Mark W. Johnson, Joseph V. Sinfield, and Elizabeth J. Altman, *The Innovator's Guide to Growth: Putting Disruptive Innovation to Work* (Boston: Harvard Business Press, 2008), pp. 148–154.

3. Data from the 2009 Pearson Annual Report.

4. See www.pearson.com/about-us/our-history/.

5. For a good overview of this research, see Clayton M. Christensen, Michael Horn, and Curtis Johnson, *Disrupting Class: How Disruptive Innovation Will Change the Way the World Learns* (New York: McGraw-Hill, 2008).

6. Background and quotes on Pearson's effort are drawn from my interview with Patrick Supanc on June 15, 2010.

7. My interview with Tom Polen, president of BD Preanalytical Systems, July 7, 2010.

8. See www.time.com/time/magazine/article/0,9171,987979,00.html.

9. See Niraj Sheth and Roger Cheng, "HTC Gives Apple a Run for Its Money," *Wall Street Journal*, June 6, 2010.

10. The CEO of the design firm IDEO, Tim Brown, relates many examples of gaining customer feedback in Chapter 4 of *Change by Design: How Design Thinking Transforms Organizations and Inspires Innovation* (New York: HarperBusiness, 2009).

11. Elaine Wong, "What Mountain Dew Learned from DEWmocracy," *Brandweek*, June 16, 2010. While energy drinks can be seen as a new market because they create new consumption, the point of this section is that the beverage which was invented through social media appealed to current users and so probably had little net effect on demand.

12. See the comment by Babson College's Professor Steven Gordon to my blog post: "Using Social Media for Innovation: Different Rules for New Markets," *New Markets Advisors Blog*, July 8, 2010.

13. Background is from my conversation with Greg Fleming of the Air Liquide project team, June 15, 2010.

14. Some of the project's outputs may be viewed at www.ericsson.com/campaign/2020_search_application/index.html. Background is from my conversation with Magnus Karlsson of the project team on May 4, 2010, as well as from Mr. Karlsson's presentation at the 2010 Front End of Innovation conference in Boston, MA.

15. For a thorough treatment of this approach, see Rita Gunther McGrath and Ian C. McMillan, *Discovery-Driven Growth: A Breakthrough Process to Reduce Risk and Seize Opportunity* (Boston: Harvard Business School Press, 2009). See also Clayton M. Christensen, Stephen P. Kaufman, and Willy C. Shih, "Innovation Killers: How Financial Tools Destroy Your Capacity to Do New Things," *Harvard Business Review*, January 2008.

16. An article from Liberia's *The News* about this interesting state of affairs can be found at www.balancingact-africa.com/news/en/issue-no-208/telecoms/liberia-s-president-and-minister-at-odds-over-cell-phone-licences.

17. An earlier approach I took to these issues appeared in Steve Wunker, "Choosing the Path the Market Penetration," *Strategy & Innovation*, November–December 2006.

18. See http://en.wikipedia.org/wiki/Knossos.

19. See www.time.com/time/arts/article/0,8599,1882569,00.html.

20. See www.theplumber.com/closet.html.

21. See http://inventors.about.com/od/pstartinventions/a/Plumbing_3.htm.

22. See www.sushimasters.com/history-pioneers.htm.

23. I am indebted for this example and for some foundational thinking to Bhaskar Chakravorti, *The Slow Pace of Fast Change: Bringing Innovations to Market in a Connected World* (Boston: Harvard Business School Press, 2003). It is recommended to readers seeking a much more extensive treatment of why change occurs at the pace it does.

24. See www.pedalinghistory.com/PHhistory.html.

25. A fascinating article on the service can be found in *Telephony*, December 18, 1909; available at http://earlyradiohistory.us/1909musi.htm.

26. See http://en.wikipedia.org/wiki/History_of_the_bicycle.

27. See Everett M. Rogers, *Diffusion of Innovations*, 5th ed. (New York: Free Press, 2003).

28. See http://en.wikipedia.org/wiki/CompuServe.

29. See http://en.wikipedia.org/wiki/Personal_digital_assistant. Smartphone data is from Lance Whitney, "Android Tops Global Smartphone Ranks," CNET, January 31, 2011 citing market research from Canalys. The Symbian operating system that was an outgrowth of Psion software's division became the clear market leader in units of smartphones sold for the next decade, until late 2010.

30. Interested readers can view prototypes of these devices and some initial specifications at http://mobileopera.com/odin.

31. My conversation with Sercomm CEO James Wang, December 9, 2010,

32. Wikipedia reports 92 3D movies being released in 1953 and only 2 such movies being released just five years later. See http://en.wikipedia.org/wiki/3D_movies.

33. A good discussion of strategy iteration for new ventures is in an article by my former Innosight colleagues, Clark G. Gilbert and Matt Eyring, "Beating the Odds When You Launch a New Venture," *Harvard Business Review*, May 2010.

34. There is a very extensive literature on these topics that is well beyond the scope of this book. Interested readers can refer to Michael Porter, *Competitive Advantage: Creating and Sustaining Superior Performance* (New York: Free Press, 1985), and Adrian Slywotzky, *Value Migration: How to Think Several Moves Ahead of the Competition* (Boston: Harvard Business Press, 1995).

35. See the profile on Eastman in Richard S. Tedlow, *Giants of Enterprise: Seven Business Innovators and the Empires They Built* (New York: HarperCollins, 2001).

36. See www.telecareaware.com/index.php/mhealth-telehealth-mobile-health.html.

Chapter 4

1. For an analysis of how Iridium went so awry, see http://mba.tuck.dartmouth.edu/pages/faculty/syd.finkelstein/articles/Iridium.pdf.

2. Pet food by mail is not a new market. Mail delivery did not change the amount of food pets were consuming (one hopes).

3. See www.reuters.com/article/idUSTRE58T70920090930.

4. This staged approach to investment and growth is explored in Rita Gunther McGrath and Ian C. Macmillan, *Discovery-Driven Growth: A Breakthrough Process to Reduce Risk and Seize Opportunity* (Boston: Harvard Business School Press, 2009).

5. Another African mobile commerce venture, Vodafone's m-pesa, subsequently has had good success in Kenya pursuing the different foothold market of person-to-person money transfers. This proposition is clearly compelling in an African context, with people holding a job in the city often sending money to relatives in their native villages. However at Celpay we were daunted by some basic challenges in this model, particularly the cost of getting money loaded into the system if people did not have their salaries paid electronically into their accounts. An even more pressing issue was that Zambia's financial regulator worried about the threat of money laundering through a transfer system, despite our numerous assurances that we could cap the amount of money transacted and flag suspicious behavior. Rather than engage in a protracted fight with powerful officials, we opted for the practical alternative of a different foothold market.

6. Bryce Ryan and Neal C. Gross, "The Diffusion of Hybrid Seed Corn in Two Iowa Communities," *Rural Sociology* 8:15–24, 1943. This example, along with a great many others, is discussed in Everett Rogers, *Diffusion of Innovations*, 5th ed. (New York: Free Press, 2003). Rogers' work can be classified more as a sociology than as business text, but its nearly 500 pages provide seminal and highly useful reading for businesspeople targeting new markets.

7. Another key book in this vein is Geoffrey Moore, *Crossing the Chasm: Marketing and Selling Technology Products to Mainstream Customers* (New York: HarperCollins, 1991). Moore's work studies the various phases of innovation adoption. One of Moore's key theses, that initial adopters may be quite distinct from mainstream customers, tends to apply most in the high-tech industries that are his focus. He suggests that this "chasm" can be bridged by targeting customer segments one by one, using a "bowling pin" strategy in which success in one segment tees up penetration of another. This finding is broadly consistent with taking a foothold approach to new markets.

Chapter 5

1. The shift from integration to modularity has been explored in several penetrating works by Clayton Christensen and colleagues starting with Clayton M. Christensen, Michael Raynor, and Matt Verlinden, "Skate to Where the Money Will Be," *Harvard Business Review*, November 2001. See also Chapter 7 of Clayton M. Christensen, Erik A. Roth, and Scott D. Anthony,

Seeing What's Next: Using Theories of Innovation to Predict Industry Change (Boston: Harvard Business School Press, 2004).

2. Interview with the author, August 5, 2010.

3. The term *value chain* was coined by Michael Porter in *Competitive Advantage: Creating and Sustaining Superior Performance* (New York: Free Press, 1985).

4. There are of course gradations between the pure forms of superhighway and country road, such as combining direct sales with industry alliances or combining direct and indirect salesforces. Some of these hybrid approaches are explored later in this chapter. It is helpful to understand the pure form of the strategy before assessing how it can be adapted.

5. The story of IBM outsourcing the elements of the PC industry that eventually made most of the profits has been laid out well by Clayton M. Christensen and Michael Raynor in *The Innovator's Solution: Creating and Sustaining Successful Growth* (Boston: Harvard Business School Press, 2003).

6. See http://insurancenewsnet.com/article.aspx?id=221766&type=breaking news.

7. For a perspective on how insurance agents can use the jobs-to-be-done approach to find new avenues for growth, see Stephen Wunker, "Disruptive Innovation: Keys to Surviving It and Thriving from It," *Insurance Journal*, January 29, 2007.

8. Interview with the author, July 7, 2010.

9. See www.insuranceheadlines.com/Life-Insurance/3273.html.

10. Interview with the author, August 18, 2010.

11. A text devoted to sales approaches on the country road is Brian C. Burns and Tom U. Synder, *Selling in a New Market Space: Getting Customers to Buy Your Innovative and Disruptive Products* (New York: McGraw-Hill, 2010).

12. See Jim Duffy, "Is Cisco's SAN Share Loss Due to Server Entry?" *Network World*, May 28, 2009.

13. See "Coach to Acquire Greater China Retail Businesses from Distributor," *China Retail News*, May 30, 2008.

14. See www.fundinguniverse.com/company-histories/The-Vanguard-Group-Inc-Company-History.html and http://en.wikipedia.org/wiki/The_Vanguard_Group.

Chapter 6

1. Data from the U.S. National Venture Capital Association at http://nvca.org/index.php?option=com_docman&task=cat_view&gid=58&Itemid=317.

2. There is an extensive academic literature on first-mover advantages that this chapter does not attempt to summarize. Readers interested in the genesis of the theory should see Marvin B. Lieberman and David B. Montgomery, "First-Mover Advantages," Stanford Business School Research Paper Number 969, October 1987. These authors revisited their enormously influential paper in "First-Mover (Dis)Advantages: Retrospective and Link with the Resource-Based View," *Strategic Management Journal* 19(12), 1998. A skeptical view toward first-mover advantage is put forth in Peter N. Golder and Gerard J. Tellis, "Pioneer Advantage: Marketing Logic or Marketing Legend?," *Journal of Marketing Research* 30, May 1993, as well as in Dennis J. Cahill, "Pioneer Advantage: Is It Real? Does It Matter?" *Marketing Intelligence & Planning* 14(4), 1996. A paper that explores some of the circumstances favoring leadership and fast following is Mark Perry, "When To Lead or Follow? It Depends," *Marketing Letters* 1(3), 1990. For a more detailed view and a thesis that favors fast following, see Constantinos C. Markides and Paul A. Geroski, *Fast Second: How Smart Companies Bypass Radical Innovation to Enter and Dominate New Markets* (San Francisco: Jossey-Bass, 2005). An earlier book in this vein that looks across 28 consumer-oriented industries is Steven P. Schnaars, *Managing Imitation Strategies: How Later Entrants Seize Markets from Pioneers* (New York: Free Press, 1994).

3. A framework about early mover advantages in the context of the flux in technology and customer demand has been nicely developed in Fernando Suarez and Gianvito Lanzolla, "The Half-Truth of First-Mover Advantage," *Harvard Business Review*, April 2005. Suarez and Lanzolla focus on a wide range of circumstances, from slow-moving industries such as vacuum cleaners to ones amid rapid change, which they call "rough waters." This chapter's focus is on those rough waters. These authors expand on their arguments in "Considerations for a Stronger First-Mover Advantage Theory," *Academy of Management Review*, January 2008.

4. Material for this section is drawn from sources including Steven L. Kent, *The Ultimate History of Videogames: The Story Behind the Craze That Touched Our Lives and Changed the World* (New York: Prima Publishing, 2001) and Wikipedia entries on Atari, Intellivision, ColecoVision, and the video game crash of 1983.

5. This commercial, for the Commodore VIC20, is kept alive at www.youtube.com/watch?v=0pYMHm_Y60s&eurl=/. YouTube also hosts several entertaining commercials for the Magnavox Odyssey and other early games systems.

6. See "Zynga's Value at $5.5 Billion Tops Electronic Arts on Virtual Goods Surge," *Bloomberg*, October 26, 2010.

7. Atari's game version of the movie "E.T.: The Extra Terrestrial" resulted from a major licensing deal, but unfortunately it was so bad that it won a nod

from PC World magazine in 2006 as the worst videogame of all time. In fact, it was so bad that Atari sent several million copies to a landfill in New Mexico to be crushed, encased in concrete, and buried forever. This led to a headline in the Alamogordo Daily News proclaiming, "City to Atari: 'E.T.' trash go home."

8. Material for these case studies is drawn from the organizations' Web sites, Wikipedia entries, conversations in October 2010 with Bosch Healthcare executives, and yes, the album liner for *Hot Potatoes: The Best of the Wiggles* (2009).

9. The Wiggles' income made them Australia's highest-paid entertainers, ahead of stars such as Russell Crowe and Hugh Jackman. See "Wiggles Still Australia's Highest-Paid Entertainers," *Australian Broadcasting Corporation News*, September 10, 2008.

10. Tom Peterson, Victory Music Review, July 2005.

11. Readers interested in a deeper exploration of these three business models are urged to consult Clayton M. Christensen, Jerome H. Grossman, and Jason Hwang, *The Innovator's Prescription: A Disruptive Solution for Health Care* (New York: McGraw-Hill, 2009), as well as Charles B. Stabell and Øystein Fjeldstad, "Configuring Value for Competitive Advantage: On Chains, Shops, and Networks," *Strategic Management Journal* 19, 1998. This section draws on the author's blog post "Three Business Models to Profit from Being an Early Mover," *New Markets Advisors Blog* April 6, 2010.

12. Microsoft's very first product was a form of the computer language BASIC that ran on the Altair, and Bill Gates visited Ed Roberts, the Altair's inventor, as he was about to pass away in 2010. However, it was the IBM PC that made Microsoft into the huge enterprise that it became.

13. There is a large literature on standard setting that lies beyond the scope of this book. Interested readers may wish to consult Stanley M. Besen and Joseph Farrell, "Choosing How to Compete: Strategies and Tactics in Standardization," *Journal of Economic Perspectives* 8(2), 1994. A more recent article applying some of this theory is Gregory Unruh and Richard Ettenson, "Winning in the Green Frenzy," *Harvard Business Review*, November 2010.

14. There is also a substantial literature on network effects that this book cannot summarize. Interested readers may wish to refer to Gerard J. Tellis, Eden Yin, and Rakesh Niraj, "Does Quality Win? Network Effects versus Quality in High-Tech Markets," *Journal of Marketing Research* 46(2), 2009. An earlier article that focuses on the apparel industry is Brian Uzzi, "The Sources and Consequences of Embeddedness for the Economic Performance of Organizations: The Network Effect," *American Sociological Review* 61, 1996. A far shallower treatment of this topic is my blog post "Network Effects in

New Markets—Who Profits Most?" *New Markets Advisors Blog*, May 25, 2010.

15. For further on this argument, see my blog post, "When Does It Make Sense to be a Fast Follower?" *Innoblog*, April 7, 2009.

16. Johnson & Johnson Web site.

17. The section on Sharp draws on my blog post "Fast Follower Strategy—Three Options for Success," *New Markets Advisors Blog*, July 29, 2010.

18. LG and Samsung entered the cell phone market in 1996 and 1993, respectively. Their initial emphasis was on the Korean market. Samsung did produce a car phone in 1986 but production was soon halted.

19. Information for this section is taken from an interview with Meredith Baratz, UnitedHealthcare's vice president for market solutions, August 24, 2010.

Chapter 7

1. International Monetary Fund, *World Economic Outlook*, October 2010. Data projection is for growth 2010 through 2015.

2. Data on this growth are presented in very accessible form at www.chinability.com/GDP.htm. The economy has grown by a factor of 82 times since 1978, part of which is accounted for by fluctuating exchange rates and inflation as well as population growth.

3. Morgan Stanley Dean Witter research as cited in John C. Bogle, *Common Sense on Mutual Funds: Fully Updated 10th Anniversary Edition* New York: John C. Wiley, 2009. I have conducted research showing that the proportion of S&P 500 revenues from emerging markets is no more than 12 percent—regardless, the actual figure is a small number. See Clayton M. Christensen, Stephen Wunker, and Hari Nair, "Innovation vs. Poverty," *Forbes*, October 13, 2008.

4. For details on Celtel's story, see Russell Southwood, *Less Walk More Talk: How Celtel and the Mobile Phone Changed Africa* (Hoboken, NJ: Wiley, 2009). For details on how mobile phones lead to economic growth, see, for example, "To Do with the Price of Fish," *The Economist*, May 10, 2007.

5. As quoted in Andrew McNulty, "In the Fast Lane: Behind Capitec's Successful Model," *Financial Mail*, November 6, 2009. Other quotes in this section are taken from this article. Additional in-depth profiles of Capitec include Maya Fisher-French, "Bringing in the Competition," *Mail & Guardian*, April 23, 2010; Gerhard Coetzee, "Innovative Approach to Delivering Microfinance Services: The Case of Capitec Bank," Microsave Working Paper, August 2003; and Marc Ashton, "Capitec Shifts Its Client Base," *Fin24*, April 1, 2009.

6. In their most recent fiscal years, Capitec's return on equity (ROE) was 32 percent, and SKS had an ROE of nearly 22 percent. According to the financial Web site Seeking Alpha, these figures exceed the estimated 2010 ROE of every major bank in North America. In 2010, SKS and other Indian microlenders encountered major problems when some government officials urged borrowers to stop repayments because of the industry's high profits. SKS has boasted of having some of the lowest interest rates alongside one of the biggest businesses in the Indian microlending industry, so its difficulties came about because of its high-profile success rather than through an unsustainable model.

7. McKinsey analysis cited in Diana Farrell and Eric Beinhocker, "Next Big Spenders: India's Middle Class," *BusinessWeek*, May 19, 2007, and Professor Mark J. Perry, "Capitalism and the Rising Middle Class in India," *Carpe Diem blog*, October 20, 2007. In separate research, McKinsey has built on data from the Economist Intelligence Unit, Euromonitor, and the World Bank to estimate that of the total $9.7 trillion in consumer spending in 24 leading emerging markets for 2010, 28 percent will be from households making less than $13,500 a year, 23 percent will be from households making $13,500 to $22,499, 32 percent will be from households making $22,500 to $56,499, 15 percent will be from households making $56,500 to $113,000, and 2 percent will be from households making more than $113,000 (*McKinsey Quarterly*, September 2010). In this chapter, the notion of abject poverty falls well under the threshold of $13,500 in household income, which in many developing countries is an income that would be considered solidly middle class.

8. See, for example, C. K. Prahalad, *The Fortune at the Bottom of the Pyramid: Eradicating Poverty through Profits*, rev. 5th ann. ed (Upper Saddle River, NJ: Wharton School Publishing, 2010).

9. For more information, see www.aleutia.com/about-us.

10. This line of thought is central to Clayton Christensen's theory of disruptive innovation, as cited many times elsewhere in this book. See, for example, Clayton M. Christensen, *The Innovator's Dilemma: When New Technologies Cause Great Firms to Fail* (Boston: Harvard Business School Press, 1997).

11. Lotus Energy was funded by E+Co, a nonprofit investor in renewable energy projects for whom I wrote the business plan back in 1995. E+Co has since gone on to invest in over 250 projects in the ensuing 15 years, often with the aim of creating local capacity to scale up distribution of these ever-improving technologies. Some of the barriers to distributing solar cells are addressed in a paper in which I was intimately involved: "Selling Solar: Financing

Household Solar Energy in the Developing World," Rockefeller Brothers Fund, 1995.

12. Further information about Adecoagro is available in Lucia Kassai, "Soros Weighs IPO to Fund Brazil Mill," *Bloomberg*, February 2, 2010.

13. The issue of institutional voids and the opportunities they create is covered in depth in Tarun Khanna and Krishna G. Palepu, *Winning in Emerging Markets: A Road Map for Strategy and Execution* (Boston: Harvard Business Press, 2010).

14. Full rankings are available at www.doingbusiness.org/rankings. The figures quoted are the 2011 rankings.

Chapter 8

1. A useful metastudy of VC success is Steven N. Kaplan and Josh Lerner, "It Ain't Broke: The Past, Present, and Future of Venture Capital," University of Chicago Booth School of Business and Harvard Business School, December 2009.

2. Interview with the author, August 5, 2010.

3. Interview with the author, August 25, 2010.

4. An article focused on why organizations tend to escalate doomed investments, including factors such as fear of harming individuals' careers, is Barry M. Staw and Jerry Ross, "Knowing When to Pull the Plug," *Harvard Business Review*, March–April 1989.

5. The dimensions of portfolio balance will vary substantially from company to company. They may include factors such as degree of support versus disruption of the core business, degree of external partnership, project cost, potential revenue or profit, time to investment payback, stage of development, and mix of new business models versus new technologies. An excellent reference for corporate venturers is Rita Gunther McGrath, Thomas Kiel, and Taina Tukiainen, "Extracting Value from Corporate Venturing," *Sloan Management Review*, Fall 2006. The authors delve deeply into Nokia's venturing efforts and lay out how the firm creates other types of portfolio balance as well, such as among positioning options, scouting options, stepping-stone options, and platform launches. None of this is to say that a portfolio plan must be slavishly adhered to—venture capitalists are opportunistic. Yet a plan shows how the actual portfolio might deviate from what is ideal in the abstract, and it can flag potential problems that might arise in the future as the portfolio's investments mature.

6. Author's correspondence with Russ Conser of Shell Gamechanger, September 30, 2010. Gamechanger's activities encompass new markets, but particularly in Exploration and Production (E&P), they focus on sustain-

ing the core business. This example draws solely from the E&P aspects of Gamechanger.

7. The dot-com era is sometimes raised as a counterpoint to this story. It is certainly true that many ventures were overfunded, but this was largely a rational response to the financial markets of the day. Because the stock market was embracing IPOs from very early stage firms and often according them huge valuations, it made compelling sense to build ventures rapidly so that they could IPO and the VCs could sell their holdings. This dynamic did not end up creating much value in the companies, but VCs could earn astounding returns during this period.

8. Author's discussion with Steve Sasson, inventor of the digital camera at Kodak, May 4, 2010.

9. See in particular Chip Heath and Dan Heath, *Switch: How to Change Things When Change Is Hard* (New York: Broadway Books, 2010).

10. For details on these archetypes, see Stephen Wunker and George Pohle, "Built for Innovation," *Forbes*, November 12, 2007. The research underlying this special report in the magazine consisted of a quantitative survey of over 90 firms. Cluster analysis revealed four general approaches to innovation. The research was conducted by me at my former consulting firm, Innosight, IBM's Institute for Business Value, and the benchmarking organization APQC.

11. The U.S. Army has made its AAR leader's guide available to the public at www.au.af.mil/au/awc/awcgate/army/tc_25-20/tc25-20.pdf.

12. For a more detailed treatment of this section, see Scott D. Anthony, Steven Fransblow, and Steve Wunker, "Measuring the Black Box: How to Design and Implement Innovation Metrics," *Chief Executive*, December 2007.

13. See in particular Vijay Govindarajan and Chris Trimble, *The Other Side of Innovation: Solving the Execution Challenge* (Boston: Harvard Business Review Press, 2010). This book also delves into many other issues relevant to leaders of incubation and innovation programs. It builds on their excellent 2005 volume *10 Rules for Strategic Innovators: From Idea to Execution* (Boston: Harvard Business School Press, 2005).

14. I worked with the benchmarking organization APQC to assess innovation practices at a wide range of companies. The Mayo Clinic example is noted in the APQC report, "The Right Failure Is an Option," July 23, 2008, which is available online.

15. The idea of breakthroughs coming from collaboration and intersection is explored in an extensive academic literature on innovation. Two recent works giving a highly readable overview of the topic are Steven Johnson, *Where Good Ideas Come From: The Natural History of Innovation* (New

York: Riverhead Books, 2010), and Frans Johansson, *The Medici Effect: What Elephants and Epidemics Can Teach Us About Innovation* (Boston: Harvard Business School Press, 2006).

16. This story, as well as the more productive path that Whirlpool eventually took, is detailed in "Creativity Overflowing," *BusinessWeek*, May 8, 2006.

17. For more on "hackathons," see my blog post "Facebook Hackathons and Innovation Capabilities," *New Markets Advisors Blog*. April 20, 2010.

18. The subject is explored at length in Christian Terwiesch and Karl Ulrich, *Innovation Tournaments: Creating and Selecting Exceptional Opportunities* (Boston: Harvard Business School Press, 2009).

19. The application of "crowdsourcing" to new markets is explored in my blog post, "Can Crowdsourcing Uncover New Markets?" *New Markets Advisors Blog*, September 16, 2010. The topic of "crowdsourcing" is covered in depth in James Surowiecki, *The Wisdom of Crowds* (New York: Anchor Books, 2004).

20. This anecdote, told via a colleague, wound up at the beginning of a *Business-Week* cover story "Companies Seek Innovation—Not Gimmicks," *Business-Week*, May 8, 2007. A few weeks later, "Innovation Man" started anchoring a series of television commercials from IBM that have since become YouTube hits. Thankfully, the name of Innovation Man's firm has remained part of his secret identity.

21. Arthur D. Little (Switzerland), "Venturing for Innovation," December 2002.

22. Timeline from "Corning's History," *Fast Company*, March 1, 2008.

23. Material for this section is drawn from my interview with Daniel Ricoult and Deb Mills, the coheads of the Exploratory Markets and Technologies Group within Strategic Growth at Corning, August 5, 2010.

24. Material for this section is drawn from my interview with Jacqueline LeSage Krause, vice president of innovation and corporate venture capital at The Hartford, September 24, 2010.

Chapter 9

1. See Julia Karow, "BGI to Receive $1.5 billion in 'Collaborative Funds' Over 10 Years from China Development Bank," *GenomeWeb*, January 12, 2010. By 2011, the institute will be able to sequence 10,000 human genomes a year compared with the 100 collectively sequenced since the science began.

2. See Andrew Higgins, "With Solar Valley Project, China Embarks on Bold Green Technology Mission," *Washington Post*, May 17, 2010.

3. See, for example, Thomas Friedman, "Their Moonshot, and Ours," *New York Times*, September 25, 2010. See also Judy Estrin's fine book, *Closing*

the Innovation Gap: Reigniting the Spark of Creativity in a Global Economy (New York: McGraw-Hill, 2009).

4. See for more detail Josh Lerner, *Boulevard of Broken Dreams: Why Public Efforts to Boost Entrepreneurship and Venture Capital Have Failed—and What to Do about It* (Princeton, NJ: Princeton University Press, 2009). Lerner spends several chapters on the drawbacks of public programs, and the challenges he addresses are far more extensive than the ones discussed in this brief section. His book is also a good source of ideas about how government can play a positive and effective role.

5. Park's comments are drawn from a discussion at West Wireless Health Care Innovation Day, October 12, 2010.

6. An extensive and elegantly written analysis of this process is in Steven Johnson, *Where Good Ideas Come From: The Natural History of Innovation* (New York: Riverhead Books, 2010). See especially Johnson's chapter on platforms.

7. Interested readers can refer to James Bessen and Michael J. Meurer, *Patent Failure: How Judges, Bureaucrats and Lawyers Put Innovators at Risk* (Princeton, NJ: Princeton University Press, 2008), as well as Adam B. Jaffe and Josh Lerner, *Innovation and Its Discontents: How Our Broken Patent System is Endangering and Progress, and What to Do About It* (Princeton, NJ: Princeton University Press, 2004).

8. See Stephen R. Bown, *Scurvy: How a Surgeon, a Mariner, and a Gentleman Solved the Greatest Medical Mystery of the Age of Sail* (New York: St. Martin's Griffin, 2004).

9. For an article about what makes for a great innovator, see Jeffrey H. Dyer, Hal B. Gregersen, and Clayton M. Christensen, "The Innovator's DNA," *Harvard Business Review*, December 2009.

10. Sudhir Syal, "Indian Silicon Valley Startups Ride on Innovation to Beat Slowdown," *Economic Times*, January 10, 2010.

11. It should be noted that not all developed-country governments are this perverse in their immigration policy. Australia and Canada are among a handful of nations that actively seek skilled immigrants.

12. Global Mobile Suppliers Association, February 10, 2010.

13. The allocation of spectrum by metropolitan area was not totally unreasonable given that the government's local approach to allocation of other spectrum had left inconsistent patches of frequencies available in various cities. Still, Europe found it possible to move other users of spectrum out of the bands it was reserving for cellular communications, whereas the United States took years to muster the will to do so. The American approach not only led to operational complexities for national networks but also left

batches of spectrum unused, resulting in inefficiencies that bolstered the case for CDMA in the United States.

14. For more background on these differences in policy, see Neil Gandal, David Salant, and Leonard Waverman, "Standards in Wireless Telephone Networks," *Telecommunications Policy* 27, 2003, and Dave Mock, *The Qualcomm Equation: How a Fledgling Telecom Company Forged a New Path to Big Profits and Market Dominance* (New York: AMACOM, 2005). CDMA ended up being foundational for third-generation (3G) systems as well as data communications, but not before it caused turmoil in a key market during a critical phase of the industry's growth.

15. This point could be read as contradicting a key thesis behind the classic work by Geoffrey Moore, *Crossing the Chasm: Marketing and Selling Technology Products to Mainstream Customers* (New York: HarperCollins, 1991). Moore argues that the first adopters of a new technology like novel engineering that pushes performance limits. However, Moore's focus is largely on enterprise IT solutions, whereas this book has a much broader view; Moore's thesis may not apply to new types of cell phones. Moreover, my next paragraph states that standards should not be set too early in an industry's evolution. This book and Moore's are consistent in their view that an industry's fast growth depends on a mass of customers perceiving a new solution as validated and safe to adopt.

16. The history of the Internet will be old news to many readers and does not need retelling in this book. Readers interested in the central role of the U.S. military in this story can refer to http://en.wikipedia.org/wiki/History_of_the_Internet. While Al Gore played a leading role in Congress in expanding support for the Internet, including opening the network to commercial traffic, his claim of creating the Internet was overblown; he was not present in the 1960s and 1970s when several of the most significant decisions were being made.

Afterword

1. Author's correspondence with Karen O'Reilly, Lexington Insurance chief innovation officer, December 8, 2010.

2. Peter Drucker, *Managing for Results* (New York: Harper & Row, 1964).

3. Chapter 2 notes the origins of this thinking in Clayton Christensen's work. See, for example, Clayton M. Christensen, Scott Cook, and Taddy Hall, "Marketing Malpractice: The Cause and the Cure," *Harvard Business Review*, December 2005.

4. For a deeper analysis of how traditional tools of financial analysis can lead firms astray in new markets, see Clayton M. Christensen, Stephen P. Kaufman, and Willy C. Shih, "Innovation Killers: How Financial Tools

Destroy Your Capacity to Do New Things," *Harvard Business Review,* January 2008.

5. Chapter 4 also notes that footholds can signal to competitors that they should focus elsewhere. This point might seem to contradict the statement that competitors can be helpful in a market's early days, but it is really a matter of degree. A handful of competitors can be useful in educating the market and providing customers with comparison points. A boatload of competitors can depress pricing and confuse customers. Relatedly, we should not take to extremes the point that competitive strategy should be secondary to market growth strategy; companies should prioritize growing markets but of course should try to beat competitors wherever possible. Focus on a foothold gives a firm a good chance of winning battles on the turf it chooses.

6. As Chapter 6 explains, country roads are akin to solution shop business models or in some cases facilitated networks. Superhighways are a form of value-chain business model.

7. Chapter 8 notes the key work of Rita McGrath and Ian Macmillan in this field. See Rita Gunther McGrath and Ian C. Macmillan, *Discovery-Driven Growth: A Breakthrough Process to Reduce Risk and Seize Opportunity* (Boston: Harvard Business School Press, 2009).

8. Philips applies this discipline to new opportunities, emerging markets, and mature markets in a balanced portfolio. Although the mandates for teams will vary depending on the market being pursued, in each case there is the same emphasis on understanding the customer prior to developing a product. The goal is to understand stakeholders and their world as if the team lived with them in that space. Philips compares this approach to finding and treating the cause of customers' issues, not their symptoms.

9. Material on Philips is drawn from the company Web site as well as my interviews with Mary Sargent, customer insight and innovation, Philips Healthcare, August 18, 2010, and Linda Trevenen, director of marketing excellence programs, Philips Home Healthcare Solutions, July 27, 2010.

10. The recommendation to pursue a specific opportunity may seem to contradict the recommendation to have a portfolio plan, but it is a matter of sequencing. A portfolio plan is critical to sustained success, but sometimes there is no organizational will to think so broadly. Progress with a single initiative can generate support for looking more comprehensively at opportunities in new markets.

BIBLIOGRAPHY

Anthony, Scott D. *The Silver Lining: An Innovation Playbook for Uncertain Times.* Boston: Harvard Business Press, 2009.

——, Matt Eyring, and Lib Gibson. "Mapping Your Innovation Strategy." *Harvard Business Review* 84(5):104–113, 2006.

——, Steven Fransblow, and Steve Wunker. "Measuring the Black Box: How to Design and Implement Innovation Metrics." *Chief Executive*, December 2007, pp. 48–51.

——, Mark W. Johnson, Joseph V. Sinfield, and Elizabeth J. Altman. *The Innovator's Guide to Growth: Putting Disruptive Innovation to Work.* Boston: Harvard Business Press, 2008.

Ardnt, Michael. "Creativity Overflowing." *BusinessWeek*, May 8, 2006, pp. 50–53.

Ariely, Dan. *Predictably Irrational: The Hidden Forces That Shape Our Decisions,* rev. ed. New York: Harper Perennial, 2010.

Besen, Stanley M., and Joseph Farrell, "Choosing How to Compete: Strategies and Tactics in Standardization," *Journal of Economic Perspectives* 8(2):117–131, 1994.

Bessen, James, and Michael J. Meurer. *Patent Failure: How Judges, Bureaucrats and Lawyers Put Innovators at Risk.* Princeton, NJ: Princeton University Press, 2008.

Bower, Joseph L., and Clayton M. Christensen. "Disruptive Technologies: Catching the Wave." *Harvard Business Review* 73(1):43–53, 1995.

Bown, Stephen R. *Scurvy: How a Surgeon, a Mariner, and a Gentleman Solved the Greatest Medical Mystery of the Age of Sail.* New York: St. Martin's Griffin, 2004.

Brodsky, Ira. *The History of Wireless: How Creative Minds Produced Technology for the Masses.* St. Louis, MO: Telescope Books, 2008.

Brown, Tim. *Change by Design: How Design Thinking Transforms Organizations and Inspires Innovation.* New York: HarperBusiness, 2009.

Burns, Brian C., and Tom U. Snyder. *Selling In a New Market Space: Getting Customers to Buy Your Innovative and Disruptive Products.* New York: McGraw-Hill, 2010.

Dennis J. Cahill. "Pioneer Advantage: Is It Real? Does It Matter?" *Marketing Intelligence & Planning* 14(4):5, 1996.

Chakravorti, Bhaskar. *The Slow Pace of Fast Change: Bringing Innovations to Market in a Connected World.* Boston: Harvard Business School Press, 2003.

Chesbrough, Henry. *Open Innovation: The New Imperative for Creating and Profiting from Technology.* Boston: Harvard Business School Press, 2003.

Christensen, Clayton M. *The Innovator's Dilemma: When New Technologies Cause Great Firms to Fail.* Boston: Harvard Business School Press, 1997.

———, Scott D. Anthony, Gerald Berstell, and Denise Nitterhouse, "Finding the Right Job for Your Product." *MIT Sloan Management Review* 48(3):38–47, 2007.

———, Scott D. Anthony, and Erik A. Roth. *Seeing What's Next: Using Theories of Innovation to Predict Industry Change.* Boston: Harvard Business School Press, 2004.

———, Scott Cook, and Taddy Hall. "Marketing Malpractice: The Cause and the Cure." *Harvard Business Review* 83(12):127–133, 2005.

———, Jerome H. Grossman, and Jason Hwang. *The Innovator's Prescription: A Disruptive Solution for Health Care.* New York: McGraw-Hill, 2009.

———, Curtis W. Johnson, and Michael B. Horn. *Disrupting Class: How Disruptive Innovation Will Change the Way the World Learns.* New York: McGraw-Hill, 2008.

———, Stephen P. Kaufman, and Willy C. Shih. "Innovation Killers: How Financial Tools Destroy Your Capacity to Do New Things." *Harvard Business Review* 86(1):98–105, 2008.

———, Charles McLaughlin, and Steve Wunker. "The Road to Nowhere." *Pharmaceutical Executive*, April 1, 2006.

——— and Michael E. Raynor. *The Innovator's Solution: Creating and Sustaining Successful Growth.* Boston: Harvard Business School Press, 2003.

———, Michael Raynor, and Matt Verlinden, "Skate to Where the Money Will Be." *Harvard Business Review* 79(10):72–81, 2001.

———, Stephen Wunker, and Hari Nair. "Innovation vs. Poverty." *Forbes* 182(7):101–105, 2008.

"Companies Seek Innovation—Not Gimmicks." *BusinessWeek*, May 8, 2007.

Davidow, William H. *Marketing High Technology: An Insider's View.* New York: Free Press, 1986.

Davies, S., P. Geroski, M. Lund, and A. Vlassopoulos. "The Dynamics of Market Leadership in UK Manufacturing Industry, 1979–1986." London Business School Working Paper No. 93, Centre for Business Strategy, London, 1991

Drucker, Peter. *Managing for Results.* New York: Harper & Row, 1964.

Dyer, Jeffrey H., Hal B. Gregersen, and Clayton M. Christensen. "The Innovator's DNA." *Harvard Business Review* 87(12):60–67, 2009.

Estrin, Judy. *Closing the Innovation Gap: Reigniting the Spark of Creativity in a Global Economy.* New York: McGraw-Hill, 2009.

Farrell, Diana, Eric D. Beinhocker, and Adil S. Zainulbhai. "Tracking the Growth of India's Middle Class." *McKinsey Quarterly* 3:50–61, 2007.

Gadiesh, Orit, Philip Leung, and Till Vestring. "The Battle for China's Good-Enough Market." *Harvard Business Review* 85(9):80–89, 2007.

Gandal, Neil, David Salant, and Leonard Waverman. "Standards in Wireless Telephone Networks." *Telecommunications Policy* 27(5–6):325–332, 2003.

Gilbert, Clark G., and Matthew J. Eyring. "Beating the Odds When You Launch a New Venture." *Harvard Business Review* 88(5):92–98, 2010.

Golder, Peter N., and Gerard J. Tellis, "Pioneer Advantage: Marketing Logic or Marketing Legend?" *Journal of Marketing Research* 30(2):158–170, 1993.

Govindarajan, Vijay, and Chris Trimble. *10 Rules for Strategic Innovators: From Idea to Execution.* Boston: Harvard Business School Press, 2005.

———. *The Other Side of Innovation: Solving the Execution Challenge.* Boston: Harvard Business Review Press, 2010.

Hamel, Gary, and C. K. Prahalad. "Corporate Imagination and Expeditionary Marketing." *Harvard Business Review* 69(4):81–92, 1991.

Headquarters, Department of the Army. "A Leaders Guide to After-Action Reviews." Training Circular 25-20. September 1993.

Heath, Chip, and Dan Heath. *Switch: How to Change Things When Change Is Hard.* New York: Broadway Books, 2010.

Jaffe, Adam B., and Josh Lerner. *Innovation and Its Discontents: How Our Broken Patent System Is Endangering and Progress, and What to Do About It.* Princeton, NJ: Princeton University Press, 2004.

James, Peter, and Nick Thorpe. *Ancient Inventions.* New York: Ballantine Books, 1995.

Jenkins, Reese V. *Images and Enterprise: Technology and the American Photographic Industry, 1839–1925.* Baltimore, MD: Johns Hopkins University Press, 1987.

Johansson, Frans. *The Medici Effect: What Elephants and Epidemics Can Teach Us About Innovation.* Boston: Harvard Business School Press, 2006.

Johnson, Steven. *Where Good Ideas Come From: The Natural History of Innovation.* New York: Riverhead Books, 2010.

Kahneman, Daniel, Paul Slovic, and Amos Tversky. *Judgment under Uncertainty: Heuristics and Biases.* Cambridge, England: Cambridge University Press, 1982.

Kaplan, Steven N., and Josh Lerner. "It Ain't Broke: The Past, Present, and Future of Venture Capital." University of Chicago Booth School of Business and Harvard Business School, December 2009.

Kao, John. *Innovation Nation: How America is Losing Its Innovation Edge, Why It Matters, and What We Can Do to Get It Back.* New York: Free Press, 2007.

Kawasaki, Guy. *The Art of the Start: The Time-Tested, Battle-Hardened Guide for Anyone Starting Anything.* New York: Portfolio, 2004.

Kent, Steven L. *The Ultimate History of Video Games: The Story Behind the Craze that Touched Our Lives and Changed the World.* New York: Prima Publishing, 2001.

Khanna, Tarun, and Krishna G. Palepu. *Winning in Emerging Markets: A Road Map for Strategy and Execution.* Boston: Harvard Business Press, 2010.

—— and Jayant Sinha. "Strategies that Fit Emerging Markets." *Harvard Business Review* 83(6):63–76, 2005.

Kim, W. Chan, and Renée Mauborgne. *Blue Ocean Strategy: How to Create Uncontested Market Space and Make the Competition Irrelevant.* Boston: Harvard Business School Press, 2005.

Lafley, A. G., and Ram Charan. *The Game-Changer: How You Can Drive Revenue and Profit Growth with Innovation.* New York: Crown Business, 2008.

Lieberman, Marvin B., and David B. Montgomery. "First-Mover Advantages." Stanford Business School Research Paper Number 969, October 1987.

——. "First-Mover (Dis)Advantages: Retrospective and Link with the Resource-Based View." *Strategic Management Journal* 19(12):1111–1126, 1998.

Lerner, Josh. *Boulevard of Broken Dreams: Why Public Efforts to Boost Entrepreneurship and Venture Capital Have Failed—and What to Do about It.* Princeton, NJ: Princeton University Press, 2009.

Levitt, Theodore. "Marketing Myopia." *Harvard Business Review* 38(4):45–56, 1960.

Markides, Constantinos C. *Game-Changing Strategies: How to Create New Market Space in Established Industries by Breaking the Rules.* San Francisco: Jossey-Bass, 2008.

——— and Paul A. Geroski. *Fast Second: How Smart Companies Bypass Radical Innovation to Enter and Dominate New Markets*. San Francisco: Jossey-Bass, 2005.

McGrath, Rita Gunther, Thomas Kiel, and Taina Tukiainen. "Extracting Value from Corporate Venturing," *Sloan Management Review* 48(1):50–56, 2006.

——— and Ian C. Macmillan. *Discovery-Driven Growth: A Breakthrough Process to Reduce Risk and Seize Opportunity*. Boston: Harvard Business School Press, 2009.

Meyer, Peter. *Creating and Dominating New Markets*. New York: AMACOM, 2002.

Mock, Dave. *The Qualcomm Equation: How a Fledgling Telecom Company Forged a New Path to Big Profits and Market Dominance*. New York: AMACOM, 2005.

Moore, Geoffrey A. *Crossing the Chasm: Marketing and Selling Technology Products to Mainstream Customers*. New York: HarperCollins, 1991.

———. *Dealing with Darwin: How Great Companies Innovate at Every Phase of their Evolution*. New York: Portfolio, 2005.

Nagle, Thomas, John Hogan, and Joseph Zale. *The Strategy and Tactics of Pricing: A Guide to Growing More Profitably*, 5th ed. Englewood Cliffs, NJ: Prentice-Hall, 2010.

Northrop, Michael F., Peter W. Riggs, and Frances A. Raymond. "Selling Solar: A Report Based on a Workshop at the Pocantico Conference Center of the Rockefeller Brothers Fund, October 11–13, 1995."

Ojha, Nikhil Prasad, Parijat Ghosh, Sarah Stein Greenberg, and Anurag Mishra. "How Innovation Really Works." *Business Today*, May 30, 2010.

Perry, Mark. "When to Lead or Follow? It Depends." *Marketing Letters* 1(3):187–198, 1990.

Perry, Mark J. "Capitalism and the Rising Middle Class in India." *Carpe Diem blog*, October 20, 2007.

Porter, Michael. *Competitive Advantage: Creating and Sustaining Superior Performance*. New York: Free Press, 1985.

Prahalad, C. K. *The Fortune at the Bottom of the Pyramid: Eradicating Poverty through Profits*, rev. 5th ann. ed. Upper Saddle River, NJ: Wharton School Publishing, 2010.

——— and Allen Hammond. "Serving the World's Poor, Profitably." *Harvard Business Review* 80(9):48–57, 2002.

Rogers, Everett M. *Diffusion of Innovations*, 5th ed. New York: Free Press, 2003.

Schnaars, Steven P. *Managing Imitation Strategies: How Later Entrants Seize Markets from Pioneers*. New York: Free Press, 1994.

Sidhu, Inder. *Doing Both: How Cisco Captures Today's Profit and Drives Tomorrow's Growth.* Upper Saddle River, NJ: FT Press, 2010.

Skarzynski, Peter, and Rowan Gibson. *Innovation to the Core: A Blueprint for Transforming the Way Your Company Innovates.* Boston: Harvard Business Press, 2008.

Slywotzky, Adrian. *Value Migration: How to Think Several Moves Ahead of the Competition.* Boston: Harvard Business Press, 1995.

Southwood, Russell. *Less Walk More Talk: How Celtel and the Mobile Phone Changed Africa.* Hoboken, NJ: Wiley, 2009.

Stabell, Charles B., and Øystein Fjeldstad, "Configuring Value for Competitive Advantage: On Chains, Shops, and Networks." *Strategic Management Journal* 19(5):413–438, 1998.

Staw, Barry M., and Jerry Ross, "Knowing When to Pull the Plug." *Harvard Business Review* 65(2):68–74, 1989.

Suarez, Fernando, and Gianvito Lanzolla. "Considerations for a Stronger First-Mover Advantage Theory." *Academy of Management Review* 33(1):269–270, 2008.

———. "The Half-Truth of First-Mover Advantage." *Harvard Business Review* 83(4):121–127, 2005.

Surowiecki, James. *The Wisdom of Crowds.* New York: Anchor Books, 2004.

Tedlow, Richard S. *Giants of Enterprise: Seven Business Innovators and the Empires They Built.* New York: HarperCollins, 2001.

Tellis, Gerard J., Eden Yin, and Rakesh Niraj. "Does Quality Win? Network Effects versus Quality in High-Tech Markets." *Journal of Marketing Research* 46(2):135–149, 2009.

Terwiesch, Christian, and Karl Ulrich, *Innovation Tournaments: Creating and Selecting Exceptional Opportunities.* Boston: Harvard Business School Press, 2009.

"To Do with the Price of Fish." *The Economist,* May 10, 2007, p. 84.

Ulwick, Anthony. *What Customers Want: Using Outcome-Driven Innovation to Create Breakthrough Products and Services.* New York: McGraw-Hill, 2005.

Unruh, Gregory, and Richard Ettenson. "Winning in the Green Frenzy." *Harvard Business Review* 88(11):110–115, 2010.

Uzzi, Brian. "The Sources and Consequences of Embeddedness for the Economic Performance of Organizations: The Network Effect." *American Sociological Review* 61:674–698, 1996.

"Venturing for Innovation— Developments in the Area of Corporate Venturing Based on a Global Arthur D. Little Study." Thalwil, Switzerland: Arthur D. Little, 2002.

Weisberger, Bernard. "You Press the Button, We Do the Rest." *American Heritage Magazine* 23(6):82–91, 1972.

Wunker, Stephen. "3 Business Models to Profit from Being an Early Mover." *New Markets Advisors Blog*, April 6, 2010.

———. "Can Crowdsourcing Uncover New Markets?" *New Markets Advisors Blog*, September 16, 2010.

———. Disruptive Innovation: Keys to Surviving It and Thriving from It." *Insurance Journal*, January 29, 2007, pp. 150–152.

———. "Facebook Hackathons and Innovation Capabilities." *New Markets Advisors Blog*, April 20, 2010.

———. "Fast Follower Strategy—Three Options for Success." *New Markets Advisors Blog*, July 29, 2010.

———. "Get the Job Done." *Harvard Business Online*. August 2005.

———. "Network Effects in New Markets—Who Profits Most?" *New Markets Advisors Blog*, May 25, 2010.

———. "When Does It Make Sense to be a Fast Follower?" *Innoblog*, April 7, 2009.

——— and George Pohle. "Built for Innovation." *Forbes* 180(10):137–143, 2007.

——— and Joe Sinfield, "Early Market Testing Can Benefit Healthcare." *BusinessWeek online*, November 18, 2009.

Zook, Chris. *Beyond the Core: Expand Your Market Without Abandoning Your Roots.* Boston: Harvard Business Press, 2004.

INDEX

ABOUT THE AUTHOR

Stephen Wunker is a specialist in finding and entering new markets. He helps companies develop new ideas, evaluate growth opportunities, and improve how they organize to pursue innovation. His clients have ranged from start-ups to many of the world's largest corporations. He worked for five years with Harvard Business School Professor Clayton Christensen to create consulting practices around disruptive innovation in healthcare, telecom, and financial services. He now heads New Markets Advisors, a firm operating from offices in the United States, United Kingdom, and South Africa.

Prior to becoming a consultant in this field, he launched Celpay, a mobile payments start-up that has become one of the most successful such firms in the world. He was also CEO of Brainstorm, a developer of mobile middleware software that acquired a start-up he founded, Saverfone. Additionally, he was responsible for taking the leading British electronics firm Psion into the cellphone industry, creating joint ventures with Ericsson and Motorola and bringing to market one of the world's first mobile Internet devices. He is a cofounder of the influential Mobile Marketing Association.

Before his entrepreneurial career, Wunker was a strategy consultant for several years with Bain & Company in their Boston and London offices. He also helped to establish George Soros' philanthropies in Czechoslovakia after the end of communism, and he worked at the

United Nations to finance alternative energy projects in emerging markets.

Wunker has written dozens of articles for publications including *Forbes* and *BusinessWeek,* and his television appearances include Bloomberg and the BBC. He is a frequent speaker at industry and corporate events, and he has been a Visiting Executive at Dartmouth's Tuck School of Business. He has an MBA from Harvard Business School, a master's in public administration from Columbia University, and a BA in public policy, *cum laude,* from Princeton.

Wunker is a citizen of the United States and France, and he has also lived in the United Kingdom, Netherlands, Japan, Ecuador, and Zambia. He resides near Boston, Massachusetts.